DAME NITA
Caribbean Woman,
World Citizen

To my Friends
Lorraine & Keith. Thanks!

Woodie

Official photo of Her Excellency Dame Nita Barrow, GCMG, DA, Governor-General of Barbados

DAME NITA
Caribbean Woman,
— World Citizen —

■ FRANCIS 'WOODIE' BLACKMAN ■

IAN RANDLE PUBLISHERS
KINGSTON

To my wife, Cynthia,
for her support and interest
and to all women
'Who hold up more than half the sky'.

© Francis W. Blackman 1995

Published in Jamaica by
Ian Randle Publishers Limited
206 Old Hope Road, Box 686
Kingston 6, Jamaica

All rights reserved. No part of this publication may be reproduced, stored in a retrieval system or transmitted in any form or by any means, electronic, mechanical, photocopying or otherwise without the prior permission of the publishers.

First published 1995

ISBN   976–8100–74–5 Paperback
       976–8100–56–7 Hardback

A catalogue record for this book is available from the National Library of Jamaica.

Designed by Susie Home
Typeset by M Rules
Printed in Great Britain by Cromwell Press

Contents

Foreword Sir Shirdath Ramphal vi
Preface x
Acknowledgements xii
1. The Early years 1
2. Nurse-in-Training 21
3. The Jamaica Years 37
4. The Christian Medical Commission 65
5. Advancing the Status of Women 91
6. International Council of Adult Education (ICAE) 110
7. South African Mission and Later 123
8. Service with the YWCA 144
9. Resident Representative to the UN 158
10. The People's Governor-General 169
Index 183

Foreword
Sir Shridath Ramphal

In February 1986, the people of the township of Alexandra in South Africa were the victims of a horrifying onslaught by the apartheid regime. Many people in the township were being brutally killed by the police as they confronted live ammunition with stones and home-made weapons. A Commonwealth Mission of Eminent Persons was in South Africa at the time; understandably, its members felt a need to go there immediately to see the situation for themselves. They were prevented from doing so by the South African military which had sealed off the township. But the Mission was determined not to be thwarted, and it did not take it long to get to the scene of terror — in the person of one of its members swathed in African garb, including matching head-gear, and escorted discreetly by a team of young ANC militants.

That Commonwealth 'eminent person' was Nita Barrow. No camera captured her entry into Alexandra. No Commonwealth news release recorded the Mission's defiance of the apartheid ban. But the people of Alexandra knew, the ANC knew, that the Commonwealth Mission had shared their moment of sorrow and outrage. When the Mission eventually spoke of these events, its credibility was enhanced by its having been in the field of combat.

As this excellent biography documents, Nita Barrow has been in the field of social and economic combat all her life. Her adversaries did not all wear uniforms or carry arms; most of them did not. They were faceless opponents with hidden agendas; systems fighting rearguard actions; attitudes standing in the way of change; prejudice barring progress. Nor is Nita Barrow a warrior figure; but this gentle woman has been in the frontline of the movement for change – mainly social change, but not infrequently related economic and even political change.

Nita Barrow's early work in nursing was to be typical of her life's work, both in its breath and its innovative quality. Pioneering public health work in Jamaica was quickly followed by her position as the first West Indian Matron of the new University College Hospital of the incipient University of the West Indies – a medical school that was to produce the first truly West Indian doctors and, more generally, to set the standard of excellence of the University to come.

The dedication to health care and an intuitive commitment to the improvement of the position of women in society ('feminism' had not yet entered the vocabulary) led to Nita Barrow's involvement in the YWCA where, again, she quickly rose to the highest positions, ultimately becoming the YWCA's world president. There followed further service to social development as the president of the International Council of Adult Education. It was the same combination of the quality of caring and of capacity for leadership that led to her being director of the Christian Medical Commission of the World Council of Churches, where her work in alternative health care was to be globally acclaimed; and later to her becoming a president of the World Council of Churches itself.

It seemed the most natural thing then that Nita Barrow should head the NGO Forum at the Third World Assembly of Women in Nairobi in 1985, a leadership role for which she was eminently equipped by those years of international service. Her proven leadership and her later unifying work with Caribbean delegations at the United Nations in New York have led to her being acclaimed as the best president the General Assembly never had. Through all these years of achievement, comprehensively and sensitively explored in the pages of this biography, Nita Barrow remained a person of humility and integrity, winning respect and admiration on all sides.

When Commonwealth leaders asked me in October 1988 to establish the Commonwealth Eminent Persons Group and organize its mission to South Africa, we were breaking new ground. Commonwealth policy had been to isolate South Africa with a view to forcing change. Sanctions were working; in trade, in finance, and very specially in sport. The time had now come to press home the advantage by exploring the prospects of ending the abomination of apartheid. We needed to talk to Nelson Mandela – still a prisoner of the apartheid regime; to explore with the ANC a basis for the start of negotiations; and of course to convince Pretoria that apartheid could no longer be sustained and had to be dismantled. And we needed to carry the by then global anti-apartheid movement with us.

It was a courageous Commonwealth move; everything would turn on the credibility of the persons engaged on the mission. I asked two former heads of government of Commonwealth countries with strong personal credentials as opponents of apartheid – Malcolm Fraser of Australia and General Obasanjo of Nigeria – to head the mission. I turned next to Nita Barrow; she was to be the only woman on the team.

Why Nita? The answer: integrity and courage, two attributes that had marked her life's work as she campaigned for justice over all those many years, fearlessly promoting the cause of enlightened change – whether it was in bringing health care to the poor or dragging the World YWCA into the 20th century, fighting innumerable battles in the World Council of Churches or in campaigning for the third world at the United Nations. Those credits, as her biography attests, were substantial. But there was something else too.

Nita Barrow was West Indian, and our region was in the forefront of the international struggle against apartheid. In the Commonwealth, at the United Nations, in international NGO movements, the West Indies – governments and people at all levels – stood in total solidarity with black South Africa. Nita Barrow embodied that passionate commitment; she carried it with her into Alexandra that said afternoon in February 1986.

There is a lesson here for all the people of our region. A new generation is coming forward with many of the old battles fought and won. Discrimination against women, lack of health care for the poor, racism in all its manifestations, and several other evils of yesterday are largely, if not entirely, overcome. There is a tendency to believe that the only task now is to consolidate the gains of the past. Nita Barrow would be the first to warn against such complacency. The issues may be different, or at least appear in different guise; but the struggle is not over. The need remains to overcome barriers to enlightened progress, to mark out a clear path to social and economic justice in the countries of our region and in our larger country, the planet.

What Nita Barrow's life confirms is how much the individual person can do to bring about change: to improve Barbados, to upgrade our Caribbean community – with, now, its wider reach to the entire Caribbean Basin – and to secure change in the wider world as well.

Nita Barrow was helped by being Barbadian, the product of a society not without social and economic imbalances to rectify, but one whose steady progress as a working democracy ensured that they would be rectified. Nita Barrow in turn enhanced Barbados and the West Indies by the many contributions she made to her country and her region.

Foremost among her attributes was, is, her commitment to service. From her earliest days, from an age when, today, many youngsters 'join the rat race', Nita Barrow's highest yearning, her largest ambition, was to have an opportunity to serve; to serve society and especially those within society whose lives most needed betterment. Within her island society, in Barbados, this devotion to service might be thought natural in one growing up close to a brother committed to the same goals through political action. But we are each of us individuals; the choices we make are our own. When we pursue untrodden paths, we mark them out for ourselves. Nita Barrow did just that. Her way was a different one, less adversarial but no less determined and committed.

And inevitably for Nita Barrow the 'society' to be served kept enlarging. She was of a generation that came to West Indian identity as a natural, even compulsive, dimension of enlightenment. I am also of that generation; it was unthinkable not to be 'West Indian' – certainly if one looked beyond 'island' horizons. And how could one not do so in the '40s and '50s – in the years of federal ambition before all our countries became independent separately. Nita Barrow embraced that regional identity with a naturalness that had a special quality. She was never less a Barbadian for it; but she was supremely, quintessentially, West Indian.

In those earliest days of building the University of the West Indies and especially the University College Hospital, Nita was as West Indian on its Mona Campus as was any of the generation of pioneers of which Phillip Sherlock became so much a symbol. Decades later, when I was privileged to be invited by Caribbean leaders to head the West Indian Commission, we turned to Nita Barrow to be the Commission's Patron – a symbol of our aspiration to 'oneness'. She received the first copy of *Time for Action* – a title that might have been her personal credo through most of her life's work.

Being West Indian is much more than following an intellectual fashion. For one thing, it is not always, or everywhere, fashionable. It involves a deep emotional change – a maturing, really – which makes each of us a worthier person and prepare us for the next step on the path away from 'otherness'.

Nita Barrow had to be a good Barbadian to be a good West Indian; just as it was being a good West Indian that fitted her supremely for the world roles to which she was called. Here, too, are lessons for young West Indians. We have to free ourselves from narrow identities if we are, as individuals, to serve in a wider world. To do so has now become a duty – to ourselves, to our homelands, to our region, no less than to the international community which, because of contributions like Nita Barrow's, looks to us to play important roles. To any who doubt, or merely wonder, let Nita Barrow's life be testimony to the world's need for leadership from the smallest of countries, to the least powerful of states. But to fulfill that need we must first believe in and assert our belonging to the human family – a sense of belonging transcending countries and governments, nationalism and separatism – and affirm our wider loyalties while remaining ourselves.

Remaining ourselves is particularly important to West Indians, for West Indianness is a unique strength. Walking with kings yet keeping the common touch comes easily to West Indians who remain true to themselves – for the common touch is our natural condition. For all the grandeur of her positions of state, Nita Barrow is always true to herself. Over the last few years she has been leaving Government House in Bridgetown about once a week to join an art class for beginners. For a few hours, she is what she most wants to be – a people's person; without fuss, or rank or special airs – just Nita. In that, too, she sets a lesson for future generations who will, I hope, read this biography with enjoyment and with pride, but also with enlightenment.

In May 1994 I was with Dame Nita in Pretoria as we attended Nelson Mandela's inauguration as president of the new South Africa. As befitted the governor-general of Barbados, Nita's clothes and headgear this time were distinctly more elegant than those she wore as a furtive visitor to a troubled township in 1986. But she was the same Nita Barrow. As she applauded the new president, she would have recalled that earlier visit when she shared the anguish of South Africa and became the first West Indian to talk with Nelson Mandela in Pollsmoor Prison. We both reflected on the line that history had already drawn between those two events – and how gratifying it was that West Indians were part of that continuum.

Woodie Blackman has done us all a great service in setting down the story of a great human being from Barbados – a great Bajan West Indian who has so consistently made us feel proud.

Preface

In 1988, while in the USA, my wife Cynthia and I visited Dame Nita Barrow who was at the time, Barbados' Resident Representative at the UN. So it happened that one Sunday we were caught up in the excitement surrounding Dame Nita's pending nomination as a candidate for the Presidency of the 1988–89 Session of the UN General Assembly. It was supposed to be the turn of the Caribbean sub-group of the Group of the Latin American and Caribbean Countries to have its candidate become the President. Dame Nita would be the candidate. While some of Dame Nita's luncheon guests were discussing the subtleties of diplomacy of moment, others speculated on the relative merits of one strategy or another. Others like myself simply tried to absorb it all.

Some months later as I recalled the pleasantries of that Sunday visit, it struck me that there must be few West Indians whose work and interests have involved them in as many local, regional and international organisations as Dame Nita. So what! So what indeed! Here was a West Indian woman who has spent much of her life serving other people, especially under-privileged women. She was a real feminist, a champion of women's rights, a determined woman, fair and firm, an achiever, one who seemed to have the support of all with whom she came into contact, including men. Many vignettes had been published about her, but should there not be something more? She helps to make the world go round.

Like some other persons I was a bit tired of seeing young women of ability, but with little commitment, being presented to an unsuspecting public displaying nothing but shallow mediocrity masquerading as excellence. Perhaps a brief account of Dame Nita's life might help to show them and others what living is really about and help them to distinguish between active giving of self and its false companion, serving of self

The result of those thoughts is this book. Because of rising costs of books, a deliberate effort was made to limit the size of this one without losing too much of what makes Dame Nita real to so many persons. Writing about her strong sense of family which regularly guides her to supervise the homework and piano exercises of her great-nieces could not be omitted from any description of Barrow/Springer family relationship. Details of Dame Nita's association and involvement with co-workers and close friends have been omitted. How would it be possible to 'write' pictures of moments of Nita with any one member of what is really her extended family, which includes Carmen Lusan, Ken and Evelyn Standard of Jamaica, Marie Matthews (Barbados), Helen Mussalem (Canada), Arne and Ruth Sovik (France) and Sylvia Talbot (St. Croix) and exclude any of the many others on five continents. Little has therefore been written about Dame Nita's social life. I do hope, however, that her high sociability, a quality which is common to the Barrow family, does show through. That sociability is more than the ordinary and continuing desire to have people of all ages near her; it includes the sudden surprises which all her friends, acquaintances and relatives have learnt not to be surprised about — like sending or bringing a tray with a full meal to a home because there is sudden illness there which will cause effort to be diverted from such ordinary activity as cooking.

In limiting the writing, I have not been altogether fair to the reader and possibly to Dame Nita herself. It was not easy to omit Nita's hosting a Christmas party for the first non-Jamaican medical students to the University College in 1948. It would have taken many pages to capture the atmosphere of that and the many similar annual parties which followed and which for the past 20 years or more have had Ken and Evelyn Standard as hosts.

Nor was it easy to omit the description of Dame Nita's participation in a celebration of exuberance, itself a kind of celebration of her involvement in the Independence of Guyana when her late brother Errol Barrow, then Prime Minister of Barbados, arrived with flying fish and liquid refreshment to support a party which should have been smaller than the twenty times larger that it turned out to be?

Writing about Dame Nita was mostly writing about a friend, but it was also writing about a Head of State who is holding office. For that reason 'Nita' in Chapters 1–9 becomes 'Dame Nita' or 'Her Excellency' in Chapter 10 where she is 'The People's Governor General'.

Nita with first ladies of Nigeria, Ghana, Liberia in Accra, Ghana

Acknowledgements

I am indebted to Dame Nita for her assistance and interest, without her almost total involvement, the attempt would have been more difficult. I am very grateful to several persons who assisted by providing me with, or pointing me towards information. Among them are the members of staff at the Headquarters of the World YWCA and of the World Council of Churches, both in Geneva. There are however a few whom I must mention because each one has assisted in correcting, or in providing, a point of view. Among them are Helen Mussalem, Philip Potter, Brigalia Bam, Lucille Mair, Joyce Scroxton, Marie Assad, Arne and Ruth Sovik, Erlinda Senturias and Doreen Boyd.

I specially acknowledge the assistance of Archbishop Ted Scott of Canada, the late Porter Mc Keever, Arne and Ruth Sovik and Arthur Stock for their assistance with certain chapters. I am particularly indebted to Leonard Shorey and Keith Sandiford for their advice and criticisms, but more especially for their very real encouragement and support when I most needed a bit of 'propping up'. Finally, thanks to Cynthia, my wife, for her varying levels of communication and support, including the indescribable silent variety, when periodically the weaknesses of uncertainty and frustration appeared.

Woodie Blackman
St. George
Barbados
January 31 1995

Photos with captions appear between Chapters 1&2, 3&4, 4&5, 6&7 and 9&10.

1
The Early Years

The first-day cover had in the top right-hand corner a picture of the lady, a bust, showing the round dark brown face with its high wide forehead. Above the forehead was a full head of curled greying black hair with an almost white tuft standing forward, more to the right front than centre. Looking from under a pair of medium bushed brows were two large eyes. Simply to state that full curved lips and rounded slightly dimpled cheeks completed the picture would be to ignore what probably made the picture most attractive, if not special. There was a smile in which the face took part; it was not one of those put on like a spray of perfume for a special occasion, but one which is sometimes described as open, so describing the indescribable. What reached the viewer was a picture of a truly cheerful person who was really enjoying life. It was in fact a picture of a face known to all Barbadians, West Indians and to many people in many lands. It was that of Her Excellency, Dame Nita Barrow, GCMG, DA, Governor-General of Barbados.

The special issue of stamps had been released to mark the 25th anniversary of the island's independence. Independence had been obtained from Great Britain by Dame Nita's brother, the late Errol Walton Barrow, the first prime minister of Barbados, the 'Father of the Nation'. On that first Independence Day of 30 November 1966, Sir John Stowe, the last English governor of Barbados became the first governor-general of Barbados. Probably the most meaningful photograph of the occasion is that of John in celebration, under the flag of Barbados with its centrepiece of the broken trident raised for the first time. Sir John and Errol faced the large crowd of Barbadians and visitors. Sir John's left hand was holding Errol's right hand in the symbolic sharing of responsibility for a new Caribbean nation.

There was no reason for Barbados to prove its new status and power by requesting the Queen to recall the English governor and replace him by a native governor-general. There was no reason to deprive Sir John Stowe of the privilege of being the last governor of Barbados and its first governor-general. He deserved to have that honour now and in history. He had served Barbados and other islands in the Caribbean as one who understood his role and who could with dignity change his function from that of servant of Her Majesty's Government to Her Majesty's Representative, largely a ceremonial office. There had been no bitterness associated with the transition of the island from colony to independent nation.

Since independence Barbados has had four native governors-general. Dame Nita succeeded her cousin Sir Hugh Springer, GCMG, GCVO, KA, as governor-general in June 1990. The people of Barbados had regarded her as the most suitable person to succeed Sir Hugh. There had been a rumour that another person had been considered, but Dame Nita's appointment by the Queen, and its islandwide, indeed Caribbeanwide, acceptance indicated that any rumour about another possible candidate was merely speculation and could not really have been part of the consultative process required by the constitution. The rumour was like an uncomfortable and muffled hiccup. It had been taken seriously by some elected members of the house of assembly, that the 'king-maker' and political strategist of the ruling Democratic Labour Party, had been promised 'the highest post in the land'. When therefore the post became vacant, the people and the members of the opposition indicated that there was a person more acceptable who might be invited to be governor-general, namely Dame Nita Barrow.

Commenting on the ceremony of Dame Nita Barrow's installation, one local newspaper had, on June 7 1990, the day after the installation, described it as having been simple and elegant. A few days earlier Branford Taitt, the minister responsible for the arrangements, had promised that the ceremony would be simple. Indeed the ceremony was simple, though without any loss of the symbolism associated with the formal assumption of duty of the highest post of honour as representative of the Queen of Barbados. In his attempt to portray Dame Nita's oneness with her people, a commentator likened Her Excellency's stroll among the hundreds of spectators standing in the courtyard of the houses of parliament following her installation to that of a queen walking among some of her admiring subjects.

Part of the dignified ceremony associated with the installation was the reading and signing of the oath of office by Dame Nita. That great moment on Wednesday, 6 June 1990, was signalled by a 21-gun salute to Her Excellency. Immediately following the salute reserved for Her Majesty the Queen of Barbados or her representative, the new governor-general of Barbados ascended the dais in the senate chamber and addressed not only those who were within the chamber, but also the people of Barbados. The ceremony, which had been televised, permitted thousands more to feel that they were part of a special moment in the country's history.

In her address Dame Nita spoke, with much feeling, of the role which women have played in the building of Barbados; and she specially mentioned her close relatives, male and female, who had contributed to her own development. Then, having made a brief review of situations existing in various parts of the world, Dame Nita next pointed to the challenges which faced our young people. She ended by pledging to serve the nation faithfully.

Later in the evening the celebration of the installation of the fourth Barbadian, the first female, governor-general took the form of a reception on the grounds of Government House, the official residence of the governor-general. A cross-section of Barbados, consisting of some 500 people, gathered to share a feeling of satisfaction, a sense of pride, a oneness of community. The coming together of so many residents and visitors appeared to be more than just another reception, another opportunity to meet friends, exchange the niceties of polite conversation and indulge in social intercourse. Many persons felt that since the general elections for a new house of assembly were soon due, Dame Nita's appointment would do much to reunite the society which had already been divided and exploited by extreme utterances and some vilification associated with political partisanship.

As Dame Nita circulated among her guests on the lawns of Government House a press photographer caught her in conversation with two female guests, Mrs Berinda Cox and Ms Candy Holder, owners of a fishing boat at Oistins, a base for part of the fishing industry in the parish of Christ Church. The two women supplied fish to Dame Nita and, until his death in 1987, had done the same to her late brother, the prime minister. When he died, the two women selected a quantity of fish and sent it as a gift to the Barrow household where they knew that there were many overseas visitors who had arrived to pay final tribute to Errol. Nita had never forgotten that special touch of domestic kindness. As she greeted Mrs Cox, nicknamed Baby Toots, Mrs Cox expressed her appreciation at having been invited to the celebration garden party, said to Dame Nita: 'The Skipper dead and lef' the water to wash me.' Errol had been affectionately known as the Skipper. Mrs Cox's colloquial turn of phrase was meant to convey that Errol had bequeathed to her his goodwill and affection, which she obviously valued much more highly than money or material things. In reply to a question about her relationship with the two women, Dame Nita explained:

> Errol had introduced me to Baby Toots and Candy. In recent times when leaving Barbados after a visit, I would stop on my way to the airport and pick up, from one or the other, fish ready packaged and awaiting me. When Errol was alive, it was always made clear to me that the Skipper's requirements took first place. I was welcome to the left-overs.

The anecdote reminded us of the number of times that one would find Errol in the kitchen of Culloden Farm, at that time the official residence of the prime minister, preparing dinner for his guests. His expertise as a cook is confirmed in a West Indian cook book, co-authored by him and published posthumously. Apparently it is a family tradition that Nita and her sister Sybil, both invariably resident at Government House, do not only supervise the preparation of specialties for the table for their guests, but indeed undertake the actual preparation and cooking of some of the dishes. There is one occasion when the sisters Nita, Sybil and Ena, together with a special selection of relatives, prepare and serve a full dinner to about 70 persons. That is at Christmas time when Her Excellency invites the Government House-based and other staff, including all those who have served her during the year, to join her at dinner. To ensure a family atmosphere, no professional caterer of any sort is used. Clearly one or other, or both, of the Barrow parents must have been good amateur cooks. Certainly Mrs Ruth Barrow was. Perhaps this is where we might take a brief look at Nita's progenitors.

Nita's paternal grandfather, Robert Barrow, lived in Jamaica in the late 1870s as a member of the West India Regiment, where he met his first wife, a Jamaican. While he was serving with his regiment in West Africa, his wife died, leaving two children. On his return from West Africa he was appointed to the post of Superintendent of Prisons in St Vincent, an island about 100 miles south-west of Barbados. Not too long after resettling in St Vincent, Robert Barrow married Frances, a Vincentian of Carib descent. Of that marriage there were four children: Reginald, Florence, Jonathan and Bellingham.

In 1897, when Reginald was not quite nine years old, Robert retired from the post in St Vincent and returned to Barbados with his wife and six children, including the two from his first marriage. On reaching maturity Florence married Charles Wilkinson Springer, who is best remembered as an assistant master at Combermere, a secondary grammar school for boys, where he started the first scout troop in Barbados and thus became affectionately known as the father of scouting in the island.

The children of Charles and Florence were Robert Christopher, Hugh Worrell and Charles Reginald, the first two of whom became Barbados Scholars. Christopher was a distinguished scholar in mathematics. Hugh Worrell, a classical scholar, became in turn a barrister-at-law, trade unionist and legislator in the Caribbean and on the international stage, first registrar of the University of the West Indies, secretary of the Universities and Colleges of the Commonwealth, and Dame Nita's immediate predecessor as governor-general of Barbados. Charles Reginald, a brilliant mathematician, served with distinction as a civil servant in Barbados and in the short-lived Federation of the West Indies. He subsequently became a barrister-at-law and legal adviser to a family business management research firm.

But what of the other Barrow children? Jonathan emigrated to Nigeria and subsequently lost contact with his relatives in Barbados. Nita made contact with Jonathan's widow during her visits to Africa in the 1970s-1980s. It was not, however, until 1988 that Nita's efforts were rewarded. Robert, the youngest of Jonathan's children, made the first visit to Barbados to meet his cousins and give them news of his sister, Edith Oritserudede, and his two brothers Oritebesimi and Jonathan, thus re-establishing family contacts.

Bellingham Barrow, the youngest of Robert Barrow's sons, married Clyne Hope who of necessity became an entrepreneur in the cottage industry, thus helping to maintain the stability of the home and to educate the children Griselda, Lucy and Barbara.

Robert's eldest son, Reginald, married Ruth Alberta O'Neal of St Lucy and became the father of Graham, Nita, Ena, Errol and Sybil. Ruth Barrow (née O'Neal) had her roots in St Lucy, Barbados' most northern parish, where her grandfather, Thomas Whitford O'Neal, had established himself as owner of Friendship Plantation.[1] There his son, Joseph Jathan Chaderton O'Neal, was born in July 1851. Joseph grew up on the estate, where he became a superintendent, or in twentieth-century plantation language, overseer. He also learnt the skills of a blacksmith, which were needed, not only to keep the shoes of horses in good shape and repair, but to make wheels for cane carts, for other commercial vehicles, carriages and buggies, and to maintain them. A practical knowledge of metallurgy, especially as it related to the tempering of steel and the relative rates of expansion and contraction of ferrous metals, was what separated the real blacksmith from the aspirant to that profession.

Nita's mother was Ruth, daughter of Catherine (née Prescod) and Joseph J.C. O'Neal. Catherine was a native of Tobago, who together with her siblings had been brought by her mother to Barbados to benefit from the education which was considered to be the best available in the eastern Caribbean. In order to maintain his wife and family in Barbados, her father despatched regularly by schooner or sloop agricultural produce most of which was sold by Catherine. This entrepreneurship did more than maintain an immigrant family. It established the Prescods in Barbados as part of the growing black community of small, but stable, business people.

The children of Catherine and Joseph O'Neal were Charles Duncan, Ruth Alberta, Ebenezer Walton, Thomas Prescod, Inez Malvina and Joseph Edwin. Charles Duncan we shall meet later as a scholar, social activist and medical practitioner. Ebenezer emigrated to the USA and Inez to Trinidad, but both maintained contact with other family members. Thomas became one of the two successful black merchant tailors in Bridgetown in the 1920s and 1930s. Joseph, the head of the family, learnt early that real estate would provide, as its name implies, the greatest financial security. Early in his working life, therefore, he bought what seems to have been his first properties, Nesfield and The Garden in St Lucy. His next venture was more ambitious, for he became one of the earliest shareholders in the Barbados Building and Loan Society, registered in 1889, one of the few such organisations ever to exist in Barbados. In Bridgetown Joseph later secured by purchase four other properties. In 1895 he mortgaged one of his properties and purchased Mount Pleasant Estate, one of some 39 acres and with sugar works. Within 4 years, however, he borrowed £208, a very large sum in those days. It is possible that he used it to purchase real estate which his will, probated in 1921, showed was fairly considerable.[2]

In 1905, when sugar was on the decline, Joseph sold some lands which he owned in St Peter. He also mortgaged Mount Pleasant estate. About 15 years later he sold Mount Pleasant Estate for some £3,700. The rental from the Bridgetown properties would later maintain his widow, Catherine, and provide part support for her grandchildren, including Nita. Even in such reduced financial circumstances and in widowhood, Catherine and her grandchildren were still among the privileged blacks of Barbados.

The classes making up the population of Barbados, of less than 200,000 during the latter half of the nineteenth century and at the turn of the twentieth, were virtually three: the planter and merchant (of Bridgetown) class, accounting for but a fraction of the overall community; a small and impoverished middle class, slightly more numerous than the plantocracy; and the remainder, a large number of manual labourers. The planter and merchant class was small in number and white in colour. Their economic and political power was derived from ownership of virtually all of the most fertile land and from the control of all imports and exports of this agricultural community. It monopolised the seats in the House of Assembly and provided the bulk of the Legislative Council, nominated by the governor. It also controlled the vestries, the church, the law courts, the press and the academic institutions.

The other classes consisted almost entirely of persons of mixed race and blacks. By far the largest proportion (over 90 per cent) was the blacks, nearly all of whom were dependent upon plantation owners and managers for employment and for the privilege of renting a small portion of estate-owned land in order to grow ground provisions for themselves and their families. They subsisted on very low wages and without the benefit of any kind of welfare system. Only the most destitute among them could find refuge in the parochial almshouses that had gradually sprung up in the post-emancipation age.

The franchise was limited to those who possessed land which yielded not less than £5 produce, or had an annual income of £50, or a university education. The number of persons who were thus enfranchised was less than 2,000 in a total population of more than 182,000. According to the census of 1891 there were 15,600 whites, 44,000 coloureds and 123,000 blacks in Barbados.[3]

The government of the country therefore lay almost entirely in the hands of the few who constituted the most privileged class in the society. The structure of the government of the time consisted of a bicameral legislature: the Legislative Council, as the Upper House and the House of Assembly of 24 members made up of two elected representatives from each of the 11 parishes and 2 for the city of Bridgetown. In addition, there was an executive council where authority was somewhat similar to that of a modern cabinet in ministerial government.

Such was the system of government existing in 1916 when Nita Barrow was born. The economy of the island and the material welfare of the people, including the landed gentry and the merchants, remained almost entirely dependent upon the status of sugar produced in Barbados and sold on the markets in England to which it was shipped. As the price of sugar was routinely set by England, the producers of sugar were then at the mercy of its main consumers. This was true of all of the British West Indian colonies. Since about the middle of the nineteenth century, West Indian sugar had been forced to compete with subsidised beet sugar in Europe and with more cheaply produced sugar from Cuba. The resulting fall in the price of West Indian sugar during the last quarter of the nineteenth century and the subsequent ill-effects on the sugar-producing islands led to the establishment of the West Indian Royal Commission of 1897. One of the results of the report of that commission was the grant of a sum of money by the British government for the rehabilitation of the sugar industry.

Because of the inequalities, social and other, already identified, little benefit of the British government's financial assistance to the sugar industry filtered down to the blacks. The survival, and indeed the subsequent improvement, of the lot of many of the black families was based on money sent back to the islands by fathers, brothers and other close relatives who had migrated to the French Islands and to Panama in the 1890s and later, in the 1920s, to the USA in search of work and better rewards. During the nearly 30 years or so while the Panama opportunity existed, it is estimated that more than 40,000 Barbadians migrated to Panama. Between 1906 and 1915 about 20,000 returned. By the early 1920s therefore, a relatively new, but small class of black Barbadians had evolved. That group comprised the artisan or the less skilled worker, who had emigrated and had later returned with enough money to set himself up as an independent artisan, a shop-keeper, or owner of a small plot of land on which he built a house. The plot size varied from one-quarter of an acre to 2 or 3 acres.

This was the sociocultural context in which Reginald Barrow had to function. He had received his early education at Miss Comissiong's private school in St Vincent and later, in Barbados, at the private school of Rev. and Mrs Alexander Pilgrim of Mount Tabor, St John, one of the north-eastern parishes of Barbados. The Pilgrims were themselves part of a distinguished Barbadian Moravian family and were numbered among the earliest middle-class coloureds in Barbados. Reginald subsequently attended Combermere School just before Charles Springer joined its staff. In 1909 he gained entry to Codrington College in St John at a time when few blacks attended that institution. At the end of two years he gained a Licentiate in Theology (LTh) from Durham University, to which Codrington College was affiliated.

Codrington College was then the highest institution of learning in Barbados and throughout the British West Indies. It had been established some 190 years earlier at the bequest of Christopher Codrington, a landowner of considerable wealth. Codrington's bequest read:

> Item: I give and bequeath my two plantations (Society and Codrington) in the island of Barbados to the Society for the Propagation of Christian Religion in Forreighn parts Erected and Established on by my late good master King William the Third and my desire is to have the Plantations Continued Intire and three hundred negroes at Least Kept always thereon, and A convenient number of Professors and Scholars maintained there, all of them to be under the vows of Poverty Chastity and obedience, who shall be obligded to Studdy and Practice Physick and Chyrurgery as well as divinity, that by the apparent usefulness of the former to all mankind, they may Both indear themselves to the People and have the better opportunitys of doeing good to mens Souls whilst they are Taking Care of their Bodys. But the Particulars of the Constitution leave to the Society of good and wise men.[4]

During 1909–11 when Reginald Barrow was a student at Codrington College he assisted the principal, Canon T.H. Bindley, as clerk or secretary. It appears that Reginald received rewards in money or in kind which assisted in his maintenance at the college. Reginald apparently had some hope of being allowed to continue at the college for a third year in order to complete studies for the BA (Dunelm). On what such hope was based is not known, but Reginald later said that Bindley's successor (who took office in 1910), Bishop Anstey, was not as charitable towards him as Bindley had been. Reginald attributed this to the racial prejudice common to, and demonstrated by, the privileged local white people. He supported this view by stating that the new principal had expressed a preference not only for priests of non-African origin, but indeed for those from England.

On leaving Codrington College, Reginald became the lay assistant to the rector at St George's parish church. He was ordained sometime afterwards and appointed to a cure in the St Vincent diocese which included the islands of Bequia, Union Island, Mustique, Carriacou and Canouan.

Before taking up his appointment in the St Vincent diocese, Reginald married Ruth O'Neal, who therefore accompanied him to his new post. Such a simple statement does not indicate the real hazards of the traveller in those times. Taking up residence in Bequia meant that the newlyweds travelled from Barbados to St Vincent, some 100 miles, and then to the island of Bequia, a further ten miles, both journeys by schooner. Although the Barrow couple arrived safely in Bequia, all of their personal belongings did not. Most of their personal effects were left in St Vincent to be transshipped to Bequia at a later date. It appears that they were lost when the vessel in which they were being transshipped foundered in the channel between the 2 islands known as Kick-'em jenny.

Rev. Reginald Barrow found the inter-island travel associated with his duties in the St Vincent Grenadines, not only demanding, but also uncomfortable, to say the least. The travel affected his health – probably a euphemism for a chronic tendency to seasickness or motion sickness. He therefore sought the first convenient opportunity to return to Barbados. On returning in 1916, the young Barrow family, which by that time included the baby Graham, took up residence at Fairmount in St Lucy, the home of the O'Neal parents of Ruth Barrow. Nita was born there while Reginald was curate of the St Lucy parish church, to which he had been appointed in Barbados but which did not offer the young and ambitious priest a living which could be considered reasonably substantial.

The sermons of Rev. Reginald Barrow often pointed to the inequalities of Barbadian society. Such preaching was disturbing to the privileged class and therefore the rulers of the church and of Barbados. He was also at that time an oddity in that he was a black priest. Among all the British institutions, the Anglican church had remained the most staunchly sexist, the most overtly racist and the most rigidly conservative. Predictably, therefore, it was subtly indicated to Rev. Barrow that his unorthodox, if not radical (and not yet identified as socialist) views were disturbing. Consequently, when the post of headmaster of the Alleyne School, a grammar school for boys situated in St Andrew, a north-eastern parish some 12 miles from Bridgetown, became vacant, Reginald applied for the post and was appointed. As headmaster of the Alleyne School Reginald also performed duties as an assistant priest in the parish of St Andrew.

In a review, however brief, of secondary education in Barbados or in the Caribbean, in any period before 1900–25, it should be noted that such education was mostly provided for the white children of the not so wealthy whites who could not afford to send them to schools in England. When Reginald Barrow became the headmaster of the Alleyne School in 1917, there were fewer than 20 boys. There had not been much real change in the racial make-up of the students since the establishment of the school. Reginald therefore encouraged the parents and teachers of bright black children attending elementary schools nearby to direct the children towards the Alleyne School where they would have some opportunity of overcoming the educational limit imposed on them by the elite of Barbados.

Reginald also saw the need for secondary education for girls, although under the terms of the school's establishment girls could not be admitted.

With the assistance of his wife, Reginald introduced some of the girls in the neighbourhood to secondary school subjects. The teaching took place in the living quarters provided for the headmaster. Apparently that kind of backdoor entry of girls to secondary education was not quite acceptable to the establishment. The late Senator Esme Rock, of St Andrew, has publicly expressed her gratitude to Rev. Reginald Barrow for having introduced her to secondary education, which she is sure she would not otherwise have had.

Reginald soon became more restless and more dissatisfied with social conditions. It was at this time that the bishop of the Episcopalian diocese of Puerto Rico asked the bishop of Barbados to find a suitable priest to assist in the work of the church in the Virgin Islands, which was part of his diocese. Reginald was recommended and was accepted for the post. His removal from Barbados, it was felt, would bring some peace to that diocese.

Reginald was posted to St Croix, one of the three Virgin Islands which had been bought by the USA from Denmark in 1917. Within a short time and again because of his willingness to draw attention to the inhuman conditions of black people in the Caribbean, he was apparently forced to vacate his post in the Episcopalian church. He therefore joined some local people in founding a local branch of the African Methodist Episcopal (AME) church. The new and relatively independent vehicle of the AME church pulpit and the associated pastoral work provided him with a yet greater opportunity to speak out against the continuing social ills which initially had their origin in the institution of slavery. Slavery had supposedly been abolished in 1834 but its oppressive influence survived for well over a century throughout the Caribbean islands.

Reginald Barrow seemed destined to pay the price, in his home island of Barbados and elsewhere, for daring to point to the inequalities within societies based on the sugar plantation. Indeed, he would eventually become the victim of the repressive power at the hands of the governor of St Croix and his advisers for publicly criticising the administration.

Reginald's criticism had appeared in the *Herald*, a local newspaper. He criticised an administrative officer of the government for lack of reasonable judgement in the execution of his duties. Because of the results which Reginald's punishment had upon Nita and the Barrow family, it is worthwhile giving in some detail the circumstances in St Croix which led to the enforced separation of Reginald from his wife and young family.

Within 2 years of his arrival in St Croix, Reginald Barrow was deported without trial from that island on 22 December 1922, on the order of Governor Henry Hough. The law under which Henry Hough deported Barrow from St Croix was a Danish law of 1827 which allowed such penalty to be taken against aliens whose behaviour rendered them 'undesirable'.

Isaac Dookham summarised the events leading up to Reginald's deportation and the maladministration of justice thus:

> By an order on December 9 1922, Rev. Reginald Barrow, Anglican Priest from Barbados, and acting Editor of the 'Herald' Newspaper, was deported without trial as an undesirable alien for an editorial critical of the Administration. When Barrow emigrated to the United States the Administration with vengeance pursued him there and governor Henry Hough tried desperately but unnecessarily to have the Department of Immigration and the Department of Labour deport him from the United States to indicate support for the Naval Administration's action. Then under an order dated January 31 1923, Thomas Hugh Morenga-Bonaparte, Grenadian and associate editor of the 'Emancipator', was deported for an editorial.[5]

The USA had purchased the Virgin Islands of St Croix, St Thomas and St John because of their strategic importance. Having had no previous experience in governing such colonies, the American administration found it convenient to retain the Danish laws and system of administration. The historian Gordon K. Lewis, discussing the status of the Virgin Islanders which resulted from the American ownership of the islands, noted that there was no provision made in the transaction for rights to American citizenship. Lewis commented in this manner on the administration following the change of ownership:

> The machinery of Government set up by Congress reflected this humiliating second-class status. It bore all the marks of hasty wartime improvisation. In fact the basic statute of March, 1917, by continuing, in effect, most of the provisions of the Danish colonial system of 1906, perpetuated a Danish constitutional system that went back to 1863 and conferred upon the Virgin Islanders the further anomaly of being governed by an odd combination of American sovereignty and Danish institutions, with the minority of modification, of course, of a changed nomenclature to conform to American usage.[6]

Sometime in 1919 or 1920, the sugar plantation workers had become united under a black native of St Croix, David Hamilton Jackson. Jackson, having formed a labour union, recognised the need for a newspaper and managed to establish the *Herald*. As trade union leader and as editor of the Herald, Jackson was the main force behind the demand of the workers for an increase in the daily wage from 20 cents to 35 cents. The request was denied by the plantation owners. A strike lasting 4 or 5 weeks ensued, with eventual victory for the labour union.

The role played by the *Herald* was immeasurable. Jackson, as editor, exposed the dehumanising influences, inequalities and cruelties associated with the plantation system and continued to attack the plantation owners and the Danish, pseudo-American administrators, much to their discomfort. Inevitably, Jackson paid the price for so-called libel by imprisonment on more than one occasion.

Jackson soon realised that if he was to be an effective labour leader and bring about changes in the conditions of the people, he should be able to challenge the Danish administrators and land-owners within the law. He therefore set out to study law in the USA.

On his departure for the USA, Jackson left the *Herald* newspaper in the hands of Rev. Reginald Barrow, who acted as editor and pursued the policies of Jackson. He no doubt used his experience of the Barbados situation, which was not unlike that of St Croix, to assist him in his regular criticisms of the St Croix administration. Within a year, however, Jackson was forced to return to deal with certain alleged irregularities in the union administration and with another conflict between the union and the plantation owners.

A second and new set of demands from the sugar workers included a further increase in the daily wage. The demand was for a maximum daily wage of not less than $1, to be derived from the increase in the price being paid for sugar in Europe. Other Danish masters were also being put under some pressure in the neighbouring island of St Thomas, where Rothschild Francis, the labour leader, had also established a newspaper, the *Emancipator*, as the medium through which he could inform readers of the legitimate and reasonable requests of labourers, and challenge the arrogant authority of the Danish land-owners.

The *Emancipator* in St Thomas and the *Herald* in St Croix proved to be worthwhile and effective instruments in upsetting the seasoned insensitivity of the administration, the members of which were not reluctant to use all the power available in their own defence.

> The terms, Agitators, Reds and Bolsheviks were used frequently by Government officers to refer to the dissenting editors, particularly to Hamilton Jackson, editor of the St Croix 'Herald' and Rothschild Francis, editor of the St Thomas 'Emancipator'. In 1922 Jackson after mildly criticising the St Croix Road Commissioner in an editorial, was cited for contempt of court by imprisonment for six days. While serving this sentence, he was elected to the Colonial Council by overwhelmingly defeating the government candidate. Also in 1922, Francis was threatened with censorship by the local officials because of his article criticising the conduct of the United States marines in Santo Domingo.
>
> Charging the dissenting editors as being 'self-seeking leaders' and 'fresh malcontents' who all set the 'unthinking masses' against the insular, and who carry 'no weight with the good thinking people' Navy governor Sumner Kittle complained in his annual report for 1922:
>
> 'The leaders and their sub-leaders teach that the insular Government is inefficient and oppressive, and the rights of the people are trampled upon, that free speech and a free press are inhibited, that the courts are conducted with prejudice . . . they are un-American in thought and action and practice a form of race hatred.'[7]

During his 2 years' residence in St Croix, Reginald's concern for the improvement of his people had led him to choose additional means for providing some social security for them by creating a form of unity other than that based on opposition to the local sugar barons. Using his base, the newly founded branch of the AME church, Reginald formed the St Croix Benevolent Society, the membership of which included a small number of non-Crucians. The object of the society was to provide benefits which were not ordinarily available to them. The society, a mutual benefit one, appears to have been based on the Friendly Society structure of Barbados. In view of the opposition to the Danes of St Croix and of the price which Reginald paid for that opposition, it is somewhat ironic that 64 years later, on 25 July 1986, his eldest daughter, Nita Barrow, should have been invited by the chief secretary of the Danish Peace Foundation to be one of the 'Eight Eminent Women' selected to form a council 'to inspire the participants of the Foundation and to the degree possible, to give the Foundation ideas. The Council would preside over the Forum of the Foundation.'

When Nita's father was transferred to St Croix in 1920, the family consisted of four children, Graham, Nita, Ena and Errol. The last two, like Nita, were born in Barbados, Ena at the residence attached to the Alleyne School and Errol at The Garden in St Lucy, a property of the O'Neal family. Sybil, the fifth and last child of the family, was born in St Croix.

The first school attended by Nita was of course in St Croix. It was privately owned and run by a Miss Lada. It was called a dame school.[8] Nita remembers Miss Lada as being always attired in a white high-necked blouse and a black skirt. There were about 20 children in the school, one of whom was her older brother, Graham. Nita could only be separated from Graham on school mornings by coercion. Indeed it was this attachment which caused her to be formally entered as a pupil of the dame school the day after she celebrated her fifth birthday, although her parents may have intended her to begin school at five years old anyway.

Having received a sun bonnet as part of a new outfit for her birthday, Nita insisted on accompanying Graham to school the following day with the clear intention of showing off the newly acquired decorative wear. When she reached the school, she was unable to separate herself either from her sun bonnet or from her brother. She therefore remained and became enrolled into Miss Lada's school and continued there until the family's return to Barbados.

The compulsory exodus of Reginald Barrow from St Croix did not result in the financial distress of the Barrow family which one would normally have expected. Ruth Barrow's father, Joseph O'Neal, had died in 1920, leaving to his daughter, Ruth, a property in Barbados.[9] It was this property which Ruth sold and with the proceeds bought a three-storey property in St Croix in the commercial area of the city. With the residue from the sale and from the rental income from part of the property, Ruth was able to maintain her family for the next four or five years. The family therefore did not return to Barbados until it was decided that the four young Barrows should be given educational opportunities which were not available in St Croix.

On their return to Barbados the Barrows set up residence at Park Lodge in Bridgetown, a property owned and occupied by widow Catherine (O'Neal). The social demands of the time and the requirements for an assumed and possibly spurious gentility, even among the very poor middle class, required that daughters of middle- and upper-class parents should not be educated with girls supposedly socially inferior. Otherwise stated, in educating middle-class girls, care was taken that they were not exposed to influences or associations which might in later life become embarrassing. It was quite in order for sons of middle- and upper-class families to go to school with the sons of the less privileged, but not so the daughters.

There were a few private schools run by young women, themselves middle-class, white, brown or black, who through necessity or lack of other opportunity or vocation, undertook to provide a form of education which included much of what is now provided by primary schools and the lower sections of secondary schools. Such an education was considered adequate for girls whose future lay in the few opportunities available at maturity. There were a limited number of jobs as clerks in the Bridgetown stores of the dry goods merchants of Swan Street, such as O.R. Grannum and R.S. Nicholls. Similar jobs in the more prestigious stores of Broad Street were reserved for white, or nearly white, young women. Jobs in the mercantile community being therefore reserved for the privileged few, the more popular sources of employment open to middle-class blacks were teaching and nursing. Failing those two occupations, marriage remained a possibility, but marriage for young women and teaching could seldom be combined successfully, for as soon as there was evidence of a family being started, the mother-to-be was required to resign her post. Similar rules applied to nursing. On becoming married a nurse-in-training was required to resign; if she was a graduate nurse then there was little hope of her holding a senior position.

One of the private schools in Bridgetown for white children was owned and run by the Ince sisters, daughters of a successful merchant of Roebuck Street, Bridgetown. The education provided seemed to bridge both primary and secondary. Known as the Grassfield School, it was probably the most commodious private school of the time with accommodation for 100 day pupils and 18 boarders. It stood on 4 acres of land, 3 acres of which were given over to lawns for tennis courts and other games. In 1921 its buildings and grounds, abandoned by the owners, became the one and only site of the St Michael Girls' School, now the St Michael School. Other private schools for brown and black girls included those of Miss Grannum, Miss Cumberbatch, Miss Bellamy and Miss Nella Taitt. Miss Taitt was the daughter of H.F. Taitt, a black businessman of some substance and standing in the community, being also a member of St Michael's vestry[10].

Nita's mother, Ruth, and her aunt, Inez, had both attended as fee-paying pupils the prestigious Queens College, established in the early 1880s as a first-grade secondary school mainly for the daughters of rich white families. Ruth was determined that her daughters should attend the same school. Since entry of pupils was not then limited to the age of 11 years, as is the case today, she felt that the entry of Nita and Ena to Queens College could be delayed until the family finances improved. Ruth and her family were being partially supported by income from the rental of properties inherited by Catherine from her late husband Joseph. Ruth's sense of independence and concern for her children's future eventually led her to leave the five young Barrows with their grandmother and seek employment in the USA.

The two young Barrow boys, Graham and Errol, were sent off to Wesley Hall Boys' (Primary) School under the management of its Headmaster, Rawle Parkinson. Parkinson had introduced a new educational philosophy into his school. The ideas were those which Parkinson had learnt in 1912 when, together with two other prominent and progressive black citizens, Washington Harper and Elliot Durant, he visited the Tuskegee Institute in Alabama, USA.

The Tuskegee Institute was providing an education for black people which taught that the acquisition of saleable skills, together with training of the intellect, were necessary as initial steps to real freedom and more than a tenuous striving towards manhood. The institute taught that a man was half a man who could only use his hands, that a real man must be skilled and resolute in his actions and in his purpose. The ideas of Booker T. Washington and the institute took root in Barbados through Parkinson.

Within a couple of years, Wesley Hall Boys' School had become famous not only for the three Rs taught along with history and geography, but for the skills of printing, brush-making, shoe-making and tailoring which had been added to the curriculum. Every boy had to learn one or more of those skills.

Nita and Ena were enrolled at Miss Taitt's school and Sybil attended Miss Bellamy's school which catered for younger children. Within 2 years, however, both Nita and Sybil had become 2 of the 79 girls who were the first pupils of the St Michael's Girls' School. This new school had filled the need for a good secondary school for the daughters of the less wealthy, for black and brown girls. The fees would be less than those of Queens College.

Ideas about the need for more educational opportunity had become associated with those about the meaning of freedom, real freedom, freedom to aspire, freedom to achieve by one's own efforts. Such ideas would alarm the plantocracy and the members of the merchant class rulers, the virtual owners of Barbados. If genuine progress was going to be made in the society, then the real rulers would have to be made to agree or to accept the legitimate aspirations of the black people. But the new ideas were also about people's rights, for which some had risked or had given their lives during the recently ended First World War of 1914-18. Among those who had returned from rendering patriotic service was Clennell Wilsden Wickham. Within a year of his return, he had joined Clement Inniss at the *Herald*, a newspaper which, by 1924, had become a formidable force in the life of the island. It had worked in and out of season to arouse the political consciousness of the people.[11]

Because of the early death of Clement Inniss, Wickham became the lone scribe using his skills to inform Barbadians of the weaknesses of the social fabric and of the thinness of the veneer of civilisation which was effective in denying ordinary human rights to one section of the society. Wickham's methods did not always fall within the description of persuasion, for when necessary he would use his pen as a weapon, and with devastating effect; or he would apply it as a scalpel to the seat of incipient social gangrene. However, he never allowed his strong feelings about issues to cause his journalistic standards to be other than the highest.

Dr Duncan O'Neal, one of Nita's uncles, later joined Clennell Wickham. He had been more fortunate than Wickham in the benefits of his early life. He had been educated at Harrison College, the most distinguished secondary grammar school for boys in Barbados, where he had been placed second in the Barbados Scholarship in 1899. The Barbados Scholarship was the only scholarship which provided the winner with the opportunity to pursue further studies at a university in England. It also identified the winner for the remainder of his life as the outstanding scholar of his year.

Since Duncan had not won the coveted and prestigious scholarship, his mother, Catherine O'Neal, wished to have her son exposed to no less a quality of university education than that which the winner of the Barbados Scholarship had earned. Such thinking for many blacks would be over ambitious and unrealistic, but Catherine and her husband, Joseph, had worked hard and had prospered and were ready to make the necessary effort to ensure its realisation. Catherine had herself benefitted educationally from the persistent and sacrificial labours of her own Tobago parents, and so understood that social mobility and the achievement of a proper place in the sun could best be gained through education. Catherine and her husband therefore sought admission for Duncan at Edinburgh University where, he read medicine and where he distinguished himself as a Gold Medalist in Surgery.

On graduating, Duncan O'Neal set up a practice in Newcastle, England, where he saw poverty such as he had never seen before: poverty which deprived its victims of all self-respect, poverty which resulted in hungry children attending school in the depths of winter and where prostitution was not a social convenience but a livelihood. His sensitivity and commitment to assisting the less fortunate in retaining dignity led him to become a representative on the Sunderland County Council. Duncan, however, soon heard the call of home where there was equally important and similar work to be done among his own people. He therefore returned to the Caribbean and worked in Trinidad and Dominica before settling finally in Barbados in 1924.

Through discussion with Wickham and going through back numbers of the *Herald*, he came to see that the situation in Barbados had changed considerably during his absence. He learnt that quite a number of people were waking up and he saw the need for unifying the efforts of all those who were prepared to work for the new order. It was in the *Herald* office, and to Wickham, that O'Neal made the suggestion that was to lead to the birth of the Democratic League.

But there were also the thoughts and influence of the Jamaican Marcus Garvey, who virtually alone through his Universal Negro Improvement Association (UNIA) sought to unify the blacks of America, who even in the northern states of the USA were worse off and more badly treated than those in the West Indies. Garvey also sought to establish Pan-Africanism, the objective of which was to create a state in Africa for all blacks. As a black Moses, he taught that black economic power was the sole means of liberation for his people. The movement in the form in which it had caught the imagination of the blacks in the USA, never became popular in the West Indies, including Garvey's native Jamaica. The movement did, however, succeed in establishing a sense of pride in being black and in reducing the effects of persistent acts of degradation.

The period after the First World War was a time when a few blacks and browns were redefining democracy and attempting to make it more real to those who were not among the more privileged in Barbados. Besides the new thinking about democracy, led by the writings of Clennell Wickham and by the activities of the Democratic League founded by Dr Duncan O'Neal, there were other brown and black leaders in the community who had absorbed the teachings of Garvey or who had themselves discovered that it was possible to challenge the white plantocracy and wrest some of the political power from them. But blacks could only really be free if greater educational opportunities were available to them.

Among the black thinkers and potential leaders in Barbados in the early 1920s were John Beresford Beckles, Nathaniel Bullen, Christopher A. Brathwaite, Aurelius Washington Harper, Beresford Branford and his brother William, Nathaniel Clairmonte, and the brothers Duncan and Thomas P. O'Neal. All of these men, except Duncan, were engaged in business.

Duncan O'Neal appeared to be in no doubt about the price which he would be required to pay for his involvement with the poor and depressed people of Barbados. In material terms, his private medical practice would be reduced. Socially, he would be ostracised, regarded as a virtual outcast for associating closely with the poor. As Nita put it:

> Uncle Duncan turned his attention from a good private practice to look after the poor. I remember one of our matriarchs who 'held court' every afternoon, even after she had a stroke, saying 'he is a traitor to his class'. . . . I remember him much earlier being quite affluent. He lived in a large house in The Ivy[12] with a beautiful rose garden which he looked after himself. He lost all that when he began to champion the poor. He came to live at 'Park House' where he had his surgery. On Christmas he would himself cook enough to feed all who came, which to me seemed to be never less than 500.

Duncan had indeed become the champion of the poor and had early, that is, by June 1924 founded the Democratic League and was its first president. But those whom he championed had no vote. The franchise was at the time limited mainly to those with an annual income of at least £50. Duncan's anger and aggressive approach found favour neither with the white oligarchy nor with the coloured conservative professionals, including F.W. Holder, W.W. Reece, D. Lee Sargeant and E.R.L. Ward, all of whom became members of the house of assembly partly through the help of the Democratic League. They, however, did not join those who attached such damning labels to Duncan as Communist, Bolshevist and activist. In spite of the difficulties which his style caused him, he would not change it in order to gain votes, and he repeatedly failed to gain a seat in the house of assembly until 1932.

Beckles, Bullen and Brathwaite were among the first black men to seek and gain places on the vestry of St Michael through the annual elections which took place in January. In 1923 when Nathaniel Bullen was elected churchwarden, he moved a motion in the vestry that a secondary school for girls be established in Bridgetown. Such a revolutionary idea would require the support of some of the liberal white law makers, among whom was Sir Frederick Clarke, speaker of the house of assembly. To ensure that the proposal received the support of the house of assembly, it was important that the approval of as many of the electors as possible be clearly demonstrated. To this end, therefore, a meeting of electors was held at the YMCA hall in Bridgetown when the proposal met with overwhelming support. In addition, the dean of the St Michael Cathedral, Alfred Shankland, was totally involved in the ambitious undertaking. It is believed that it was he who influenced the Ince family to sell the property (formerly the Grassfield School) to the trustees of the proposed new secondary school for girls.

The school was opened on 7 May 1928, with Miss Helen Catlow as its first headmistress. Miss Catlow was supported by Miss Nella Taitt and Miss Norah Burton as senior assistant mistresses. Among the junior assistant staff was Nita's first form mistress, Miss Grace Thorne, later Grace Lady Adams, wife of Sir Grantley Adams, premier of Barbados and the only prime minister of the defunct Federation of the West Indies, and mother of the late J.M.G.M. (Tom Adams), the second prime minister of Barbados. Miss Taitt transferred her pupils to the new school, amongst whom were Nita and Ena Barrow. Miss Taitt's pupils therefore formed the nucleus of the new school. Miss Taitt later became one of the School's distinguished headmistresses.

During the 6 years of Nita's attendance at St Michael's Girls' School, her mother had emigrated to the USA and had taken Sybil, her last child, with her. When the family's financial situation improved, Ruth sought to have Nita and Ena transferred to Queens College where she had herself received her secondary education. As neither Nita nor Ena liked the proposal, they eventually managed to persuade their mother to forego that ambition.

The loyalty of the two Barrow girls to their school remains undiminished. In the school magazine, published to commemorate the first 21 years of the school's existence, is to be found these greetings from Nita:

> From Jamaica, I send greetings to my old school on its twenty-first anniversary. It is not good to begin with regrets, but I am sincerely sorry that time, distance, and other circumstances prevent my being there in person. As one of the oldest old girls of St Michael's, my years begin to weigh heavily when the laying of the corner stone, the opening of the school doors to us its first students, and now, the attainment of its majority unfold like a picture before me.
>
> St Michael's and its fine staff under such able Heads as Miss Catlow, Miss Cowper, and Miss Lucy Brown have had an immeasurable effect on my present career. It is pleasing to think, not only that some of the old staff still remain to shape the destiny of the school, but that many old girls have now joined them. We hope that girls of St Michael's School will, as they have done in the past, contribute in ever increasing numbers to the welfare of their community, for, to paraphrase an educator, the wealth of a nation depends on the advancement of its women.
>
> It is obvious that in the West Indies of tomorrow, the women must play a leading part in the struggle for progress. May the next twenty one years of the school's life be even richer and fuller than the first have been in the preparation of future West Indian citizens.

Nita completed her secondary school career at St Michael's School in July 1934 after successfully writing the Cambridge School Certificate, in which she gained a Grade I standing. Having been invited by the headmistress to act as a junior assistant mistress, she taught at the school for the next two terms, that is, until the end of March 1935. On 1 April 1935 Nita became a student nurse at the Barbados General Hospital.

---

1. Barbados Police, *Magistrate's Returns*, 1847.
2. Morris, Robert, 'Father of Democracy in Barbados', unpublished research paper, 1980.
3. Richardson, B., *Panama Money in Barbados, 1900-1920*, University of Tennessee, 20.
4. Harlow, Vincent, *Christopher Codrington*, Hurst & Co., London; St Martin's Press, New York, 2nd impression, 218.

5. Dookham, Isaac, 'Search for an Identity, Political Aspirations and Frustrations', *Journal of Caribbean History*, Vol. 12, 21.

6. Lewis, Gordon K., *The Virgin Islands, a Caribbean Lilliput*, Northern University Press, 1972, 45.

7. Boyer, William, *American Virgin Islands, Human Rights and Wrongs*, Caroline Academic Press, Durham, NC, 1983, 129.

8. Joseph O'Neal, in his will registered 7 January 1921, left £200 and a half share in 'Park Lodge', Bridgetown to his son Ebenezer; the other half to widow Catherine with ¼ acres land in St Peter and the dwelling house 'Nesfield' in St Lucy. To Inez Forde, 'Westneath', a property at the corner of Whitepark Road and Chapman St, Bridgetown; 'Wave Cottage' in St James to Ruth; £50 to Duncan whom he had already educated at Edinburgh University.

9. The vestry was a kind of local government at the time.

10. *Builders of Barbados, op. cit.* 118 *et seq.*

11. A suburb of Bridgetown.

First Day set of stamps of 25th anniversary of independence of Barbados

Dame Nita leaving Houses of Parliament after inauguration ceremony, accompanied by E.L. Sandiford, Mrs Sandiford and Lt.-Col. Deighton Maynard

Dame Nita with section of guests at reception after inauguration as Governor-General

Front and rear views of Codrington College, Barbados, where Dame Nita's father studied theology

2
Nurse-in-training

Before the changes which took place in Barbados and other parts of the British West Indies following the social unrest of 1937-40, there were few opportunities for employment open to educated blacks. Social mobility and success were possible only through the professions, such as medicine, engineering and law. Even engineering was effectively closed, for on graduation from an overseas university, employment still had to be sought from a local engineering firm, owned and managed by whites, who were not yet ready to accept any but whites amongst them. For blacks and browns who had been fortunate enough to pursue secondary education to the limit available in Barbados, the employment available was confined to teaching, mainly in primary schools, and the civil service. There were more openings in the civil service for men than for women, as Barbados was still perhaps the most sexist among Caribbean communities. The few stenographers or female clerks in the government service were white or light brown. The opportunities for black women were therefore even more limited still than for black men or white women.

The nursing profession, although it had not yet been designated as such, or elevated to that status, was attractive to many girls who had completed primary school and who would have done well in secondary school, but who had been denied the opportunity because they could not pay the fees. In any case, there were not enough second-grade secondary schools for girls in Barbados in those days. Apart from the St. Michael's Girls' School, which Nita Barrow had attended, there were spaces only in the Alexandra and Codrington high schools, which then attracted mainly the daughters of the wealthy whites. The only first-grade secondary school for Barbadian girls in those days was Queens College which also tended to be elitist. There were, however, a few girls who had managed to obtain a secondary education and sought to enter the nursing service. Among them were the Barrow sisters, Nita and Ena.

In her choice of a career in nursing, Nita was not supported by her uncle, Dr Duncan O'Neal, who was at the time an elected member of the House of Assembly and a member of the board of trustees and directors of the hospital. What he could not convey to his niece was that the inner workings of the Barbados General Hospital were fraught with difficulties which had nothing to do with commitment to study or performance of duty. Most of these difficulties were associated with the attitude on the part of the white Barbadian and English staff that any black person performing a service for a wage was, in effect, rendering servitude a remnant of the slave and master relationship of a period less than 100 years past. Injustice towards and humiliation of nurses and trainee nurses were openly practised. Duncan had been present at board meetings when accreditation had been unjustly withheld from a nurse who had successfully completed her five-year course of training.[1]

Nita also received little encouragement from her mother, Ruth, in her search for employment as a nurse-in-training. Being the pragmatist that she was, Ruth recognised that the death of her own father, Joseph, 15 years earlier and the enforced absence of her husband, Reginald, had deprived her children of sources of advice which would have been most useful. Living and working in the USA did not make it easy for Ruth to give advice to her eldest daughter on the choice of employment or career. Nita recalls that her mother, though not enthusiastic about her choice of career, nevertheless recognised the importance of self-confidence as a stimulus to achieving a full life. Ruth therefore said to Nita, 'I know a little about nursing as a career. One thing I shall insist on, is that if you enter the course, you shall finish it.'

Ruth's charge to Nita, almost a warning, was not given without sound reason. Ruth knew of the difficulties of the five-year course, mainly the conditions of service, which had led some young women of ability to quit the training without completing the course. They had found the accommodation poor and other conditions unsuitable and degrading. Indeed, having been attracted to the profession as a result of a discussion with Maggie Sealy (now Williams), Nita owed her persistence with the five-year training programme not only to her own determination, which faltered when the bad effects became almost unbearable, but to the encouragement of Eunice Griffith (now Chandler) who was Nita's first ward sister and supervisor.

On the very first day of duty on the wards Nita discovered that there were duties required of her which seemed to her to have nothing to do with gaining knowledge about caring for the sick. She was called upon to sweep the floor of the ward to which she was posted. Nita considered herself competent, if not expert, in the art of sweeping and thought that she would finish the job in no time, especially since she did not like doing it in a public place. On one occasion Eunice, the ward sister, was looking on somewhat amused at Nita's genuine, though amateurish, efforts, and being unable to remain silent any longer, said to her: 'Little nurse, you are holding that broom like a tennis racquet. Let me show you how to sweep under and around the beds.' Later when the going became really tough and Nita began to despair of becoming a trained nurse, Eunice encouraged her to remain and not to quit like some of her trainee colleagues.

The Barbados General Hospital was managed by a statutory board, the board of trustees and directors. Its responsibilities included the employment of professional and ancillary staff. Its membership was, *ex officio*: the bishop of Barbados, the president of the legislative council, the speaker of the house of assembly, the attorney-general, the solicitor-general, and about four other members of the house of assembly or vestry of the parish of St Michael. The day-to-day running of the hospital was the business of a subcommittee of the board, that is, the house committee which included the senior medical staff, resident and visiting, and about half of the members of the board of trustees and directors.

The composition of the board of directors and trustees had changed little since 1839 when the management was vested in a court of trustees and directors named at the meeting of the 'Inhabitants of the Island' held in October 1839 to form the Barbados Hospital Society for Relief of the Sick Poor. Incorporated in 1840, the society's name was soon changed to the Barbados General Hospital. In 1965 a new hospital replacing the general hospital was built on the present site at Martindales Road, Bridgetown, and was named the Queen Elizabeth Hospital.

As a first entrant in training Nita became what would nowadays be called a trainee or student nurse, clearly indicating her status. But such a dignified term was not then used. The student nurse was designated a probationer. The regulations for nurses which existed in 1935 when Nita became a probationer were not much different from those summarised below after they had been revised in January 1938. The regulations defined the status of nurses. Probationers were those who were in the first and second years of training; those of more senior years were third-year and fourth-year nurses-in-training. The term nurses was applied to those in their fifth year; a trained nurse was one who had successfully completed the five-year course.

Fixed rates of pay, an improvement on the previous system, were 18s. ($4.32) per month for probationers and 24s. ($5.76) per month for those in their third and fourth years. The nurses received £2 1s. 8d ($10).[2] It would be difficult to find an adjective suitable to describe the wage of 14s. ($3.36) per month which a probationer received in 1924. This was the salary which Eunice received as a probationer. Eunice outlined other conditions of service during the mid-1930s.

> All nurses, whether in training or not, were required to reside, 'live in'. Until 1938, when the George Nightingale Home for Nurses was erected,[3] nurses were accommodated within the hospital in dormitories which were open areas with no provision for privacy. In order to begin daytime duty at 8.00 a.m.,

breakfast was served at 7.00 a.m. That meal on two days of the week would be salt(ed) fish cakes, bakes[4] and a cup of tea; on the other five days it would be simply biscuits and tea. Eunice recalls that the bakes were often uncooked in the middle, when she would 'peel' hers, leaving the uncooked inner portion on her plate. The evening meal was invariably split peas and rice, and salt(ed) fish, except on Sundays, when chicken was substituted for the fish. Fresh green vegetables, except for the occasional banana, were not part of the diet. A nurse or probationer whose relatives could manage to do so, would on Sundays, and sometimes during the week, send a small basket with a snack or a substantial meal to the 'gate' of the hospital where it would be collected and its contents shared with peers. Nita's brother, Errol, often performed the role of messenger bearing a basket of 'goodies' which would serve to punctuate for Nita and her colleagues, the regularity of the monotony and proverbial tastelessness of hospital fare. The 'goodies' often consisted of a substantial meal of peas and rice and fried pork, a popular Sunday meal.

According to the shift, or rota arrangement, the day duty might end at 2.00 p.m. or 4.00 p.m., when a period of off-duty began. Whether off duty or not, all nurses had to be on the hospital premises by 9.00 p.m. Absence, if detected, would result in a fine. Nurses on night duty were permitted to be off the premises from 9.00 a.m. to 12.00 noon, after which time they were required to be in the dormitory resting until they prepared to go on duty. There was no chance whatever of avoiding the compulsory rest period. The senior nurse in the dormitory, who would herself be on night duty, was responsible for securing the door of the dormitory. She would lock the door of the dormitory and put the key under her pillow.

The 9.00 p.m. curfew imposed an unnatural, if not an unreasonable, limitation on the freedom of the active young nurses and nurses-in-training who must have often felt their freedom so curtailed as to consider their lot not much different from that of prisoners, especially on Saturday nights. But youth will establish its own priorities and balance a penalty against the illegal benefit. Eunice relates how fond she was of dancing. Although in the mid-1930s, there were not many social clubs in Bridgetown, the few that existed, as well as the cricket clubs, often held dances at the Drill Hall on Saturday nights.[5] The dances hardly got started before 8.00 p.m. Eunice neither explained nor did the writer ask at what time her escort conducted her to the gate. She did confirm, however, that although breach of curfew was not commonplace, she was not alone in circumventing the rules.[6] Nita was not asked about her views or action on this matter. Protocol and regard for the dignity of the post currently held by Nita precluded such questioning. What we do know is that Nita still enjoys a turn or two on the dance floor.

The meagre salaries of nurses and those in training was never their take-home pay. The probationer's salary of $4.32 per month was subject to deductions. The amount of 2s. (48 cents) was deducted monthly and placed in the Nurses Institution Fund. A nurse's contribution was usually returned at the end of the training period or when she left the nursing service. The remaining 16s. was often reduced further. In order to encourage careful use of equipment, fines were instituted for damage to, or loss of, hospital property. It was indeed possible to receive no salary at the end of a month simply because the fines exceeded or were equal to the monthly remuneration. Nita recalls that: 'Quite often one would sign for one's salary at the end of a month, but actually receive no pay at all. For a broken thermometer a trainee was charged 6d (12 cents); for a broken bed pan the amount deducted was 18s. ($4.32).

Nita tells the story of a probationer colleague, whom she met one afternoon returning from the hospital secretary's office where salaries were paid. Nita was herself on her way to receive hers. Noting the look of despondency on her friend Dolly Gittens' (later Lady Springer's) face, Nita asked: 'How much did you draw?' Back came Dolly's reply: 'I only drew my breath!'

But fines were not imposed for loss or damage of hospital property within the wards only; the practice was extended to the Nightingale Home, the nurses' hostel where nurses were also fined for loss of, or damage to, items in the hostel, including plates broken supposedly while in use in the dining room. There was at least one occasion when all the nurses in residence at the hostel had 2s. 6d (60 cents) deducted from their pay for plates which had been broken during the month. Apparently no allowance was made for the possibility that some of the breakages might have occurred in the kitchen. On returning from the paymaster with her small salary reduced by the amount deducted, a penalty which Nita considered she did not merit, she went into the kitchen, took up a plate which could then be bought in any city store for 6d (12 cents), went outside, placed it on the ground, and with the aid of a large stone, broke it while remarking to her amazed colleagues and onlookers: 'That is my plate which I have been charged for and which I have now broken!' Needless to say, many of them followed suit.

It is surprising that Nita was not charged for leading a rebellion. A few months earlier, 20 nurses had protested against a change of rota, the lateness of communication and the manner in which they had been informed of the change. The matron had, contrary to established custom, simply sent an oral message about the proposed change by a probationer to the nurses a couple of hours before the time for change of duty. The nurses had already made arrangements under the existing rota.

The incident was probably more of the nature of aggravation of the low status forced upon them than the real cause for the confrontation. The matron, an Englishwoman, was known for her low regard for local staff. It was quite common for English whites on arrival in Barbados to find themselves absorbed into sections of the local white society where they associated with socially superior people. They made pathetic attempts at copying their new associates' attitudes. Their newfound social status seduced them into mistaking a crude display of snobbery and colour prejudice for patronage so that they ignored the subtleties which avoided confrontation.

The 20 nurses wrote a letter to the board of trustees and directors about the matter. Such action could not be encouraged nor tolerated, so the matron suspended the leader of the protest. During the discussion of the matter by the board, one white professional member of the committee deemed the action rebellious and deserving of dismissal. The nurse in question would have been dismissed had not D. Lee Sargeant and Charlie Elder, two brown men, not intervened. Indeed, when they asked for a full investigation of the part played by each of the nurses, the chairman, threatened to resign and himself supported the proposal for dismissal. However, Dr Phillips, MLC (later Sir Randall Phillips, president of the legislative council) a man secure in his status and well-known for his sense of justice and humanity, intervened and proposed the penalty of one year's loss of seniority instead. The bishop lent his support to Dr Phillips' proposal, a more equitable approach which also appeared to recognise the right to protest. It was eventually agreed that the penalty should be the loss of one month's salary.

The medical staff of the hospital during Nita's five-year training period included doctors who practised what is today called family medicine and exercised a competence which would probably surprise many specialists today. Included among them were Dr Gerald Manning, Dr Bancroft, Dr J.A. Massiah, Dr Harold Johnson, Dr Bertie Carter and Dr Harold Skeete. All were white, non-resident and visiting staff. The permanent posts included the senior house surgeon, usually an experienced person recruited from England, junior house surgeons, visiting surgeons, an ophthalmic surgeon and specialists in nose and throat (ENT) radiology and dental surgery. Among the doctors appointed first as junior house surgeons were Dr Phil Edwards of British Guiana (now Guyana), the 1932 and 1936 800 metre Olympic bronze medalist, Dr A.S. Cato (now Sir Arnot Cato), Dr Lionel Stuart, Dr A.S. Ashby and Dr R. Charles of Dominica. The salary of a house surgeon was £325 p.a. or per annum ($130 per month), that of the matron £250 p.a. ($100 per month) and sisters received £175 p.a. ($70 per month).

Nita was soon joined at the hospital by her younger sister, Ena, and by Ilene Stewart (Murray-Ainsley). Ilene recalls the rigid routine especially in nursing patients who had fever. In those days, when living standards were lower and there were not many homes with water toilets, there would be occasional outbreaks of typhoid fever in spite of the efforts of the members of the sanitation department. When these outbreaks occurred, the demands on the hospital staff, especially the nurses, were extreme particularly since there were no antibiotics.

In the hospital system, where monetary rewards for services rendered by staff were so small, status met the human need for greater recognition and recompense. Seniority, real or imagined, became more important than it might have been. As Evelyn Francis (Lady Standard) put it: 'In those days if someone walked through the Hospital gate-way just ahead of you, so long as you did not see them entering, that person was your senior.' The nature of the responsibilities thrust upon nurses in training and qualified nurses required that seniority be real and acknowledged. Evelyn Standard confirmed that the responsibilities which senior trainees were required to undertake were similar to those which today would only be undertaken by a ward sister. Evelyn also recalls that having entered as a probationer two years after Nita, she was very much Nita's junior and did not look forward to the time when she would inevitably have to work with her. The latter's reputation for hard work and high performance had evoked from one of the junior trainees a comment not intended to give encouragement to the lazy: 'That Nita Barrow, she is a hard person to work with, my dear, she does work too hard, she will kill you with work.' It was not usual for a new trainee during the first six months of her training to be required to undertake night duty on a firm rota. The senior trainee who was in charge of a ward during the night would have a very junior probationer as her assistant, or in today's parlance a "gofer", more euphemistically called at the time a "runner". The "runner" would not necessarily be allocated to one ward, but was often expected to serve two or more.

Around midnight on the first occasion when Evelyn was runner, working with Nita, Nita said to Evelyn: 'Nurse Francis, a snack is there for you.'

Evelyn replied: 'Thank you very much Nurse Barrow, but I do not eat late at night.'

Nita made no comment and since there was no one else to whom the refreshment might be offered, the late snack remained uneaten. On the second night, at about the same time, Nita once again informed Evelyn that there was a late supper snack prepared for her. Evelyn once again with some dignity declined the offer, saying: 'Please, Nurse Barrow, I do not eat late at night.' Nita, while appreciating Evelyn's concern for the welfare of her digestive system, clearly indicated that Evelyn's priorities needed some rearrangement. She therefore quietly but very firmly said: 'Listen to me little nurse, you will eat at night if you are working with me, because you have to work; if you do not, then the next thing the nurses will say is that I starve you out.'[7]

'So,' says Evelyn, 'I had to eat at night. I survived.'

The night duty shift ran from 7.30 p.m. to 6.30 a.m. without any period off duty. Since supper was served at 7.00 p.m., the long periods did require that nurses on duty should have a snack during the night. The snack provided from the kitchen was called 'nourishment' and was prepared in the nurses' kitchen. It consisted of a hunk of bread (only) and coffee. The portion allocated to each nurse on night duty was put into a small basket owned and provided by the nurse. Whoever gave the name 'nourishment' to the tasteless and monotonous fare had a strange sense of humour.

The five-year training course had been designed and approved by the Barbados Nursing Council which had some time earlier agreed that the training then provided was inadequate. The council had sister-tutors, trained in England, whose main responsibility was supervising the training of the hospital nurses. Other islands in the Caribbean had their own training schemes, but there appears to have been no inter-island exchange of ideas or methods on the subject and therefore no common standards. Such would come later, much later. Among the fully qualified nurses or sisters recruited from England were Miss Purvis, Miss Fletcher, Miss Pocock and Miss Jones. Later Miss Nora Cotton, from Canada joined the staff. They were all referred to as supervisors.

Resident and visiting senior doctors gave lectures from time to time. There was, however, no real midwifery training in the programme. The trainees during their last year attended lectures at the St Michael Almshouse and were required to assist in a stipulated number of deliveries at the same institution. It was to the maternity wards at the almshouses in the island that many of the poor women went to give birth to their babies. If there were abnormalities or pre-natal difficulties, then the expectant mother would be transferred to the general hospital. If the mother-to-be preferred to have her baby at home, she might engage the services of an itinerant midwife whose fee was about 60 cents.

The arrangement for providing training in midwifery at the St Michael Almshouse seems to have been haphazard, for during 1935 the matron had reported to the hospital board that the nurses were very keen to do midwifery, but no classes had been held at the St Michael Almshouse for the preceding three years. The absence of a proper midwifery course at the Barbados General Hospital within the five-year training programme had been a source of dissatisfaction to the nursing council for some time. Since there appeared to be no local means of improving the situation, the Barbados Nurses Association had made arrangements with the Trinidad General Hospital whereby graduate nurses from Barbados could undertake a six-month attachment there, during which they would study midwifery. At the end of the period they would return to Barbados.

Having received all the training that was available, Nita and those who had completed the five years of training with her thought that they should receive their certificates of training. They therefore requested them of the matron. It was not the practice of the hospital authorities (in effect, the matron) simply to hand over certificates to those who had earned them. That would never do. The newly qualified nurses must not be so easily allowed to assume any dignity associated with professional status. Such pride in achievement might excite their ambitions and make them unmanageable. To avoid such disruption of the existing matron/trainee relationship, the newly qualified nurses must be made to await the pleasure of the hospital administration, and that with much fear and trepidation. They must be made to show due gratitude for the privilege of having been trained. Another possible reason for withholding certificates might have been to ensure that graduate nurses remained at the hospital, for they could not be employed elsewhere at any of the local almshouses, nor outside Barbados, without having certificates of training.

Neither the matron nor the sister tutor had anticipated the reply which they received from the nurses when they were asked why they wanted their certificates. The answer was simply: 'We want them because we have earned them.' Such a reply was not acceptable to either of the two English women. The matter eventually reached the hospital board which no longer had only white Barbadians as members. Oppression and colour prejudice or bias could not be openly displayed as in previous years. Nor could reasonable demands of the kind made be ignored as before. Since no proper reason could be given to the hospital board for denying the certificates, the board directed that the certificates be prepared and handed to those qualified to receive them.

Once again it seems that the direct method used by Nita and some of her peers in dealing with the vagaries of authority introduced an element of surprise which the matron had some difficulty in handling. Only a few months earlier, a nurse who had been offered a post at the St Michael Almshouse had been denied her certificate by the acting matron, also an Englishwoman. The nurse had appealed the acting matron's decision in a letter to the board of trustees and directors. Without the certificate of qualification the nurse could not be appointed to the post offered. The acting matron confirmed to the board that the nurse had completed her five-year course and that she had passed all the prescribed examinations, but that she would give the nurse no certificate. Her contemporaries, Nurses M. Byer, C. Lavine and M. Sealy, who had also completed their courses had been given their certificates. Nurses were growing tired of this kind of callousness and whimsical behaviour.

Nita's successful completion of five years of study at the Barbados General Hospital was an achievement worthy of celebration, as it was to her colleague Grace Thorne. Deciding to make an occasion of the award of the certificates, they organised a presentation ceremony, a graduation entertainment, and invited all of those who had lectured them. It was the first graduation ceremony of Hospital Nurses held in Barbados.

It is somewhat ironic that because of the war, opportunities became available to blacks in the West Indies. As a direct result of the war, English trained ward sisters were no longer available for employment at the Barbados General Hospital as supervisors. The hospital authorities therefore turned to Canada for nursing supervisory staff.

One of the first Canadians to accept an offer and serve in one of the ward sisters' posts was Miss Nora Cotton, who was a post-basic graduate student of the School of Nursing of the University of Toronto, where she had met students from Latin America and from other countries, pursuing post basic courses in Public Health and Teaching. All or most of them had been sponsored in their training by the Rockefeller Foundation, based in the USA.

A short time after completing her training at the hospital, and before she went off to Trinidad to begin her midwifery training, Nita discussed with Miss Cotton ways and means by which she might enter a programme of advanced training. Miss Cotton mentioned her contact with the School of Nursing of Toronto University and of her admiration for the school's innovative approach, led by the Dean of Studies, Dr Kathleen Russell. In her search for further training, the idea that she should consider going to Canada had not entered Nita's head at all. It had long been an established custom in all fields of professional study that education or training beyond that available in Barbados should be sought in the UK. Because of the war, Nita could not travel to the UK nor gain financial assistance from the UK Colonial Office for the kind of programme she sought. In addition, the hazards of travel were very real. For all these reasons, therefore, Nita's dreams of advanced training would remain dreams, or so it appeared at the time.

The possibility that she might benefit from a Rockefeller fellowship as nurses from South and Central America were doing caused Nita to write to her uncle, Ebenezer O'Neal, who had many years earlier emigrated to the USA. Nita told Ebenezer what she had learned about the support which the Rockefeller Foundation was providing for citizens of other countries for advanced training. Ebenezer made enquiries and learnt that the foundation had up to that time only awarded fellowships to nurses from Latin America, but that they would consider a formal application from Nita. Nita submitted an application to the foundation and went off to Trinidad to begin her six-month midwifery course.

The Rockefeller Foundation's reply to Nita's application came within a week or two of her return from her training in Trinidad. The foundation requested that she go to Trinidad to be interviewed by one of their staff members or associates, Dr Dowens, head of the epidemiological unit there.[8]

Once again Nita travelled to Trinidad. There was no such thing as a commercial flight. Inter-island travel was done by schooner, sloop, or one of the ships of the Canadian National Steamship Co., *Lady Nelson*, *Lady Drake* and *Lady Rodney*, which sailed between Canada and the West Indies. If schooner or sloop were chosen, then a day and a half's adventure with the sea, salt spray and meals of fish could be anticipated. If one were subject to motion sickness, travel became a miserable experience undertaken with resignation and some fear. If a 'Lady boat' were available, the length of the adventure – or ordeal – was reduced by about 12 hours. The extra cost of a cabin would provide some comfort. Otherwise, people travelled 'deck' or 'steerage'. More often than not, it was by 'deck', where comradeship in adversity led to the sharing of food and drink among total strangers. During the night the demands of sleep and the discomfort of unaccustomed exposure to the chill temporarily made all equal and a neighbour's blanket or body warmth were shared.

The 'Lady boats' brought from Canada lumber, salt fish and other commodities to Barbados and to many of its island neighbours. They also provided a means of shipping freight between the islands. On their return trip to Canada, they would take Barbados rum, some sugar and other agricultural products. The 'Lady boats' served the Caribbean islands well. Their loss during the war, mainly through enemy action, was very real.

Nita gained a Rockefeller Foundation fellowship to take a course of post-basic nursing education at the School of Nursing at Toronto University. Once again she travelled to Trinidad by a 'Lady boat'. In order to reach Canada she had to travel by air first to the USA and then take another flight to reach her destination. During the few days of her stay in Trinidad, awaiting the plane which would take her to the USA, Nita was enrolled by Miss Phyllis Haslam, the secretary of the YWCA, as a member of the Trinidad Young Women's Christian Association (YWCA), at the Bishop Anstey High School in Port-of-Spain. The very new Trinidad branch of the YWCA had established close links with the YWCA of Canada. Nita's enrolment would become useful when she became settled. There were YWCA facilities near the university which she was able to use when she became an associate member of the local YWCA. From such an ordinary beginning in Trinidad, Nita has had a long and active involvement in the work of the YWCA.

In the early 1940s (the war years) there were no regular commercial flights in the Caribbean. On leaving Trinidad, therefore, Nita's flight took her to Haiti, where for some reason, she was delayed for a few days. Instead of being taken to New York on the next leg of the flight, she was taken to Miami, a place where - until the early 1970s – no black West Indian would choose to spend any length of time. In Miami there were only two hotels available to blacks, the Elizabeth and the Mary Dawson. Nita went to each in turn and found them not quite what she had hoped. Fortunately, her friends the Procopes in Trinidad had given her the name and address of a Madame McNeil, who usually lived in Chicago, but who resided in Miami and accommodated paying guests during the colder months of the year. Nita appealed to Madame McNeil and was accommodated in the guest room of the McNeil household. But here Nita came face to face with the incivility of southern American racial prejudice and the extreme damage done to the self esteem of non-white people. She would experience, at first hand, assaults by the uncivilised, mainly American citizens, designed to degrade all blacks. No subtlety was used in the application of the degradation and inhuman treatment visited daily on the members of her race by the white people of the southern USA.

Nita experienced an incident of precisely the same kind as took place 14 years later on 1 December 1955 in the state of Alabama, and which precipitated protests which eventually led to integration (real or otherwise) in the American South. On that occasion, the insult was directed towards Mrs Rosa Parks in her own country and in her own state. Because she refused to sit in the back of a bus, she was prosecuted and fined.

Madame McNeil provided lodging accommodation at her home for Nita, but could not conveniently arrange to provide regular meals. She therefore told Nita of restaurants where she would be served. One day after leaving a restaurant she went to the bus terminus nearby, entered a bus, paid the fare and took a seat near the front of the bus as she would have done in any island in the Caribbean. The driver took his seat at the appointed time but did not move the bus. Instead he kept repeating: 'Go to the back of the bus.' Not realising that the driver was addressing her, Nita paid no attention. The driver eventually left his seat approached Nita and said: 'I cannot move this bus until you go to the back.' The affront to Nita and the assault on her sensitivities did not induce the fear intended. In defence of her pride, she replied sharply: 'The back of the bus is full.' Whereupon the driver extended towards her the dime fare which she had paid on entering the bus. 'This is yours,' he said. Discomforted by the whole incident, Nita suggested: 'You can keep it.' With that, she got off the bus and walked away.

Nita related the incident to Madame McNeil, who became quite alarmed and told her that she had indeed not only exposed herself to the injustices of the law and the indecencies of the uncivilised whites of the South, but that she had endangered her very life, for blacks had been killed in Miami and elsewhere in the southern USA for a lot less.

In 1986, just after Nita had taken up the post of Resident Representative of Barbados at the UN in New York, she was invited to attend the American Jewish Committee meeting in Miami. Her brother Errol was also invited to attend and witness the presentation to her of an award in recognition of her contribution to peace, with special reference to the Nairobi meeting the previous year. Nita could not resist saying to Errol: 'You would not think that this is the same city where I got off a bus and left my ten cents fare because the man said that I could not sit in the front of the bus.'

Arriving in Toronto, Canada, in the autumn of 1941, Nita found the weather cool but her reception from the West Indians who had preceded her or who were resident there was warm. Her meeting with Ivy Baxter, Eugenia Charles (Dame Eugenia) and Ivy Lawrence (Maynier) turned out to be a meeting of about one-third of the female members of the West Indian component of the student body of the University of Toronto. Ivy Baxter was studying physical education under the sponsorship of the

Canadian YWCA; Eugenia Charles was pursuing a degree before going to London to read law. The other female West Indians resident in Toronto at the time were Gloria Cumper and Muriel Carpenter (Carnegie). Except for Eugenia Charles, who was Dominican, and Ivy Lawrence, who was a first-generation Canadian, born of Trinidadian parents, all the others were Jamaican.

The West Indian students, possibly because they were very much a minority group, became closely knit. Some West Indians who had taken up permanent residence in Toronto virtually turned their homes into meeting places for male and female West Indian students. One such home was that of Mr and Mrs Charles Mills. Mrs Mills, formerly Ray Jordan, was Barbadian. She was a close friend of Donald Moore, a Barbadian who initiated the formation of the Home Services Association which was dedicated to assisting West Indians in getting to Canada, the new land of opportunity. Much later, in 1950, the association became very involved in promoting the emigration of West Indian nurses to Canada, where many of them subsequently settled. Donald Moore lived for more than a century and had the rare honour of attending many functions in 1992 to mark his 100th birthday. He is still highly regarded in Toronto as the father of all postwar West Indian migrants. Another home which was open to the few resident West Indians was that of Rev. and Mrs Reynolds, whose daughter Betty became one of the first black nurses to be trained in the Toronto General Hospital.

That the Rockefeller Foundation, an American body, assisted students of nursing from third world countries to study in Canada and not in the USA requires some explanation. The School of Nursing of the University of Toronto was one of the very few institutions in North America at that time that provided a comprehensive training programme in post-basic nursing and which also accepted an applicant's certificate in basic training done outside Canada as an entry qualification. Among the programmes available at the school was one which led to an undergraduate degree, combining liberal arts with nursing education. The four-year programme was the brain child of Dr Kathleen Russell, Director of the School of Nursing. Another programme was available to post-basic students which qualified them for leadership positions in the profession. It was this pioneering approach to education in the nursing profession which had encouraged the Rockefeller Foundation to provide funding for the training of nurses from countries outside Canada who would in time hold positions of responsibility in institutions in their own countries.

Since Nita had already done five years' training in Barbados, she was permitted, based on an assessment made of her knowledge, to enter the School of Nursing to take the one-year course in public health, which was identified as a need in the Caribbean. She was due to return to Barbados at the end of the 1943/44 academic year. But that was not to be. At the end of the year's training she was one of three international students invited to speak at a gathering of students and other members of the university community. Nita chose a theme for her speech related to the training of nurses in Barbados and to the practice of public health there.

Nita briefly identified Barbados' geography, topography and people's origins. The island of 166 square miles with a population of over 200,000 people was one of the most densely populated places in the world. She gave a brief account of social and administrative changes which were taking place. For some, living was extremely pleasant, but unfortunately the chief industry, sugar production, made for seasonal employment, and therefore many people were unemployed for a portion of the year. This did not make for a reasonable standard of living for the majority of the people.

On public health, Nita said that there was much yet to be done, although there was some social and health legislation, including compulsory primary education. However, bad housing conditions and extreme poverty rendered much of the education ineffectual. Referring to some of the work of the Barbados Registered Nurses Association, founded seven years previously, Nita mentioned that some of its members had volunteered to give of their services for one month without remuneration, in rotation, throughout the year. Private subscriptions and annual flag days had subsequently provided funds for the venture and had made possible the payment of a nominal salary of $30 per month to the volunteer nurses.

Miss Tennant, adviser to the Rockefeller Foundation on the training programme for nurses, was on a routine visit to the School of Nursing in Toronto and was present at Nita's lecture. She was also aware of Nita's good performance as a student. After the lecture, Miss Tennant invited Nita to meet her the following day, when she advised Nita to apply to the foundation for a second year of support in order to undertake the nursing education programme which prepared students for teaching and administration.

Before Nita took up the Rockefeller Foundation Fellowship, it had been expected that the newly created Colonial Development and Welfare Corporation (CD&W), based in Barbados, would provide her with employment at the end of the one-year training course.

Miss Tennant's proposal therefore presented Nita with a difficulty. There was no formal commitment to CD&W on her part. It was her own opinion and that of her advisers that it would be unwise to forego the unique opportunity offered for further training. Nita therefore accepted the foundation's offer of sponsorship for a second year and enrolled for the 1944/45 academic year. At the end of the academic year, Nita was advised by her sponsors to spend one month doing field work in Jamaica to observe what was being done in public health training there. Nita found the experience very enlightening. The conditions in Jamaica were quite different from those in Trinidad or Barbados. The areas in Kingston and in the rural districts, where the less privileged lived, were quite depressed.

At Toronto University, black and brown West Indians appeared to experience little or no colour prejudice. In the School of Nursing there was one other black, Ruth Dash from Meharry Medical College in Tennessee, apart from Nita, from a small island in the Caribbean. Ruth Dash was also taking the one-year course in nursing education. Their training included instructing Canadian trainee nurses. The resulting situation was as much a learning experience for Nita and Ruth as it was for the Canadian trainees. The tolerance developed among the racial groups was considered low but not superficial. There were incidents in the community based on colour prejudice but nothing similar had occurred on the university campus and its environs.

Nurse Chatterjee, an Indian who was taking an undergraduate programme, and Nita fulfilled an invitation one evening, as international students, to address the Women's Medical Society at the Granite Club. After the lecture Dr Marion Hillyard invited them to her flat for refreshment. When they returned to the nurses' residence very much later than expected, they found Ruth Dash and another student sitting on the steps quite concerned. They had imagined that Nita and Nurse Chatterjee, might have had some unpleasant experience based on colour prejudice. This concern was not unreasonable, for a few weeks previously, Marion Anderson, the famous black American contralto singer, had been refused permission to sing at the same club, allegedly because of her colour.

Having completed her training in May 1945, Nita thought that she had earned a vacation and went off to Trinidad to visit her cousins there, intending to follow up the vacation with a brief visit to her native land, Barbados, in order to view the prospects for employment. Nita's Trinidad visit coincided with the end of the war in Europe and with the local celebrations of V-J Day on 14 August 1945. While enjoying the celebrations she received a cable from her cousin, Hugh (later Sir Hugh) Springer stating that the Rockefeller Foundation had made her an offer of the post of Assistant Nursing Instructress at the West Indies School of Public Health in Jamaica. For good measure and in case Nita found the carnival atmosphere of Trinidad irresistible, Hugh reminded her that acceptance of the offer should be taken seriously. Hugh's advice was taken.

Public health training in the West Indies was not new, but it had not previously received the attention which it deserved. Health care, as a preventive approach, had been limited more or less to the maintenance of good sanitation, especially in and around homes. There had been courses of three or four months' duration for those who were at the time designated sanitary inspectors and were all men. There had never been any formal training of female personnel, that is, nurses who served communities outside hospitals. The term public health nurse was new and was probably applied for the first time in the Caribbean to the graduates of the West Indies School of Public Health.

1. In January 1934 a qualified nurse was offered a post at what is now a district hospital, subject to her certificate being submitted. The acting matron, an Englishwoman, refused the nurse her certificate. But for the intervention of the board of management a great injustice would have been done.
2. Minutes of the Board of Management.
3. The George Nightingale Fund was established from the sale of the property of his brother David Skeete Nightingale according to the latter's will (1928). The fund would be divided equally among the general hospital, the Goodrich Home and the St Paul's Soup Kitchen.
4. Bakes is the Barbadian term for a batter of flour, sugar and baking powder fried in oil.
5. The Drill Hall was the large recreation room of the Barbados Volunteer Force (military).
6. In January 1938 the attention of the board was drawn to the discrepancies existing between the gatekeeper's (guard) record of nurses' re-entry on Saturday nights and that of the nurses themselves.
7. 'Starve out' is a Barbadian colloquialism meaning 'undernourished' or 'hungry looking'.
8. From about 1919 the Rockefeller Foundation had been providing technical and financial support for the improvement of public health in the Caribbean. One of the first programmes supported was the eradication of yaws in Jamaica. Somewhat later was the establishment of the Epidemiological Unit in Trinidad.

3

The Jamaica Years

The appointment of Nita Barrow as assistant instructress at the Public Health Training Station in Jamaica was in direct response to a recommendation of the Moyne Royal Commission which enquired into the disturbances during the period 1935-37 in the British West Indies.

The commission recommended that a medical adviser for the West Indies should be appointed who would undertake the unification of the medical services. The Commission stated:

> We are impressed by the fact that very few West Indian nurses hold senior positions in nursing services. We consider it a real grievance which should be remedied as soon as possible. The present training of nurses in small hospitals and their accommodation and condition of service are . . . unsatisfactory.
>
> It would be far better to have a few good training centres in large hospitals with adequate residential quarters. Above all, a good type of sister tutorship should be appointed and a training syllabus of lectures and practical work suitable to the health conditions of those colonies should be carefully arranged at each centre.
>
> Particular attention should be paid to preparing student nurses to assume responsibility by gradual promotion to higher grades. We also recommend that a few scholarships should be instituted to enable those nurses, who have shown such skills and especial capability, to take training overseas. The registration of midwives and formation of Nursing Boards are also important matters which in the colonies should be given attention.

The establishment of a school of hygiene was also recommended.

The British government hastened to repair as far as possible its neglect of its subjects in the Caribbean by passing the Colonial Development and Welfare (CD&W) Act of 1940, under which a fund was set up. A headquarters with qualified and experienced staff for the administration of the fund and services was established in Barbados.

Nita Barrow assumed her new post as assistant instructress in September 1945, but was soon called upon to take on much more serious responsibilities than she had been employed to undertake. The nursing instructress of the institution was Mrs Mary Wolfe, a Canadian, whose husband was a commissioned officer in the British regiment stationed in Jamaica. He had been recalled to England just before Nita arrived to assume duty as assistant instructress and so Mrs Wolfe had left the island too. As a result Nita was given the responsibility for the training of public health nurses as well as for part of the training of public health inspectors. Fortunately, Mr Smith, the Scottish instructor of the public health inspectors, was still there. Together with Frank Gordon Somers, an experienced Jamaican member of the staff, they both gave her all possible support to ensure that she did not falter for lack of the local expertise that they possessed.

In Kingston there were only two hostels organised as residences for young working women, one run by the Methodist church and the other attached to the YWCA. The phenomenon of young women leaving their homes in the rural parishes and migrating to the city of Kingston in search of employment was not new. Most of the new arrivals tended to live with relatives or friends because other accommodation was scarce or too expensive.

When Nita arrived in Kingston to take up her new post, she found that by coincidence, her younger sister Ena was also there attending a course in midwifery at the Jubilee Hospital, there being no such course available in Barbados. She had recently completed the training programme in public health. Ena was preparing to take up the post of matron in charge of the Public Health Centre in St Vincent in the Windward Islands. She was based at the YWCA hostel in Kingston but unfortunately at the time there was no available room there which Nita might occupy. Such an obstacle could not overcome sibling affection nor the inventiveness of Marjorie Stewart, a native of the UK and general-secretary of the YWCA of Jamaica. The patio of Marjorie's bedroom was rearranged temporarily to accommodate a bed for Nita, who shared a clothes cupboard and other facilities with her sister. This continued for a few weeks until a suitable room fell vacant when Nita settled in as a resident of the Kingston YWCA hostel.

This renewed contact with the YWCA and the ready response of its administration to the needs of young women caused Nita to associate herself more closely with the day-to-day services and activities provided by the association. She soon found herself a member of some of the committees, a member of the board of the Kingston YWCA and shortly thereafter chairperson of the local branch. Not long afterwards she was elected vice-president of the Kingston branch of the YWCA.

Nita also became a member of the Council of the Jamaica YWCA, the national body. It was at about this time that Lady Foot, the governor's wife (later Lady Caradon) and president of the Jamaica YWCA thought that a Jamaican should become the general-secretary of the Central YWCA in succession to Gwen Panter whose secondment from the

YWCA of Great Britain was about to end. Sister Jessie Kerridge, the Methodist deaconess resident in Jamaica, who was also a member of the YWCA council, had first hand knowledge of Carmen Lusan and her voluntary work and recommended her as a suitable candidate. If Carmen was found acceptable, however, she should receive some training before taking up the post. Carmen Lusan was at that time president of the Girls' League of Jamaica. She was an active church leader in the Lyndhurst Methodist Church, Kingston, and a committed voluntary social worker.[1]

Some of the other members of the YWCA council thought that Carmen might not be attracted to the post of general-secretary since the remuneration attached to the post would be far less than that which she was probably then receiving in the public service. Such opinion, however, did not deter Lady Foot and Sister Jessie Kerridge from approaching Carmen.

The approach was timely, because Carmen had herself been thinking about how she might become a full-time social worker. The post she held in the government service was really a temporary one. It was one of several created in each of the islands of the British Caribbean during the Second World War to meet the additional special services required by the wartime emergency. Many of those posts in Jamaica, like similar ones throughout the Caribbean, remained temporary for some time after the war had ended, though some were later added to the permanent establishment.

Carmen's initial reservation about the offer did not last after she had discussed the proposal with Nita. The latter was enthusiastic, not only because Carmen would be a worthy successor to Gwen, but also because Carmen's appointment would be clear recognition given to a Jamaican and acknowledgement that a West Indian could perform in the post of general-secretary of the YWCA in Jamaica. Carmen accepted the post and went to Great Britain for training.

The Kingston branch of the YWCA, like that in many cities in other Caribbean islands, not only provided a home for some young women, but assisted in their development which enabled many of them not only to survive, but to also to excel. Joyce Robinson, a distinguished Jamaican, summarising the role of the YWCA and the social structure of Jamaica 50 years ago, describes her own experience with the YWCA in these words:

> the 1940s was a critical period when young men and women were expected to be of mature understanding and be involved in some activity outside their homes. In 1940, I was a teenager, young and impressionable. I have a clear memory of people of influence making things work, of them giving willing voluntary service and of my coming into contact with the YWCA.
>
> I had come to Kingston to go to secondary school. Not that secondary education was not available outside of Kingston, there were indeed Grammar Schools in some parishes, for example, St Elizabeth, but those (Munroe College for boys and Hampton college for girls) were for the sons and daughters of the whites and wealthy blacks and browns.

Secondary education for some of the children of ambitious parents was therefore sought in Kingston where there were private secondary schools of varying quality. Probably the two most popular and successful were St Simons and Excelsior College.

The social situation in Jamaica in the late 1940s was not much different from that in other West Indian islands. In terms of educational opportunities, most young people completed their education at the primary school level. Secondary education was available to those few who could afford to pay the fees required by secondary schools, or who were fortunate enough to gain places in those schools through the few scholarships available and for which hundreds of primary school pupils competed annually. Perhaps the hardest lesson in discrimination learnt by the young people in secondary schools was the exclusion of the private secondary schools from the secondary schools inter-schools sports and games competitions. It was similar discrimination which forced private schools to seek common ground and unity. It was partly to help some of those schools that the YWCA allowed some of their pupils the use of their grounds.[2]

Since much of Nita's involvement with people has been made through her voluntary work with the YWCA and other organisations with branches all over the world, a comment made in 1972 by Michael Manley, former prime minister of Jamaica, about the role and function of voluntary organisations in a developing society is particularly applicable. Manley considered that:

> whatever the motivation (for persons participating in voluntary service in a community) it is the tradition of intrinsic value and one which can be organised and mobilised to great effect in a strategy for change. In the presence of such a tradition, for example, the appeal for volunteers to man a national literacy campaign has an instinctively receptive audience because it is part of the tradition of the society to respond.
>
> Where resources are limited and the tasks immense, no society in search of justice through democratic means can afford to ignore the voluntary spirit. Furthermore, the spirit is not only of value as a factor which can be mobilised to work for change, but is itself a creative avenue through which men and women can express their instinct for service. When the more and the less privileged of the society come together on a project like literacy or work together to provide an infant school . . . they educate each other in the dynamics of social unity.[3]

Because of the limited resources available to the School of Public Health, real success could only be achieved if executive, administrative officers and staff were innovative and resourceful. The school suffered from inadequate funds for the purchase of equipment and supplies, insufficient teaching space and irregular maintenance. By example Nita taught everyone to cut and contrive and yet maintain quality. When classroom space became scarce, she showed them that outdoor tree shadow was plentiful, available and suitable.

Training in public health was delivered not only in the classrooms and under the trees at the Kingston site for students. There was also in-service training for those staff members already working in the field. Together with her assistants, therefore, Nita travelled around the island to the health centres supervising and teaching staff. It soon became clear that there was a need for a demonstration project in a rural area to support the practical teaching of the Public Health School in Kingston. The Rockefeller Foundation had agreed to fund a new building to be erected on a site near to the Spanish Town/St Jago Health Centre, quite near to the then newly built hospital.

In order to gain field practice, the health workers in training at the School of Public Health were required to perform complete public health activity under supervision. The Spanish Town/St Jago district was selected as suitable and convenient with its moderate-sized town and surrounding villages and small communities, some of which extended into the hills. One community was a small Rastafarian group (Rastas for short), small in number, living in virtual isolation on the Pinnacle, so named because it was part of the mountainous area nearby. The isolation had been forced upon them by the residents of the town who found their way of life unusual and disturbing. The Rastas were made to feel quite unwelcome by the town dwellers and by other village people. Acknowledging that it is human to fear what is not understood, Nita nevertheless thought the action was inhumane and in discussion with her assistants and students she called it 'a lot of foolishness'. Further inquiry into the ways of the Pinnacle dwellers proved that they were a law-abiding and closely-knit group. They probably did grow and smoke marijuana (commonly called ganja in Jamaica), which they considered part of their religious practice. They were industrious. Some of them came to market every Saturday to sell their agricultural produce, mainly peas and their handmade goods (rubber slippers) made from discarded motorcar tyres.

The time came for the Rastafarian group to be immunised. Offering the respect which any self-sufficient and industrious group deserves, Nita sent an advance party to get permission for herself and the immunising team to enter the compound, but they first had to pass a sentry at the entrance. Having obtained the required permission, they found the compound to consist of a clearing in the centre with individual dwellings, including a school, surrounding it. The residents were summoned by drumbeat. The community seemed well organised. Everyone was quite courteous and readily agreed to participate in the immunisation programme. After further amicable association with the Rastafarians, the health team found it easy to provide them with antenatal care and to introduce them to other preventive and community health practices.

Later Nita was able to identify the layout of the compound as basically African. The Rastas showed their gratitude and appreciation for the services provided and for the genuine respect which they had received from the visiting health team. The leader sent gifts of peas regularly to the team of nurses and kept them fully supplied with wood for their stove.

Nita's concern for the social difficulties which this nonconforming group experienced has never been forgotten. Without any prompting she has time and again returned to the subject, as follows

> I learnt much about the local culture from the people. I could not just walk in and start immunising. I had to try and learn what social behaviour was acceptable. Their display of several multi-coloured flags was part of their symbolism. In one or two cases I witnessed their dances, one of which I related to Ivy Baxter who identified it as a ritualistic healing dance.

Ivy Baxter, one of the earliest Jamaican choreographers, had only been able to identify 12 Jamaican folk dances. Some 40 years later, she expressed regret that she had not done more research on the origin of the dances, as Beryl McBurnie of Trinidad had done in her own country. Nita also remembered her professional visits to other Rastafarian communities like that at Trench Town in West Kingston where her students and health personnel thought that they had found Pocomania, which like Shango in Trinidad appeared to be closely related to religious rituals in some parts of Africa.

Simultaneously with the expansion of the health services, with which Nita was so involved, the British government introduced formal or organised social development. The less privileged people of each island of the Caribbean had from time to time benefited from forms of social concern from other members or groups of the society. Such assistance could be regarded as a kind of charity. What was being introduced had no claim to being charity, but was part of the improvements for which West Indian governments would have responsibility, with the support of trained professional and experienced personnel and funds from the CD&W fund. Professor Simey and Ms Dora Ibbotson were appointed from the UK to develop social welfare courses. Ms Ibbotson was based in Jamaica, where she came into contact with Nita as she trained her students and health workers in the field and led them to practise in depressed areas of Kingston, such as Tivoli Gardens, the Dungle and Denham Town among the cardboard boxes and discarded motorcar bodies, some people's only shelter. Dora's students were selected from among adult Jamaican and other West Indian men and women with demonstrated interests in the field of social welfare.

In 1950, having served for five years at the West Indies School of Public Health, Nita was offered a CD&W fellowship to Edinburgh to do a sister tutor's course. The one-year programme was arranged by the Royal College of Nursing in Scotland. The programme would introduce Nita to the British system of training. Part was taken at the Faculty of Medicine of Edinburgh University and part at Moray House Teacher Training College also in Edinburgh. Fieldwork was done at Queen's

University in Ireland. One of the most profitable periods, at the end of the year, was six weeks under the auspices of the International Nursing Council, which soon after the end of the Second World War had arranged with nursing associations in Scandinavia and Finland to provide travelling fellowships for nurses who were suitably qualified. The six-week experience provided opportunities for the study of advanced training in public health and in the administration of schools of nursing. During her stay in the UK Nita was awarded one of these fellowships, which enabled her to visit hospitals in the host countries. The programme of the fellowship was coordinated by the International Nursing Council and accommodation was provided by the host institutions. The recipient was only required to meet the cost of travel.

The one-year stay in Europe provided other experiences for Nita. The YWCA in Jamaica, which was affiliated to the World YWCA, was entitled to be represented at council meetings of the world body. One such meeting was due to be held in Beirut, Lebanon. The Jamaica association was unable to pay the passage as well as meet the other costs of a representative. Since Nita, a member of the Jamaica YWCA council, was at the time resident in the UK and therefore virtually halfway to Lebanon, the Jamaica YWCA nominated her as its representative to attend the meeting of the world council. Costs of travel were met by the World YWCA.

This world council YWCA meeting was the one at which the democratisation of its management began. Up to that time the council had included a disproportionate number of people of wealth and influence, including members of royal houses in Europe and women of means from other countries, all of whom made substantial, financial and other, contributions to the world organisation. They were deeply committed to the purpose and values of the YWCA. However, those same members recognised that if the appearance of patronage was to be reduced or avoided, a real attempt should be made to include on the council people who would be more representative of the rapidly growing worldwide membership. In order to meet this new objective the membership of the council was expanded. The process thus begun at the world council meeting in 1951 resulted in West Indies associations being represented at the next world council meeting in 1955 by four persons from Jamaica and one from British Guiana.

The council meeting also provided Nita with her first contact with apartheid in South Africa. There were two YWCAs in South Africa, one of which endorsed apartheid and in consequence had been denied representation on the world council some years earlier, and the other, which was multiracial, had become affiliated to the world body. During the council meeting in Lebanon one black woman, Mrs Maidie Hall Xuma, and one white woman, Mrs Agnes Neilson, both from the YWCA in South Africa which had admitted black members, were invited to address the council about the situation of the YWCA in their country and how the movement might be assisted. Mrs Xuma was a social worker through whose initiative black young women had formed themselves into Zenele or self-help clubs. The clubs later became part of what is the world-affiliated YWCA of South Africa.[4]

Mrs Xuma had begun work among black girls in townships because they needed the training in basic skills which was provided by YWCAs all over the world. She discovered that the YWCA branch in Durban, led by Mrs Neilson as its president, was willing to accept the Zenele clubs as associates. This was done and survived, even in the most difficult days of apartheid and the enforcement of the Group Areas Act, to provide the thrust needed for rapid advancement of blacks in the new South Africa. Seeing the need to have a national YWCA affiliated to the World YWCA and which would serve all sections of the community, the multiracial branch applied for affiliation to the world body and was successful. It was from the effort to form that multiracial association that the YWCA's involvement in the lives of black women in townships grew and provided not only training in basic skills supportive of self-development and independence, but moral support during the dark days of apartheid before the new day dawned.

On her return to Jamaica Nita was appointed sister tutor at the Kingston Public Hospital (KPH). It was also a time when basic training in nursing was under review. The system of training of nurses required that a trainee should spend part of her first year or part of both first and second years at a hospital in a rural area. The remainder of her training was done at KPH. The system therefore unintentionally supported varying standards of training which were directly related to the standards of hospitals and in turn depended upon the interest and competence of the medical officers and matrons of those hospitals.

The new methods placed responsibility for training on the newly-appointed sister-tutors: the English women, Misses Morrison and Felstead and Gertrude Swaby, the first Jamaican sister-tutor, and Nita. Thus what had previously been more or less apprenticeship entry to nursing became a system of nursing education and training. KPH effectively became the training centre for nurses. It was at KPH that the nurses for University College Hospital of the West Indies (UCHWI) were trained, since immediately after its establishment it also became a training centre. As Nita put it:

> there were two training schools of general nursing. One at KPH, the other at the University College Hospital. It was an exciting period because we were all working to show what could be done when people worked together. We, the Tutors had the overall responsibility for patient care as well as for the teaching, that is, for the classrooms as well as for the wards. There were blocks of time in the classroom and blocks of time on the wards. It all contributed to the students' education rather than to their training.

In 1954 Nita accepted the post of matron of the five-year old UCHWI, succeeding Miss Margaret Foster-Smith, the English matron who had been the first holder of the post. Before taking up her position, however, Nita was provided with the opportunity of visiting teaching hospitals in the UK from a temporary base at Guy's Hospital, London.

University education in the West Indies and in other former British colonial territories is less than 50 years old. The sad fact is that, historically the UK did not pay much attention to university education, even at home. It was not before the Education Act of 1902 that the government began to focus with any seriousness on tertiary training. It was long felt, indeed, that secondary education should be reserved for the élite and was entirely an individual and family matter. In any case, the limits put on the ambitions of the subject peoples of Britain for higher education were severe, whether intentionally imposed or not.

At about the time when the recommendations of the Moyne Commission's report were being given careful study in the West Indies and some were being implemented, another royal commission, chaired by Lord Asquith, was considering advanced education for the British colonies. The commission was set up in 1943: 'to consider the principles which should guide the promotion of higher education, learning and research and the development of universities in the colonies.'[5]

The Asquith Commission's report recommended that university colleges be set up in special relationships with the University of London. That London University was chosen as the degree-granting university for this proposed new network of university colleges was not by chance. London University, through its awards of external degrees by examination, had for many years provided the only opportunity for many both in Britain and throughout the old British Empire, who had brains but no money to support travel to and residence in England, the USA or Canada to obtain degrees. By studying at home one could obtain a university degree after writing three examinations of London University: the London Matriculation Examination, the Intermediate Examination and the Final Examination. The home study programme could be guided by courses from one of the correspondence colleges in England.

Some abortive attempts to meet the need for higher education had been made in Jamaica. In 1926 the West Indian colonies had established a standing conference which had this subject on its agenda. Three years later the first West Indian conference urged further consideration of the establishment of a university in the region. In 1938 the Jamaica government set up a committee to reconsider the question, but this lapsed with the outbreak of war. In 1942, following a public meeting with P.M. (later Sir Philip) Sherlock as one of the promoters, an unofficial provisional committee was set up to make plans for a local university college. In 1943 a committee was formed in Barbados to consider the possibility of enlarging the curriculum of Codrington College, an affiliate college of the University of Durham, which had long served as the only institution of higher learning in the Caribbean, but had focused exclusively on the classics and divinity. In British Guiana (now Guyana), the University of London Association of British Guiana sent a memorandum to the Colonial Office advocating provision for higher education in the West Indies.

A committee under the Asquith Commission was set up to help effect its mandate in the West Indies. That committee took the name of its chairman, Sir James Irvine, vice-chancellor of the University of Edinburgh, and included amongst its members such scholars as Margery Perham, reader in colonial administration of the University of Oxford, Raymond (later Sir Raymond) Priestley, vice-chancellor of the University of Birmingham, H.W. (later Sir Hugh) Springer, lawyer and member of the Barbados house of assembly, and P.M. (later Sir Philip) Sherlock, secretary of the Institute of Jamaica. The committee visited the West Indies in 1944. It had been appointed to examine how, when and where a University College of the West Indies might be established. As a result of the commission's report, the British government helped set up the University College of the West Indies (UCWI) at Mona, Jamaica in 1948.

The first faculty to be established was medicine, which began teaching with 33 students in October 1948. One of the first requirements of the faculty was a teaching hospital. While English supervisory staff for the hospital was being selected, senior West Indian nurses were taking administrative courses at hospitals in the UK. Initially some 14 or 15 nurses selected from all over the UK were trained. Subsequently eight or nine of them were appointed to supervisory posts at the University College Hospital of the West Indies (UCHWI).

Needless to say, Nita's appointment as matron of the UCHWI, the first West Indian to hold the post, was hailed in Jamaica and the rest of the Caribbean with enthusiasm. It was another triumph for black West Indians, as well as another huge step forward for the women of the region. That in 1954 a West Indian should be appointed matron of the hospital, with all the authority and prestige associated with the post, was an achievement and a signal that the West Indies had come of age. What was also significant was that, as matron, Nita had among her senior nursing staff one assistant matron and nine ward sisters, all of whom were from the UK. To have a West Indian in charge of an institution where the first line of subordinate staff were white and British as well as West Indian was new not only for the Caribbean but throughout the so-called non-white segments of the British empire. The novelty of the situation and the surprise shown by visiting or resident professional persons sometimes could not be concealed.

Sir Thomas Hunte was a member, possibly chairman, of the board of medical examiners for the University College at Ibadan in Africa and of the University College of the West Indies. It was therefore his duty to visit the colleges periodically. Soon after Nita's appointment in 1954 she received notice of an impending visit from Sir Thomas. On the day and at the time appointed for his visit, Nita duly awaited his arrival. Entry to the matron's office was through that of the assistant matrons'. One English assistant matron, Miss Hay, accompanied Sir Thomas, knocked on the door of the matron's office and announced his presence. On entering, Sir Thomas said: 'I am looking for the Matron.'

Nita rose from her seat and said, 'Sir Thomas, I am she.'

In obvious surprise, he exclaimed 'You?'

Sir Thomas explained to Nita some days later before ending his visit to the UCHWI that the shock on entering her office on the first day was twofold, not only that he was surprised to find a West Indian in the post, but that he had expected to see a matronly-looking English woman wearing the traditional fall. Sir Thomas' expectations were not unreasonable, since he had first met an English assistant matron. He might also have been confused since Nita's uniform as matron of the Hospital little resembled the traditional white uniform with a fall. Nita wore instead a pale blue uniform and a small cap.

Professor Gerald Ovens, resident professor of the UCHWI and a distinguished orthopaedic surgeon, originally from Guy's Hospital, London, appeared rather distant during the first year of Nita's service. However, during the year he became more comfortable with and pleasant to Nita, and near the end of the year he invited Nita to dinner, neither out of duty, nor in condescension, but apparently by way of making amends for his initial aloofness and possibly feeling that he might have been, to say the least, ungracious and slow in acknowledging her professional competence. The following year, when Nita accepted the post of principal nursing officer of Jamaica, Ovens wrote her a letter in which he stated:

> I did not welcome you when you were appointed, I feared for the standards of the institution (UCHWI) because you were too young and you had had no experience of English teaching hospitals. Now you are leaving I cannot come to tell you good-bye. It may be a promotion for you, but it is a sad loss for the University College Hospital of the West Indies.

As the University College grew and faculties were added, the young male students — especially the medical students – began to take a considerable interest in the social life of the student nurses. The proximity of the nurses' hostel to the halls of residence of the university students was a challenge to the young people. As in all nurses' hostels, there were rules which controlled the time for return to the hostel in the evening. Initially, there were schemes to circumvent the rules, and the exuberance of youth or the excitement of romance caused many student nurses to return late. Sometime they could rely on their peers' assistance to help them regain entry. It was important to avoid being seen by the gatekeeper, whose duty it was to record the names and times of return of all those passing his post. Matron Barrow heard of these evening escapades and without giving notice had bars installed in the windows of rooms on the ground floor.

The male medical students designated the nurses hostel the "Bastille" in appreciation of, or frustrated by, the security measure.

The gatekeeper's book with its record of exit and entry of staff members and student nurses was placed on the matron's desk each morning. If a student nurse was shown to have returned to the hostel after the regulation time, she would be required to appear before the matron and say why a penalty for the breach should not be imposed. One might well imagine such a meeting between a nurse caught in the act and the matron. There would be Matron Barrow putting discreet questions and receiving too few answers. Answers might be fewer still if *esprit de corps* was likely to be violated. Matron Barrow's questions seldom received satisfactory answers. The sentence of confinement to the Bastille, which was basically the loss of off-campus privileges, for a number of evenings was often the penalty.

The government, with the assistance of the Colonial Office, continued its efforts to improve and expand the health services in Jamaica by creating the post of Principal Nursing Officer (PNO) to equate with a similar senior post in the medical section, that of Principal Medical Officer. A Sunday picnic, which included rafting on the Rio Grande River (Jamaica) was given by senior nursing personnel in honour of Miss Florence Udell, visiting Chief Nursing Officer of the Colonial Office, at which Miss Udell arranged for Nita and herself to be on the same raft. In that relaxed atmosphere Miss Udell introduced the subject of the newly created post of PNO. They discussed what the appointee would be expected to do and, what is more, that the person should be a West Indian. Further discussion included the existence and availability of qualified West Indians, among them Gertrude Swaby and Eva Lowe, both Jamaicans trained overseas. Eva Lowe was at the time the public health supervisor, a post she had taken up after training in the UK. There was one other person whose suitability Nita also mentioned, Evadne Bailey, who had been trained in the USA and was at the time a public health supervisor.

Miss Udell asked Nita if she would be interested. Feeling that she was not ready for another change, Nita indicated her concerns: 'I have been in my present post only two years and I am enjoying it. I have just begun to see the results of some of the ideas which I put to work.'

Miss Udell did not pursue the matter any further at that time, the discussion ended and attention was given to less serious topics.

Nita had not taken Miss Udell's inquiry seriously, but she later discovered how carefully she had disguised her more than apparently casual or mildly professional interest in securing Nita for the post. Nita was therefore very much taken by surprise when she was offered the post, which she accepted.

The creation of the post of PNO in Jamaica was a further step in the development of nursing services and in the public health of the country.

At the time there were two doctors in charge of 256 medical personnel, with the chief medical officer as the chief executive. Their work was mainly the practice of curative medicine. The duties of the PNO would include the supervision of over 3,000 staff members attached to 26 hospitals of varying sizes, from 20 beds to more than 300 beds, more than 50 health centres around the country, rural schools of nursing, midwifery and public health and a large psychiatric hospital with more than 2,000 patients. There were only three supervisors among the public health nurses, the most senior of whom was Eva Lowe, the chief public health supervisor.

Nita's objectives in this new post were the building not only of a more efficient nursing service, but also of an integrated one. In order to achieve this, she wanted to add to the staff at least another five supervisors to function as assistant nursing officers. There should also be a revised management structure which would divide the public health staff into categories according to their responsibilities and roles. For this there was no model either in the Caribbean or elsewhere to which Nita might refer. So once again in a new post she had the opportunity for innovation and for the introduction of new structures and procedures. Above all, she had the opportunity to improve the self-image of members of the nursing service and help them to achieve the dignity of professionals, this with external support including that from the newly formed Jamaica Nurses Association.

Her major aim was to change the nursing services from being divided into public health, hospitals and school health into a coordinated unit. A department of nursing it did become, with its nursing education at appropriate stages adequately differentiated into those for public health and hospital. Such a community approach to health services was to be usefully employed later when Nita undertook the task of evaluating the nursing services in the Caribbean.

There would be real difficulties in attempting to integrate the nursing services, since it had long been established by practice rather than by decree that nurses were subject to the direction of the medical staff of the hospitals, who viewed them as handmaidens. Indeed it was not unusual to find a nurse carrying a basin of water and a towel for a doctor's use as he made his rounds. Until fairly recently, the medical officers attached to hospitals not only in Jamaica considered themselves little deities and treated the hospitals as their private domains. They not only gave medical instructions, which was within their competence, but they also directed the matron in the general running of the hospital. They chose their favourite nurses to do certain things, some of which could not possibly have been part of any job description, had there been one. In Nita's attempts to improve the status and roles of the matrons, nurses and student nurses, she attracted the opposition of at least one medical officer and she had to indicate to him that each nurse, qualified or student, was a member of the nursing staff and was therefore responsible to the matron who allocated her duties. The officer, claiming proprietary rights, informed Nita that no one could come into *his* hospital and tell him what could or could not be done. In a firm, but level tone of voice, Nita assured the doctor that she was doing exactly that; further, that the matter was not one which any opinion of his could affect. The old-established and deeply rooted system of training used to be not much different from an apprenticeship, which fostered commitment of the trainee's time to service at the expense of study, training and qualification. Supervisory personnel, on the other hand, had the difficult job of trying to fill too many slots on a duty rota with too few nursing staff and, in effect, sacrificing suitability.

Nita's plan for the reorganisation of Jamaica's nursing education was to raise the entrance qualification (over a period of time) from the level of the primary school-leaving certificate to the Cambridge or Oxford and Cambridge School Certificate, which was in effect the secondary school-leaving certificate accepted in the British Commonwealth. All trainee or student nurses would undergo a general nursing course, including psychiatric care, public health, some obstetrics and gynaecological nursing. This programme would provide basic skills, to which she might add specialisations. The trainee nurse became known as the student nurse. Simultaneously with the new nomenclature came the introduction of student days in which the nurses studied in a school with regular lectures and with the supervision of a sister-tutor. The changes combined to improve and to shorten the training period for some from three to two years.

In order to achieve Nita's objectives of health care for all, the government of Jamaica agreed that there should be a health centre or hospital within eight miles of any village or small community. This could only be achieved by reorganising the services on a parochial basis, so that in any one parish there would be all the necessary services administered by one senior person of supervisory level whose job it would be to maintain and coordinate them.

The reorganisation and extension of the public health services required that funds be available for constructing new buildings such as hospitals, nursing homes and health centres and for repairing existing ones. Additional funding would also be required to meet the increasing day-to-day expenses. Included in the recurrent expenditure would be the cost of revision of salaries and purchase of materials as well as the provision of services associated with the delivery and teaching of curative and preventive methods. Other matters which would require attention included changes in procedures for making transfers and new appointments within the nursing service. Consideration had to be given to adverse effects which transfers of staff between posts might have on persons with family responsibilities. In addition, there was the human dislike of change to be considered.

Nita found fairly easy acceptance for most of the reorganisation. In 1956, at the beginning of her tour of duty, the budget for the nursing services was less than J$1 million. The next year's budget, prepared by Nita, was ten times greater, which alarmed the minister of health (Dr Eldermire), who felt that he could not present it to the prime minister and minister of finance, Norman Manley, without bringing down on his own head the latter's wrath. It was therefore agreed that Nita would be allowed to defend her draft budget at the estimates committee meeting at which the prime minister, as chairman and minister of finance, would be present. Nita's presentation and her powers of persuasion resulted in her budget being accepted. Manley had been persuaded almost against his will, but showed commendable vision in supporting a most important development for his people.

During the seven years of Nita's administration as the PNO in Jamaica, the number of health centres increased to about 100. In addition, with the strong support of the growing Jamaica Nurses Association, legislation requiring registration of nurses, including those in private practice and those employed by private companies, was introduced. With the support of ministers of health, the cooperation of the Chief Medical Officer (CMO), Dr Courtenay Wedderburn and the General Nursing Council a unity of service was created which produced a stability and sense of well-being previously unknown. Assistant nursing officers were given responsibility for supervision of a number of parishes. In each parish there was a senior nursing officer who was responsible for all public health nurses. But what was equally important in this improved training system was that training was not limited to student nurses only. Indeed, with the assistance of Pan-American/World Health Organisation (PAHO/WHO) personnel, awards were made to senior supervisory staff to take overseas courses in advanced nursing.

An experienced American nurse, Janet Thompson, graduate of Yale University, had come to the Caribbean area some years earlier and had since 1955 been resident in Venezuela where she had responsibility for a PAHO/WHO rural health project. At the end of that project, she had been offered and had accepted a post with the same regional organisation as nursing adviser in Zone 1 (the Caribbean). In that capacity her role was to examine the nursing services of the region and find ways and means of improving them. Janet understood that the system of training for nurses to which she had been accustomed in the USA was entirely different from that in the Caribbean. She also recognised that if the objectives of PAHO/WHO were to be achieved, there would have to be senior competent Caribbean personnel in the forefront of the action.

Janet had come into contact with Nita's work as PNO in Jamaica. She was also aware of the growing need for well-qualified and competent nursing professionals in the Caribbean region. Janet's knowledge of Nita and her work included the encouragement which she had given to senior nursing officers in Jamaica to take overseas training in nursing administration, public health administration and sister-tutor courses whenever and wherever such became available. Many of the fellowships through which senior nurses undertook advanced training courses were provided by PAHO/WHO. Those were tenable at Columbia University. Other fellowships were provided by the Colonial Office and were tenable in UK. Some fellows pursued undergraduate degrees, others postgraduate degrees. Among those who took the former were Gertrude Swaby and Eva Lowe. Eva proceeded to a postgraduate degree and later succeeded Nita as PNO of Jamaica. The idea that she herself should also have a university degree in nursing never seemed to have occurred to Nita. In the British system, which the Caribbean had inherited, there would be hardly any obstacle to Nita's continued professional progress, for besides her experience she had pursued post-basic study in Canada, the UK and in Scandinavia. But with the growing influence and interest of North America in the Caribbean, her competence might be questioned in future because she was not a university graduate. Such a deficiency might be regarded not as caused by lack of opportunity, but as based either on lack of discipline or of commitment to formal study.

To ensure that Nita did not suffer the indignity of having a less experienced and possibly a less competent nursing officer with a university degree supersede her in the Caribbean, Janet encouraged Nita to accept a fellowship in 1962 to attend Columbia University. At Columbia Nita gained credits for her previous training, including that in Canada and in the UK, and for her experience. She was therefore able to complete her degree in one year, the 1962-63 academic session.

Since Nita's career would now enter to an international phase within the Caribbean, it would perhaps be worthwhile to review briefly at this point the political changes which were taking place in the West Indies.

Before 1944 few aid or developmental agencies had shown any interest in the British West Indies, although the Rockefeller Foundation has already been identified as one which provided support for the development of health programmes. The foundation had assisted in the eradication of yaws, in Jamaica and elsewhere. In the early 1940s when the recommendations of the Moyne Commission were being implemented, the UK under its CD&W Act of 1940, and the WHO, for example, had been providing funds and personnel to assist in raising living standards and the professional competence of West Indians throughout the region.

Like some other European powers, the UK finally began to understand the demands for change made by her subject peoples after having mistreated them for so long. It also recognised that there was an opportunity to divest itself of those colonies which were no longer profitable, but which had become liabilities, requiring grants-in-aid for their day-to-day administration and costs of services. Directly and through the sub-agencies of CD&W, the UK provided the training and expertise required to support the aspirations and eventual independence of West Indians.

One of the results of the involvement of West Indians in the Second World War was the impetus given to the revival of a desire for genuine social change. These changes were not so much associated with the kind of social development already being implemented, but were in fact concerned with the fair and reasonable redistribution of the wealth of the individual islands among the people. Nita's work, especially in public health and in nurses' training in Jamaica, might never have been effective if it had not taken place within an atmosphere of political awakening.

The period 1958–62 witnessed the entire life-span of the Federation of the West Indies. The brevity of its life was not unexpected since during its gestation period it had already contracted the illness of the Caribbean, that of insularity. This is, in fact, the normal fate of island peoples. Separation from others, caused by geography, inevitably leaves an impact on their psyche. Thirty years after the demise of the Federation, attempts to unify the Windward and Leeward Islands have had varying degrees of success. The aim of the Federation of the West Indies, introduced and supported by the UK, was to convert the Caribbean islands group into one administrative and independent state. A federated group made up of Jamaica at the extreme north-west of the archipelago, together with the islands of the Leeward group, St Kitts-Nevis-Anguilla, Montserrat and Antigua with Barbuda; those of the Windward Islands group, Dominica, St Lucia, St Vincent and Grenada; together with Trinidad and Tobago and Barbados, was considered to be the best unit to facilitate the economic development and promote the survival of the West Indians in a highly competitive Western-oriented world.

It was doomed to failure from the beginning since the UK had always pursued a deliberate and short-sighted policy of divide and conquer within the territory. The various islands therefore existed as so many separate cocoons, having little to do with each other's life, culture, trade and politics. There was no effort (or even need) to cooperate, except on the cricket field, and in fact it was there, in 1886, that the idea of a composite West Indian team first took root. The cricketers gradually learnt how to pool their resources, but the politicians never did. The fact that the islands were too far apart geographically, before modern aviation, compounded the difficulty.

It is perhaps not as difficult as we of the Caribbean islands think it is for persons living outside the region to imagine or understand the petty jealousies which exist among the islands. Most of the latent animosities and trivialities associated with insularity and parochialism have their roots in the history of the region. The emotions are not much different from those which exist among the residents of other political entities, such as counties or states. The islands of British West Indies, from Jamaica in the north to Trinidad and Tobago in the south near the equator, form an archipelago of about 13 islands and subgroups of islands. With the exceptions of Martinique and Guadeloupe, each island became British either by so-called acquisition in the name of the British sovereign, as in the case of Barbados; or by conquest like Jamaica from the Spanish and St Vincent from the French. Until the 1940s each island was governed by a legislature, some of the members of which were elected under a limited franchise. The legislatures were unicameral in some islands, bicameral in others, all under a governor representing the British sovereign. According to the level of constitutional development (or more accurately, the whims of the metropolis), the powers of the elected representatives and those of the governor varied. The representatives were elected mainly from among planters, merchants and persons of some material substance.

Beginning in 1932 with the first conference of representatives of all the British West Indies and ending with the introduction of adult suffrage in the 1940s and 1950s, the several islands each gained a measure of autonomy and learned the intricacies of democratic government associated with the Westminster parliamentary model. Advances in social and economic affairs, however, did not keep pace with those related to the representation of the people.

In 1944 the first bicameral legislature was introduced in Jamaica, with the lower house (of representatives) elected on adult suffrage. Three parties contested the elections: Jamaica Democratic Party, of planter and commercial, mainly white interests; the People's National Party (PNP), representative of the middle class; and the Jamaica Labour Party (JLP), representing most of the disadvantaged blacks, mainly from the rural sugar-cane growing areas. The JLP, under Alexander Bustamante, who was also the head of the Trades and Labour Union, gained the majority of seats.

The next few years were turbulent, because the majority of the people had, through their representatives, the voice in government with which to protest their poverty but not yet the power to demand fair wages. Regrettably, the strike weapon was the only means available to those aggrieved for achieving their reasonable objectives. In 1947, therefore, the whole community suffered through the loss of 250,000 man-days and the 150 disputes between the trade union and sugar estates management.[6]

The 1955 elections in Jamaica were won by the PNP, led by Norman Manley, a distinguished lawyer of the upper middle-class-brown minority. Those elections were followed by the introduction of ministerial government, so that the representatives had at last the ability to make decisions for the people and to introduce programmes for change in the social structure and in the social services, including the health services.

In 1959, on the initiative of the then Federal Medical Adviser, a group of nursing administrators, educators and representatives of the General Nursing Council of England and Wales and of the Nursing Association of the Caribbean, met in Barbados. The purpose of the conference was to examine the standard of nursing in the region, including British Guiana, British Honduras and the Bahamas. Of the known 23 schools of nursing, only two were recognised by any professional body outside the region, namely the General Nursing Council for England and Wales.[7] This limitation made it difficult for most nurses to take up vacant posts in islands other than those in which they were trained or resident, usually their native islands. It also made the status of the graduate nurses of each school uncertain. There was clearly a need to determine the standing of each school of nursing and to regulate training to enable it to meet international standards and give the nursing profession the kind of fillip which it required.

There was never any intention of introducing fixed standards into the training of nurses in the Caribbean. It was thought best that there should be minimal standards which all the schools of nursing should meet. Each school would then be at liberty to develop higher and additional syllabuses. There should be no attempt to introduce a rigid system of training which would reduce a particular school's ability to relate its training to specific needs of the island or group of islands it served.

As a result of the recommendations of the 1959 conference (out of which grew the health ministers conference) an approach for funds was made to the Pan-American Sanitary Bureau Regional Office in the Americas Branch of the World Health Organisation (WHO) in support of improving the standards of training schools for nurses. Funds were made available in 1963 for the project, which would have as its first function the conduct of a survey of the existing schools of nursing. The team to conduct the survey of the 23 schools would consist of a project nurse, who would head the project, a zone nurse and a short term consultant. In addition there would be a cadre of regional visitors comprising 17 sister-tutors or matrons from the region, each of whom would, in turn, accompany the project nurse on visits and in that way become part of the survey team.

The Zone Nurse was Janet Thompson. She had the overall responsibility to PAHO/WHO for the project, which would include a review to take place at the end of the survey period. It is to Janet's credit that she recognised that West Indians should be involved in the examination of nursing education in the region. Indeed, it was clear that Janet had been on the look-out for persons competent in the field while carrying out her work in the region. She had been impressed by Nita's work in Jamaica and had been instrumental in helping Nita to attend Columbia University. From available evidence, it is clear that in doing so she was making it possible for Nita to be a leader of the project, which was due to begin in 1964. It was no surprise, therefore, when Janet recommended to the PAHO/WHO headquarters that Nita should be appointed as the project nurse.

As Janet Thompson had recognised the need to select a competent West Indian to lead the research or inquiry, so did Nita in her turn recognise her own lack of experience in participating in such a research project. Nita was also aware that there should be someone on the survey team with suitable experience in examining schools of nursing. She was therefore on the look-out for such a person, whom she discovered while at Columbia University. This was Dr Helen Mussalem,[8] a Canadian, who had successfully defended her thesis, 'A Plan for the Development of Nursing Education Systems of Canada', for a doctoral degree from Columbia University. Helen and a small group of her friends were in the university cafeteria celebrating her success, and as Helen herself recalled:

> When I left the group which had joined me at coffee after that memorable and successful event, a lady came up to me and said: 'I am Nita Barrow and I want you to come to the Caribbean to study our schools of nursing as you have done in Canada.'
>
> I have never forgotten that opening sentence nor the lovely person who was speaking to me. I replied, 'I am already committed to returning to Ottawa to work with the Canadian Nurses Association and also to return to my home in Vancouver.' I sat down for a few moments and Nita told me about the situation of nursing in the British West Indies.

Nita gave Helen a description of the existing UK system, which had been adapted for the training of nurses in the Caribbean and which was not really working to the best advantage of the West Indians. Nurses were clearly not being prepared to meet the needs of the region. Nita then identified the difficulties which she had met in the system.

After some exchange of views, Helen told Nita that she had been able to develop a plan for the training of Canadian nurses because she was herself a Canadian and knew about the education system of Canada and its impact upon nursing education. She then added: 'If you wish to have a survey done of the nurses in the Caribbean you will have to be the project director.'

Helen also recalled that: 'There had been a great deal written in Canada about Nita and her work in Jamaica, especially as Principal Nursing Officer there. I was therefore aware of her reputation as the leading nurse of the Caribbean.'

The most suitable guide for the proposed survey was the one of the Canadian Nurses Association which had been done about three years earlier and had been led by Helen. Nita and Janet quickly collaborated and secured Helen's services as consultant to the Survey team. Helen and Nita prepared the outline for the survey and visited the project for six weeks each year to advise and assist.

There had been surveys of hospitals and nursing institutions in the Caribbean region by senior British nursing personnel who had little or no knowledge of the region. The surveyors most certainly were under no obligation to divulge their findings to, or share them with, any Caribbean person. That the surveys were probably well done is not in question; but that the West Indians who had participated in and were themselves subjects of the surveys were subsequently ignored and often left to wonder about the findings and analyses is unfortunate. The West Indians felt that they did not matter and that they were not supposed to be involved in analysing their own weaknesses and those of their teaching institutions. Such was the nature of British colonial administration and the non-involvement of the Caribbean peoples in some matters directly affecting their own welfare.

There had within recent times been at least one survey of nursing education in the Caribbean. It had been undertaken by Miss MacManus, Miss Shenton and Miss Marjorie Houghton, all members of the General Nursing Council of England and Wales. In addition, Miss Florence Udell, Chief Nursing Officer of the Office of Technical Cooperation and Assistance in the UK, made regular visits to the region. The purpose of both survey and visits was to familiarise the English administrators with the conditions in the region.[9]

In some of the Caribbean islands there were a few native West Indians holding administrative positions in nursing. The number varied both in degree and in time. In the Bahamas, as late as 1966, there was only one black Bahamian nurse holding any supervisory position in the Bahamas nursing service. This was Hilda Bowen, who had been trained in the UK at her own expense. Hilda had returned with the qualification required of anyone serving, or aspiring to serve, in a senior administrative post in nursing. But there had been no rush to appoint her to any senior post. The inaction was caused by the fact that the native Bahamian was at that time perceived to be a third-class citizen in his or her country.

The certificate which most Bahamian students received on leaving secondary school more or less equated with the Junior Certificate of Cambridge and was based on an examination which had been abolished in some islands in Eastern Caribbean schools as long ago as 1938. In addition, because of the tourism-oriented economy of the Bahamas, most of the young people took up lucrative jobs in hotels on leaving school. Such jobs provided them with opportunities to improve their standards of living and obtain many of the amenities of life which would not have been possible on the salaries paid to nurses and to other government employees. It naturally followed that there would be few, if any, qualified Bahamians ready for training, appointment or promotion to supervisory posts in the nursing service. Consequently, all supervisory personnel in hospitals and in other nursing services in the Bahamas were entirely expatriate, white and British.

The supervision of the proposed survey was another first for Nita Barrow. Whenever Nita and a regional visitor arrived on an island for the survey, they interviewed the minister of health, the senior medical officer, the matron, the senior tutor, the medical superintendent and/or the hospital secretary, assistant matron(s), tutors and members of the teaching staff representing other disciplines, the department/or administrative sisters, the ward sisters, the staff nurses in the clinical area, the home sister and/or warden in charge of nurses' residences, the sister or staff nurse in charge of health services; matrons and/or sisters from community agencies or special hospitals; class representatives in schools, almost the entire student body; members of the education committee or nursing councils in some areas.

The survey of the schools of nursing was conducted by Nita and a regional visitor. The latter was one of the several senior nurses, each of whom would be appointed by her respective participating government. In this way, for example, when visiting the Bahamas, Nita, the project nurse was accompanied by the regional visitor from Jamaica Enid Lawrence and Olive Ennever. The task was often difficult. Many of the medical and nursing personnel felt their competence and professionalism were being questioned, rather than that both were under examination, the results of which would provide a base for improving the nursing profession.

The interviews and discussions provided, for the first time, the opportunity for West Indian professionals in the field to unburden their minds to other West Indians about the inadequacies, real and imagined, of the system. Some aired their animosities, petty jealousies and suspicions. The survey team of two rarely remained on an island more than one week. At the end of each survey Nita and her partner would meet representatives of the ministries of health and those of associated ministries, PNOs, matrons of hospitals, principals of schools and representatives of nurses organisations and of the several groups and levels of health delivery personnel and read to them a summary of their findings. This democratic approach permitted each island administration, through its officers, to react early and set about correcting any misconceptions and remedying any deficiencies identified. The members of the survey team were thus seen as partners in an exercise dealing with improvement rather than mere critics of existing conditions. The surveys tended to confirm what was already suspected, that the standards of recruitment and encouragement given to local personnel to enter and qualify as professional nurses varied as much as the standards of hospitals and nursing education institutions.

Speaking about her visits to the project in 1964 and 1965, Helen Mussalem found that:

> It was a fascinating experience which I have never had in my life either before or since. I have never known a person that was more highly regarded by everyone that we met or talked to in all those islands than Nita.

She noted parenthetically that:

> Although Nita's brother, Errol, was prime minister of Barbados at that time, Nita never on any occasion took advantage of that relationship. I think that was really very special because there would have been times when some kind of political clout would have helped things along.

Helen's first visit to Jamaica, where Nita was based initially (that is, before she actually began the survey of the schools), was not without its moment of self-inflicted minor indignity. When exposed to the traditional Jamaican welcome at the airport, it is quite easy to fall victim to the liquid-enticing Jamaican hospitality.

Relating a personal, if slightly embarrassing incident, Helen wrote:

> I was told that there would be someone to meet me when I arrived in Kingston, Jamaica. I got off the plane, went into the air terminal and found that they were handing out glasses of what appeared to be pineapple juice to all the passengers. I tossed back very quickly more than one of the glasses of liquid because I was so hot and it was so humid there. About two minutes later I started to see the room swim around ... I became quite worried about this. I had no idea that anybody would give away free alcoholic drinks, certainly never in Canada. I was completely taken by surprise . . . so I sat in a corner quietly in order to regain my equilibrium.
>
> Apparently during that time, Nita had been looking around for me . . . she had missed my arrival because the plane had been a little early. . . . She was about to leave the arrival lounge when I spotted her, stood a little wobbly upright or as upright as I could, and said: 'Oh Nita Barrow! Here I am!' Well Nita was very polite and told me how she had almost given me up thinking that I had decided not to come . . . the blandishments of Jamaican rum punch!

During Helen's first visit, she and Nita travelled to each of the island territories to acquaint the senior health personnel and administrators of the aims and objectives of the survey. When that was completed they returned to Antigua, which by that time had become the base of operation for the survey. It was here that Helen led the survey of the first island, so that Nita and the regional visitor could follow the methods which she had used in Canada and which were being adapted for the Caribbean survey.

The report on that first survey was difficult to write, possibly because of the number and level of the deficiencies that existed but which were not peculiar to Antigua. They managed to put together a 25-page document on the last day of the schedule for the visit, but it still had to be read to the representatives. The reading of the report had its comic relief, because a gust of wind swept through the hall just as Helen had completed the introduction and was about to pick up the looseleaf report to read it. Every page was blown through the windows and doorway on to an adjacent sloping grassed area where they were pursued by the uniformed members of the medical department present. All the pages of the report except one were finally retrieved.

As if that was not enough of a threat to the results of their week's work, that night a hurricane warning was issued and caused much uneasiness and concern. Helen was staying at an hotel near Nita's flat. Knowing how frightening and destructive a hurricane can be, Nita tried to persuade Helen to accept the offer of Dr and Mrs Luther Wynter to spend the night with them. Helen declined the kind offer, preferring instead to remain near Nita and share her companionship as danger threatened. Helen moved into Nita's flat early in the evening. With concern for the fruit of their efforts, they placed the precious report in the oven of the stove in the kitchen since it was unlikely that such a heavy piece of equipment would be blown away.

But later in the evening they thought that the oven of an electric stove was perhaps not really safe, for there was nothing to reassure either of them that some gremlin would not set the oven to work and bring the report to a crisp or fiery end. They therefore transferred the precious document to the refrigerator where its preservation would be more certain and where even partial decomposition of the paper would be inhibited. There was little which they could do to preserve their peace of mind for the howling of the wind did nothing to induce sleep but much to induce ordinary human fear. But joy did come in the morning, as there had been no hurricane during the night and the hurricane warning had been called off.

On completion of the survey of all the schools, the report of each island was submitted to the project's board of review, which consisted of the senior nursing officer from each of the participating territories. The function of the board was to read and evaluate each report. It was only human that the member of the board whose nursing school received a poor report would feel peeved. This did happen and differences of opinion threatened to disrupt the peace of the board. But Helen found that:

> Nita had that great talent of being able to put people at ease, to explain things clearly, but she also has that no-nonsense tone on her voice when she wants to get a point across.

The board, having made its evaluations, met a second time, in 1965, to review its initial appraisal of each school, make further assessments and finally draw up for each school a document stating what were its strengths and weaknesses.

In spite of the language used to describe situations requiring varying amounts of remedy, there were people who were over-sensitive and assumed defensive positions among the administrators and tutors of the schools.

Conveying the stress experienced in discussing the reports with the administrators and staff of the nursing schools, Nita wrote to Helen in Canada in April 1965:

> The final assessments are going better than the first ones in many ways, from my point of view at least. Each time I have to write a report, I bless you for (a) the 'non-patented form' of the report which helps so much; and (b) for the time which you spent with us when we did the first one. Each time after a report is read I feel like a wet rag, but after a night's sleep I recover and really feel fine again. There have been near traumatic reactions in the most unexpected places. Since we are working in small island areas we 'get it back' either through our own staff who may 'get it' from a Minister, or a Permanent

Secretary, or in a couple of instances I have 'had it' directly. I have accepted this as one of the penalties of a job which I still enjoy immensely. It has been harder sometimes for me to say things which seemed fair than for my hearers to accept them, but this they will never know.

Continuing her letter to Helen, Nita related what was her most traumatic experience to date. This was one of challenge to her purpose and competence. It came from a visiting English nursing sister who felt she had to defend her native country's position. It was the first time that any critical examination of the nursing service had taken place in the Caribbean; besides that, it was also probably the first time that a major work of its kind had taken place without being initiated and directed by UK personnel. To the English professional it was nothing less than an affront to English superiority and a display of independence not previously experienced and totally unexpected. The English sister introduced the discussion by asking Nita about the project.

> I answered the same question three times. I do not think that she heard me. . . . Quite suddenly she said, 'I want to know what really made you competent to do a study on British Training schools? I understand that you did not even do your training in Great UK.' . . . My reply by the time that my wits returned was simply that I did not feel competent at all, WHO had made the decision that my qualifications were adequate; that if we were discussing the same project, the schools which I had worked with were Caribbean Schools of Nursing. The Visitor with some condescension in her voice asked: 'Have you told those people that only three places in the area could possibly be considered for graduate nurse training: Barbados, after my two experienced tutors get there, Trinidad and Jamaica?'

'Those people' to whom she referred were clearly the government administrators who would be the decision-makers on any matter affecting the schools. Nita replied: 'It is not for me to tell them, the decision will be their own.' The visitor offered her opinion: 'Then the study is a waste of time, the GNC (General Nursing Council of Great UK) will never recognise any of the smaller territories except for Pupil Nurse training.'

Commenting on the unsought opinion Nita said, 'The question of GNC recognition does not arise; we are speaking in terms of the Caribbean.' Recovering from a kind of shocked silence, the sister said: 'I suppose that you are now proposing a Canadian or American system, if so then the territories which now have reciprocity with UK may lose it.' To which Nita replied: 'That is a decision they would have to be prepared to take.'

Seeing that she was getting nowhere with Nita, the visitor continued in a more conciliatory tone: 'Well, how do you propose to finance the schemes? My Ministry [of the UK] will give nothing.' Realising that she was winning the battle of words, Nita with greater confidence said: 'Well, we have managed so far and no doubt will continue to manage. We have many kind friends . . .' Nita ended her letter to Helen: 'I came home dripping wet and feeling wrung out. Lord give me no more hills to climb like that one . . .'

The third seminar on nursing education was held in Jamaica in 1966. It dealt with curriculum development for the Caribbean. Since this was a relatively new field, it was thought best to have another seminar as soon as possible afterwards (actually, April 1968 in Guyana). The 1966 seminar in Jamaica identified the following requirements for the participants:

> Evaluate the progress in improvement of nursing education in the countries involved
> Develop an understanding of the use of group dynamics in the improvement of nursing.
> Assist the teaching staff in curriculum through planning individual areas of the curriculum, making use of varied teaching methods . . .

The participants were senior sister-tutors from the territories previously involved, except Belize. The resource persons were PAHO/WHO personnel, headed by Nita and based in the several territories: Enid Harden, Barbados; Birgitte Haugland, UWI, Jamaica; Antonia Klimenko, Kingston, Jamaica; Stella Landauer, Trinidad; Helen Mussalem, short-term consultant, Canada; Emma Ochoa, Venezuela; Janet Thomson, PAHO, Zone 1 administrator, Venezuela.

Among the recommendations from the seminar were:

> that the process of improvement in the several fields of nursing education be continued and regularly evaluated;
> that a Regional Council of Nursing be formed as a Caribbean Commonwealth advisory body to assist in the formulation and maintenance of educational standards in the schools of nursing in the area;
> that the Regional Council should have representatives from the Advanced Nursing Education Course at the University of the West Indies.

Other seminars, which also involved the UWI, PAHO, the governments of the territories and nurses representatives, were conducted in Antigua, Barbados, St Vincent, Trinidad and Tobago, Guyana and Jamaica. Representatives from islands where seminars were not held attended seminars in islands nearest or most convenient for them.

Dr Kenneth Standard of the Department of Social and Preventive Medicine of the UWI became totally involved in the objective of improving the quality of the nursing services by using West Indian institutions and qualified West Indian personnel wherever possible, thus providing a more effective regional orientation than previously. He participated in many of the seminars and later provided the support required to begin the Advanced Nursing Education Unit at UWI.

The work in public health was more or less coincident with the intensive work being done in nursing education during the period. The nursing education work required the continuing involvement of Nita both as adviser and as participant. PAHO/WHO, acting on the results of the initial surveys and seminars and the advice of Janet Thomson, had brought into service in the area nurses from mainland USA with specialisations in nursing administration and nursing education as they related to the curative and the preventive aspects of the profession. Among them were Emma Ochoa, Stella Landauer and Antonia Klimenko, who had been among those participating in the review and planning seminars. But there were also three others – Marie Matthews, Janet Ives and Jean McKay – who became very active and particularly well known in the eastern Caribbean for their exhaustive work in administration and public health. These members of PAHO/WHO staff did not work in isolation, nor did they work simply under the supervision of the PAHO/WHO Zone 1 nurse, Janet Thomson. Together with the local West Indian administrators and trainers they formed a unique team of health personnel bound together not only by their profession but by bonds of friendship which have outlasted their professional service. This unique band of pioneers, inspired by the leadership and enthusiasm of Nita, assisted in coordinating the work in the teaching process taking place in schools of nursing and among the health nurses and other personnel.

The need for competence through training and efficiency through better organisation were the objectives. These led to further nursing education. Once again, Ken Standard, acting with colleagues in the Medical Faculty of the UWI, persuaded the university administration of the importance of an advanced nursing education programme and that it would render travel to North American universities for advanced training unnecessary. The funding was provided by some of the West Indian governments and by PAHO.

Following this review, a seminar was held after which the Regional Nursing Body was formed which would provide for: 'Voluntary accreditation of nursing schools; advice and assistance in the improvement of standards in nursing education and periodic evaluation of nursing education programmes.'

Although no formal recommendation was made about advanced nursing education, the UWI representatives at the seminar did indicate the university's interest in examining the possibilities for training tutors and sisters in the Caribbean.

As a postscript, it is worth adding that in May 1991, Queens University, Canada, conferred on Her Excellency, Dame Nita Barrow, GCMG, DA the honorary degree of Doctor of Laws. The principal of the university and chancellor invited Helen to place the hood on Nita's shoulders. That act which completes the robing in the academic regalia before the formality of conferring the degree is normally performed by the chancellor and is a carefully guarded right not lightly given to persons outside the university. Helen related this story, showing her extreme pleasure on the signal honour granted to her.

---

1. Carmen was awarded the Order of Jamaica.

2. A. Wesley Powell, OJ, founder of Excelsior College, wrote: 'The nearby YWCA provided facilities for a variety of physical and social activities for our girls and staff.' See *The Excelsior Story*, The Methodist Church of the Caribbean and the Americas, 1989.

3. Manley, Michael, *Politics of Change*, Andre Deutsch, 1972, 183–84.

4. Mrs Xuma was the wife of Dr A.B. Xuma, president-general of the African National Congress (ANC) of South Africa in the late 1940s. Dr Xuma was accused by the Youth League of the ANC of not being purposeful enough: that he was content to have the Indians, liberal whites, browns and Communists initiate action. Some years later the charge was regarded as having been unreasonable. See Fatima Meer, *Mandela, a Biography*, Mandiba Publications, Durban, 31, 51, 75.

5. Sherlock, P.M. and R. Nettleford, *The University of the West Indies*, MacMillan Caribbean, 1990, 14.

6. Munroe, Trevor, 'Politics of Constitutional Decolonisation', *Institute of Social and Economic Research Journal*, 1972, 56.

7. *Survey of Schools of Nursing in the Caribbean area, Report on Nursing No.6*, PAHO, Regional Office of WHO, 1966, 11.

8. Helen Mussalem has since been awarded the highest honour by her country, the Order of Canada.

9. See note 7 above.

Dame Nita's mother, Ruth Barrow, with children (left to right) Graham, Sybil, Ena, Errol, Nita

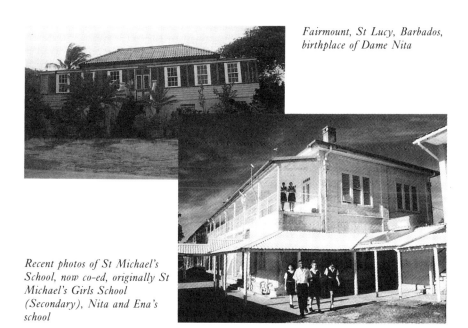

Fairmount, St Lucy, Barbados, birthplace of Dame Nita

Recent photos of St Michael's School, now co-ed, originally St Michael's Girls School (Secondary), Nita and Ena's school

Above
Portion of main building of Barbados General Hospital, 1922

Nita with health workers in Papua New Guinea, 1978

Below
Nita, as Matron of UCHWI, with part of nurses' graduation class

4

The Christian Medical Commission

Six years after Nita began her service as nursing consultant in charge of the research project in the Caribbean for PAHO/WHO, she was invited by the World Council of Churches (WCC) to attend a conference at Tubingen, West Germany, concerned with the role of the Christian church and its involvement in health care. Nita was invited as a member, that is, one of the commissioners, of the new commission of the WCC, namely the Christian Medical Commission (CMC). As a commissioner she brought with her experience in nursing education, community health work and approaches to change gained through her involvement in restructuring the nursing service in Jamaica and her role in PAHO/WHO.

The search for a suitable ecumenical agency had begun at Edinburgh as early as 1910, when representatives of the existing missions, who were mostly Anglo-Saxons, together with a few Africans and Asians, met to exchange ideas on the subject. The First World War intervened before plans could be formulated. However, in 1925, in Stockholm, with the residue of impetus of the 1910 meeting, the churches made some headway towards the creation of a possible structure.

Meetings held in 1937 onwards, mainly of church leaders and others involved in Faith and Order and Life and Work units of the churches, resulted in agreement to establish a council, which, as the WCC, was finally founded in 1948 after delays caused by the Second World War. The WCC, in conjunction with the Lutheran World Federation, one of the partners, held the first conference to discuss the churches' role on health and healing in Tubingen in 1964. It was realised that the big problem was not simply how to reorganise medical missions or Christian health care, but to try to find the meaning and the philosophy of Christian health care, and what was the church's role in attempting to provide it. There was considerable theological discussion about the matter. The degree of dissatisfaction with the existing practices of the missions can be deduced from a sharp but descriptive comment of Dr Erling Keyser, made after a visit to the churches in Asia, saying that the churches did not see medical work as a ministry, but as a matter of prestige or as a means of providing Christians with employment or with bait for fishing men.[1]

Health care had been a focus of Christian missionary work throughout the world for many years. The emphasis, however, was changing as governments took on a national responsibility for health care. Churches recognised the need to reassess the medical and health-related work which they were doing and made a survey of church medical organisations in Asia, Africa, Latin America and the Middle East. The survey revealed that there were 1,238 medical institutions with a total budget of over US$100 million. The survey indicated that if the proposed commission was to be successful, a comprehensive plan would be required for the guidance of the new agency of the WCC, since it would be expected to advise the doctors, nurses and aides who would be the field agents of delivery of community health. The survey showed that about 93 per cent of the time of professional personnel working in health care institutions supported by the church was spent in the practice of curative medicine. Since there were few centres other than hospitals for delivering health care, this meant that only about 7 per cent of the population, those mainly in cities where the hospitals were situated, received medical or health services of any kind. If the churches were to function effectively, they would have to seek the cooperation, not only of the congregations, governments and other agencies concerned in the delivery of health care, but also of the communities which they sought to serve. It therefore became important that the roles of the churches and of governments should be identified, although both might have similar objectives. The various churches had had varied and separate approaches, resulting in duplication of effort and in an uneconomical use of scarce resources.

The second Tubingen conference, designated Tubingen II and held in 1967, recommended to the WCC that there should be an organisation solely concerned with the Christian approach to health care. The WCC accepted the recommendation and set up the CMC in 1968 as the agency for putting into practice a revised Christian approach, one which would promote health, not only as the absence of illness as demonstrated in curative medicine, but as a unit within a three-part philosophy which Rev. Dr Arne Sovik would, many years later, refer to as a theology of health,[2] a suitable term for the difficult search for the true meaning of health and wholeness.

For the Tubingen II conference efforts were made to involve not only theologians but also people with experience in medicine and related fields. Included among them was the chairman, Dr John H. (Jack) Bryant, himself a well-known practitioner in community health who had done much pioneer work in Indonesia; and two female members, Dr Sophia Kruyt, a Dutch missionary doctor running a hospital in Indonesia, with community care aspects; and Nita, experienced in public health, administration and education with community emphasis as well as the coordination of hospital and clinical services.

The change in emphasis of the ecumenical church in its medical ministry from curative medicine to community health had its opponents. For example, one well-known medical missionary suggested that preventive care did not bring people in touch with the evangelistic notion of health care work or medical missions.

The director of the CMC, Dr James MacGilvray, and Dr Philip Potter, secretary-general of the WCC, were among those who thought that the CMC would do well to have Nita as a member of staff working full-time in helping to implement the new CMC ideas. Nita had also become well-known in Geneva where she had been visiting annually since 1957 as a member of the executive of the World YWCA, which also had its headquarters there.

One of the reasons for inviting Nita to Tubingen II was not only to have available at the conference the advice and expertise of the leading female advocate of the teaching of primary health care (PHC) and of its importance to a community. James MacGilvray and Philip Pottor also wanted the commissioners of the WCC to have an opportunity to meet Nita which might lead to her being invited to become part of the CMC on a full-time basis. The strategy worked.

Nita had not intended to give up her post of nursing consultant to the PAHO/WHO project which she was currently leading in the Caribbean, and indeed, her contract with PAHO/WHO had been renewed. When the contract of the CMC staff member with nursing experience expired, James McGilvray appointed Nita to the post of associate director of CMC without even consulting her. When Nita arrived in Geneva in 1970 to attend a meeting, James greeted her with these words: 'We have appointed you Associate Director of the CMC.' Taken aback by the boldness of the action, Nita protested: 'How could you do that when you knew that I was still under contract to PAHO/WHO, a contract which they might have renewed?'

However, no diplomat or psychologist could have produced a more effective balm than James, when he replied: 'You see, if we waited until you were ready, we would never get hold of you.'

The first phase of the Caribbean Nurse Training project had been successfully completed and planning for the future had taken place, so Nita felt that she could move on to the CMC post. She was, nevertheless, able to maintain a continuing interest in and contact with nursing in the Caribbean because the CMC position required her to travel extensively to all parts of the world including the Caribbean.

Very early in its existence the CMC created a bi-monthly journal, *Contact*, first published in 1970. This journal over the years continued to be circulated free of charge on request and has informed its readers of the work done in the field not only by employees of the commission, but also by many health professionals, pioneers and ordinary people. It has also served to publicise, educate and disseminate all ideas used in the delivery of community health service.

The first issue of *Contact* consisted entirely of a summary by Mr Richard Blakney, of the Hong Kong Christian Council, of a lecture given in December 1969 by Dr R.A. Lambourne, then psychiatrist at the University of Birmingham. Lambourne considered that the greatest injustice of all was inadequate health care. In his words:

> Body care is incarnated in words and that is why it is so central to the preaching of the Gospel, so neither health care nor the Church can show preference to the wealthy and to those who live in towns close to where doctors choose to live for their own convenience.

Noting that hospital medicine was becoming too expensive and that it was time to examine the crisis in medicine, which was providing an opportunity for learning, he emphasised that the CMC was therefore attempting to bring 'a new understanding of what it is to be healthy, a new understanding of how to give health care.'

From her initial contact with the commission, Nita saw that there was no simple answer, least of all for those who insisted on precise identification of a problem and equally precise solutions. In her quest for answers which could assist her in making her own philosophical contribution, Nita found some help, in a dialogue between Jack Bryant and Professor David Jenkins, Bishop of Durham and director of the WCC Human Studies.[3]

Explaining her views Nita stated:

> If you attempted to apply the CMC philosophy, you found that you had to leave behind the hierarchical structure of hospital-based care with its stratified and bureaucratic structures. You entered a situation which involved people in their own health care. You got a completely new look at what health meant, part of which was often that of traditional practice. Westerners entering such a world had to be careful to avoid denigrating some of what they did not understand, it was so easy for them to resort to a not uncommon approach that what was foreign to them appeared to be of no consequence.

The CMC philosophy for supporting community health was a stimulating experience for Nita. Asked about what changes she had to make in her own knowledge and thinking, she replied:

> I would say that CMC was itself the greatest learning experience I have ever had. For example, I saw what was probably one of the best examples of Christian medicine at work, in Chimaltenango, Guatemala, a rural district about 50 km from Guatemala City. There Dr Carroll Behrhorst had taught the Indians in that area to provide their own health care, indeed to be responsible for the community health care. He had himself learnt to supply the leadership which would permit them to maintain health on their terms and not on his . . .
> I had come from a background of professional nursing with white uniforms,

the sterile atmosphere of hospitals, the insistence on absolute standards, including those educational. In all that I had been taught and in all that I had seen related to the successful application and performance of nursing and medicine, the nurse was responsible for the patient's health.

In Chimaltenango, the people themselves had learnt from Behrhorst to be responsible for their own health – community health.

During my visit to Chimaltenango, I entered homes with beaten earth floors, one where a woman was making tortillas, plain tortillas, on a little open fire. Tortillas and nothing else would be all that family would have for the day. I discovered that that mother had been selected, by her village, for training as a health worker. She had not been selected by any medical authority, not by Behrhorst. She had exhibited more than ordinary interest in the community and in her children. Her own people had selected her as the one who should be trained to apply what would be available to her as a health worker. There was no running water, no stove to boil water for sterilisation and very little food to teach nutrition. By using basic knowledge of what was available and the people's traditional insights, successful primary health care was achieved.

In his self-appointed task, Behrhorst, an American medical practitioner from Missouri, had first tried to help the women since the men, employed as seasonal farm workers, had gone off to work for the large landowners. The latter represented only 2 per cent of the population, but owned 90 per cent of the land. At the end of the working season the labourers returned with little to show for their efforts because of the low wages and of the deductions made for their board and lodging.

Nita had gone to Chimaltenango to visit the community health project because Behrhorst had applied to the CMC for a grant to purchase chicken cholera vaccine. This request seemed absurd and to have no bearing on the delivery of community health as understood by sophisticated Western medical personnel nor to the CMC itself.

Behrhorst had been brought up in the American tradition, but changed his approach on going to Chimaltenango. He realised that he had to become acquainted with the people of the village. He would sit on a bench in the park and listen to what they perceived to be their needs. In that way he gained their confidence. Finally when he asked them what they felt was their greatest need, they said it was chicken cholera vaccine, because chicken cholera was killing off large numbers of chickens on which they depended for their livelihoods and also their own lives.

Ways and means were also found to provide loans to purchase and develop land as it became available to the villagers. An agro-cooperative was formed through which they purchased land and produced crops which were easily marketed. The men of the village no longer had to leave home for long periods to work for large landowners. Their quality of life improved considerably.

Behrhorst's total involvement and the villagers determination had to be made known elsewhere. Nita therefore arranged for him to travel to places where other indigenous peoples might hear at first hand of the success of good leadership and how other people had exercised initiative and determination which resulted in better standard of living and independence for themselves and their families. In July 1975, for example, supported by the CMC, Behrhorst visited Papua New Guinea to share his experience and knowledge with the local people.[4]

Early in her service as an associate director of the CMC, Nita also experienced another example of self-sacrifice associated with PHC. This was the work initiated, maintained and supervised by a young Indian couple, Rajanikant and Mabelle Arole. This was so impressive that they were invited to address the annual general meeting of the CMC in June 1972.

Raj and Mabelle were graduates of the prestigious Christian Medical Hospital in Vellore, India. After working for some years in the same hospital, they left for the John Hopkins Hospital in the USA to be trained in public health. While they were there they realised that the work in which they had been engaged touched only a few lives and that the majority of the population was outside the walls of the hospital. On their return to India, therefore, they did not go back to the same clinical setting in Vellore, but decided to go into rural districts where there were no medical personnel. In the village of Jamkhed, in the state of Maharashtra, they found a community of about 100,000 which required medical help. There was neither a doctor nor a trained nurse; the villagers helped one another as best they could. The Aroles did not build an institution, but worked on the principle of PHC which involved people in their own health care; some of them became health workers after training. There was some opposition from a few of the villagers who felt that PHC was second-class medicine. However, the success of the personnel in treating the prevalent though preventable conditions changed that view.

Having obtained some successful results, the Aroles increased the number of clinics and extended the practice of preventive medicine. In addition, they trained health workers in providing family planning education, reducing the mortality of children under five years old and treating chronic diseases, including leprosy. Much of this was done with the support of the CMC.

On one occasion when the Aroles returned to the village where they were then resident, they were met by a large delegation of the villagers who conveyed them in a decorated bullock cart to their residence, adjacent to which there was a new wooden building resembling a West Indian chattel house, with a large wooden cross mounted on the front. The building could be taken apart and moved to another village to serve as a centre for their work. When asked by the Aroles the meaning of the large cross, the Hindu villagers replied to the Christian Aroles: 'Is that not the reason why you have done so much for us?'

Convinced that the Aroles' work in PHC should be used to typify what

CMC was mostly about, the commission invited them to give of their expertise to other persons and groups. Mabelle Arole, co-director of the Comprehensive Rural Health Project, the name by which their work had become known, commented in a letter in 1979: 'much of my time in these past six months has been spent in sharing my experiences at Jamkhed with different study groups sponsored by CMC, churches in north America and the WHO.'

Since the CMC had no funding of its own to allocate to projects, it was necessary to approach international funding agencies for support. In order to do this, the CMC, had to prepare the documentation required and the submissions of requests to funding agencies. In this way the CMC built up considerable experience and goodwill, and earned the respect of other organisations which considered its innovative approach to its mandate worthy of emulation.

In 1974 a request was made for the CMC to evaluate the CARE/MEDICO Community Hospital Training Project in Solo, Sumatra, in Indonesia. The focus of the project was improvement of the Kabupatan district hospitals by training medical, nursing and laboratory staff and developing facilities.

Nita undertook the evaluation which included visits not only to Sumatra and Java, but also to neighbouring islands. She also found time to visit two communities that were practising PHC, based on the perception of Dr Gunawan Nugroho, who was already known to CMC.

In her report to the funding agency for the project, Nita confirmed that:

> the hospital-centred project had met a need. Most of the objectives on which it was based have been met. The most important one, however, – the improvement of the health of the people of the community – requires re-examination. A different focus of care should be developed in order to meet this need realistically.[5]'

When the first term of the CMC expired in 1976, a new commission was appointed with Nita as Director, in succession to James McGilvray. Although there had been some concern about Nita's competence as a nurse to deal with doctors she was nevertheless selected for the post from a field of three or four candidates. The initial fear was soon dispelled.

The annual meeting of the Christian Medical Commission in 1977 took place in April at Royal Holloway College, UK. This was the first time that Nita was attending this meeting as its director. It was also the first time that five commissions were meeting together and experiencing the benefits of interaction. The five were: the CMC, the Commission on Church Aid, the Commission on Inter-Church Aid Refugee and World Service (CICARWS), the Commission on the Churches' Participation in Development (CCPD), the Commission of the Churches on International Affairs (CCIA) and the Programme to Combat Racism (PCR). The common aim of the five commissions was the search for a just, participatory and sustainable society.[6]

Nita in her first report as director to the CMC commented:

> In many parts of the world, the distribution of land, the inability of the rural sector to feed itself, the scarcity of employment opportunities, the lack of basic domestic and sanitary conveniences, and other pressures arising from social injustice constitute the greatest threat to public health. Many people are still deprived by the decision makers of a reasonable chance to have healthy lives. Furthermore, the existing style of many so-called democratic governments as well as those which make no pretence of being other than authoritarian or despotic, excludes the majority of their people from participating in decisions which affect their health. The majority of the people in such countries have no opportunity of identifying their needs, of expressing them, or of determining their priorities. They have no share in the process of planning to meet those needs. They are given no share or responsibility in administering or in controlling the health care system.
>
> The subject of the people's participation in the delivery of primary health is crucial to the justice and sustainability of the social system as it relates to health. A healthy society cannot be sustained unless everyone is involved and shares the responsibility for its continuing existence. Sustainability is also closely tied to the matter of technology for healthy living.

Earlier in the same report, Nita had more precisely, but equally philosophically, stated:

> The Christian Medical Commission is primarily a resource of the Christian Churches. The Commission attempts to assist in clarifying the Churches' role in their stewardship for the health of all people and in determining priorities which it then exercises in the name of Our Lord.

In the words of Philip Potter, then Secretary-General of the WCC:

> That was how Nita saw the task. She used very much the magazine *Contact* in promoting this understanding. It was under her leadership that there was a new study process in the three elements of: traditional medicine and healing practices; human values in bio-ethical issues and the congregation as a healing community.

Nita's focus on the use of local medicine was seen as an example of the CMC's commitment to supporting existing community practices, most of which respected the dignity of the people and were part of the community's services to its members. Nita knew that many Western academics (and others) had, in their ignorance or arrogance, failed to recognise the usefulness of folk medicine because either they did not understand it or they had not taken the time to study it. They had therefore applied the pejorative term 'witch doctors' to its practitioners, a term which connoted professional snobbery and superiority. The practitioners of folk medicine were in fact traditional healers, health attendants and birth attendants.

Nita was to remember that the use of herbal medicines in the Caribbean had its origin in its African background. In the training of doctors and nurses, folk medical knowledge was replaced – though not in memory – by modern medicinal practice. Nita felt that when she was confronted by traditional medicine she had no difficulty in acknowledging that there were forms of treatment for ailments which were not conventional. Confirming the open-mindedness of the CMC on this subject, Nita said:

> the CMC published the first book on health care in China in 1970, when no one else was talking about China. When I took up my appointment with CMC the study had been started. The so-called barefoot doctors[8] were virtually introduced to the West by that CMC publication.

Nita has also commented on other examples of the direct involvement of her CMC colleagues and herself in the study of traditional medicine:

> When we first went to Tanzania, we met Dr Raimo Harjula, a Finn who had been sent to teach in Tanzania in the Theological College there. Dr Harjula, a theologian and member of the Institute for Cultural Research, University of Turku, Finland, became interested in traditional medicine and apprenticed himself to one of its practitioners, Sainaikito Mirau Massari, himself of the Meru ethnic group, better known as Mirau, who was one of the traditional doctors, herbalists or *waganga*, a Swahali term. As Harjula collected herbs, he despatched specimens to his wife, in Finland, who then had the specimens classified.[9]
>
> In support of their work and in recognition of the need to educate western medical workers about their counterparts in the so-called third world, CMC solicited funding for the continuing research and for the publication of the Harjulas' work. The publication would be a valuable contribution to the existing literature on the subject. Furthermore, it might encourage others to undertake similar work elsewhere. In his book Dr Harjula describes how Mirau practised his art and provided many of those who sought his assistance, with herbs or extracts which proved effective.

In his acknowledgement of the assistance given him by the CMC, Harjula wrote in the preface to his published research work:[10]

> In Geneva my gratitude is due Ms R. Nita Barrow, RN, RM LL.D, Director of CMC as well as to her colleagues on the Commission for their whole-hearted encouragement. Without their contributions, this book would never have come out.

Dr Harjula referred to Mirau's ethno-medicinal repertoire as:

> a totality of expert knowledge and skills which he employed in his practice as mwaanga.[11] The purpose of the Mirau study was to provide empirical material for the Tanzanian Government and on health education for Church authorities who were trying to create a more understanding and realistic attitude towards traditional medicine or to provide points of departure for experts in medicine

73

and pharmacology and botany, or for those who were interested in employing aspects of traditional herbal medicine in the changing society of Tanzania, East Africa and elsewhere.

Harjula's opinion of himself at the time was:

> At first I must have been an unusual and interesting stranger in Mirau's eyes. Our relationship developed into one of close friendship. At the end of the period, Mirau offered me one of his wives as a token of friendship and even though she was an excellent cook, I could not take her to be my second wife for reasons that were understood and accepted by Mirau.

In 1978 a conference of medical doctors and other health personnel was held in Botswana as a means of promoting the training of health personnel and for assisting in its administration. One of the biggest problems at that time was the antipathy between the Western-trained doctors and the traditional healers. The venue was chosen to improve the attendance of participants from southern Africa. However, there were no black South Africans present because of the apartheid policies of the minority white South African government although there were a very few white South African Western-trained doctors who were practising institutional care. One of them, who was engaged in some form of community medical care in his country, was quite indignant when he found that he was expected to sit down with African traditional healers.

A central theme of the Botswana conference was the African systems of religious belief, values and traditional healing. One of the papers was delivered by Dr Nartey, a Ghanaian, chemist by profession, whose father had himself been a traditional healer. After having been educated at Western universities, Dr Nartey returned to Ghana and studied local medicines. At the end of his presentation, the white South African doctor, who had earlier protested against the presence of black herbalists and had been ignored, approached Nita and said how good Dr Nartey's paper had been. Uncertain whether the South African doctor had expected the African traditional healer to fit the Verwoerd stereotype or not, Nita hastened to assure him of the identity of the African who had displayed such erudition and eloquence, saying: 'That gentleman is the head of 250,000 traditional healers.'

African traditional healers are involved in the physical, mental, social, emotional, moral and spiritual well-being of his patient. They mostly relate to good neighbourliness and to harmonious relationships with one's ancestors, local deities and the supreme being. In attempting to restore in patients the harmony needed, recourse is made to pouring libations, invocations, intercession, offering of sacrifices, confession, penance and physical touch.

Many Western-trained physicians know that there are plants growing in the wild which have medicinal properties. Some of them also know that, until comparatively recently, cultivated and wild plants were the only source of medicines. A few also know that people of African descent, including West Indians as part of their African heritage, still employ extracts of some of the less potent herbs to cure or relieve ordinary ailments such as the common cold. Among the most commonly used are wild cerasee *(momordica charantia)*, purslane or pussly *(portulaca oleracea)* and periwinkle *(vinca rosea)*. Until recently little was known of the side-effects or of real dosage in terms of the active ingredients. Such information seems to have been lost in the 'middle passage'.

Nita realised that although during Western-type medical training much of the awareness of herbal medicinal cures was lost or ignored, the use of herbs could not be entirely wrong. When she encountered its practice, the degree of precision and the knowledge of its genuine practitioners, response was enhanced by memories which had become suppressed by Western ways of thinking.

The damage done to the African culture by Western missionaries, in their ignorance, is probably best exemplified by a representative from Cameroon at the conference. He sadly observed that:

> Our names were designated pagan, our dances were proscribed, . . . everything that constituted the cultural life of our people was declared an anathema with baneful results. Mission theology became one of domestication, rather than one of liberation.

The importance of traditional healers and their role in the promotion of health and healing received much attention from the CMC which recognised them as genuine specialists in their own communities. These healers were deliberately sought after by the CMC, with Nita very much in the lead, both in thought and action, so that their specialisation might be employed in any CMC-sponsored PHC programme. A few examples are given below.

> The Lutheran World Service, a corporate member of the CMC, had a project in North Bengal which was the cultivation of medicinal plants, including lemon grass, citronella java and solanum khrysianum.
>
> Joint workshops for practitioners in traditional and modern medicine were held in several countries. One of these was held in January 1974 in Yaounde, Cameroun. A group of westerners led by Nita took time off to visit a village reached by plane and half-day's walk into the hills. There was situated a health station, which had for eight years been run by an American missionary, trained in nursing. The nearest hospital or source of medical help was in Bamenda, four days walking distance away into neighbouring Nigeria. The visitors learnt that by gaining the confidence of the traditional healers by learning from them, the missionary had been able to determine dosage of herbal extracts which she made more palatable with wild honey, the local sweetener, thus replacing virtual guesswork by measurement and reducing mortality, especially in young children. In addition, primitive bamboo knives used in preparation of food and otherwise were also used by traditional midwives in obstetrics, which increased the danger of tetanus to the newly born. Obtaining

a supply of razor blades and converting the bamboo knives into razor blade holders, and sterilising the blades by flame, the indigenous people retained practices important to their national dignity while discovering the practical benefits of elementary western technology.

Another was of the local peoples held in the Upper Volta. Professor Ki-zerbo had stimulated study groups in medicinal herbs in all parts of Africa. Two meetings of traditional healers, biologists, pharmacologists and psychiatrists were held in Lome and in Niamey, Niger, in 1976.

Also in 1976 the WHO Regional Committee for Africa at its annual meeting discussed at length how the large numbers of traditional healers might be integrated into African health services. A main advantage was the trust and faith which they enjoyed in their own regions.

The Medical Faculty of the University of Ibadan under Dr T.A. Lambo in keeping with national policy has conducted research into traditional medicine. Similar work has also been done at the Faculty of Medicine of the University of Ghana.[12]

In 1976, when the WCC renewed the life of the CMC, it gave to Nita, its new director, a mandate to establish a CMC study/enquiry programme, 'to engage in action reflection studies of the Christian understanding of health and wholeness'. In order to fulfil this requirement, a network of resource persons was created in order to find out what was being done in three areas:

- Traditional medicine and healing practices
- Human values in bioethical issues
- The congregational approach to its responsibility to be active in caring, supporting and healing of people.[13]

Interest in traditional medicine from an international organisation was not monopolised by the CMC. Indeed the WHO, during the two years following the formation of the Joint Committee (WHO/CMC) was extremely interested in the present and future roles of herbalists in community health care and held a consultation in Geneva in November 1977 on the promotion and development of traditional medicine in which the CMC was invited to participate. On this occasion Nita, as director of the CMC, was accompanied by Dr Stuart Kingma, associate director. Both took part in the discussions about the advantages of traditional medicine, namely economic, cultural, holistic, safety-serving and human resource-saving. Perhaps even more important were the proven psychotherapeutic benefits of the art.[14]

Following a conference held in South Africa on the church's role in health and healing, Nita took time out to visit Dean Michael Mokasi Molale of the Anglican Cathedral in Botswana who was supposed to attend the conference, but had not. It was learnt at the conference that he had been abducted by the South African government. Molale had left Botswana to attend but had disappeared between the point of disembarkation and the baggage claim area. He was a critic of the South African government and its apartheid policy supported by the doctrine of the Dutch Reformed Church and had over a period of time expressed his opposing views in personal letters to members of the WCC. For the agents of the South African government it was not unethical nor an infringement of personal rights to intercept and photocopy letters. Being a marked opponent of the tyranny, the dean was seized on arrival in South Africa and would probably have 'disappeared' forever had not the WCC and other church agencies been vocal in their condemnation. Nita found Dean Molale some 25 lb lighter and traumatised by the inhumanity he had experienced at the hands of the government of South Africa which had detained him.

It was natural that the headquarters of the WCC should be in Geneva, which was itself the base of many of the international non-governmental organisations (NGOs), such as WHO. It was to be foreseen that WHO and CMC would share similar purposes and philosophies, since they were both dedicated to improving worldwide health.

The WHO had been established at least 20 years before the CMC. It would have taken some time before the role of CMC and its philosophy of health, healing and wholeness would be demonstrated and accepted, but the period proved to be shorter than expected. Dr Karsten Mahler, director-general of WHO, had early in 1974 noted from *Contact* and mentioned to some of his senior staff that the CMC were genuinely involved in the business of health. As a result a meeting of WHO and the CMC was arranged. James McGilvray, director of CMC, led the CMC delegation of six persons, including Nita Barrow, Dr Helen Gideon, Dr Hakan Hellberg, Sr Gilmary Simmons (consultant), and Dr Sylvia Talbot, one of the commissioners. The WHO was represented by 32 members.

As a result of that meeting a permanent joint standing committee was established which provided for consultation and leadership for the expanded role of the WHO in community health care. A few years later, a book, *Health by the People* was published by the WHO, in which there were summaries of studies of alternative methods of providing basic health services to total populations. Of the nine projects described, three associated with CMC were included: those at Chimaltengo, Guatemala; Jamkhed, India; and Solo, Indonesia.

One year after the establishment of a working relationship between WHO and CMC, Nita became world president of the YWCA. Through this coincidence PHC became one of the instruments of the YWCA in its objective of providing a better world for women – and indeed all people.

Time, circumstance and the experience of working in yet another international organisation and indeed in an international city, Geneva, were once again providing fertile ground for Nita to develop more skills, so that others sought her help in dealing with delicate and difficult human problems.

The WCC had participated with Ethiopia in the peace settlement, which was really a ceasefire, between the Sudan south and the Sudan north. The north was effectively Muslim and the south Christian. The Anya Nya rebels of the south first sought secession from the north in 1963. At the talks between the insurgents and the government in 1972, a settlement was reached which provided for a measure of autonomy for the south which hopefully would end the civil war which had begun in 1955 with riots by southern troops.

To supervise the international assistance as part of the rehabilitation process of the south, a Kenyan, Mr Kiplagat (Kip to his friends),[15] was selected by CICARWS to establish a base in Khartoum, the capital of the Sudan situated in the north of the country, and from there to coordinate the administration of the material aid being provided by the churches and other organisations. It was then that Nita first visited the Sudan. She went to evaluate the progress made in social rehabilitation especially as it related to health care. At that time there were two ways of travelling between northern and southern Sudan: by a plane owned by the United Nations High Commission for Refugees (UNHCR), normally used to assist in returning refugees to their homes from Chad, Zaire, Uganda, Kenya and Ethiopia; or by boat on the river. The refugees during the unrest simply walked across national boundaries to their neighbours, often people of their own ethnic grouping divided on a whim by European colonialists who knew little and cared less about the cultural, ethnic and familial ties of Africans. Unable to distinguish one African nation or society from another, the Europeans lumped all Africans together under the pejorative label of 'tribes', as if that would make the natural grouping of people of similar origin any less real.

Nita and Kip travelled south from Khartoum in the UNHCR plane sitting on bags of dura (sorghum or guinea corn). But this was not the only inconvenience they underwent. Since there would be no accommodation approaching that of hotel or guest house, they travelled with their own bed rolls or sleeping bags and of course their own food. With such minimal human comforts Nita and Kip visited Malakal, Wau and Juba, some 400 and 700 miles south of Khartoum. Indeed, they often slept out of doors and on at least one occasion they slept on a verandah of a house with no roof.

Nita's second visit was in 1976 when she and Dr Martin Scheel of the German Institute for Medical Mission, Tubingen, went to the Sudan as a part of a committee of three. The other member was Peter Ring, secretary of the Sudan Christian Council (SCC). After discussion with the CMC, the WHO had instituted a programme of health services in southern Sudan with the involvement of local groups. The purpose of the visit was to evaluate the status of the programme and advise donor agencies on the level of funding required for extending, revising or maintaining it. However, a visit to the south was deemed inadvisable because of an outbreak of a virulent virus disease. Nita and Martin discovered a high commitment on the part of the Sudan government to the WHO/CMC health plan. The role and function of the SCC as the local agency for disbursement of funds from external church-oriented sources were defined by direct or by diplomatic statements.

The Caribbean region, because of its high standards of general health services, continued to attract the attention of the CMC. Nita visited Curacao in the Dutch West Indies in July 1974 to attend the Ninth Annual Meeting of the Caribbean Nurses Organisation and deliver the keynote address. She next visited the Dominican Republic, part of the island formerly known as Hispaniola, as a representative of the Commission on World Mission and Evangelism of the WCC rather than as associate director of the CMC. The purpose of her visit was to attend a meeting organised by the Movement for Evangelical Unity in Latin America. Nita had the opportunity to improve the opinion of many of the delegates about the healing ministry, since until that time their approach had been curative-oriented and did not appear to involve the congregations of churches. Large numbers of volunteers came from the USA and Canada, at their own expense, to provide health care in rural areas. As a result of that visit a Haitian doctor visited CMC headquarters in Geneva in 1975 and, on returning to Haiti, established the Christian Medical Commission of Haiti (CMCH), which was ecumenical in nature. Then in 1976, when Nita again visited Haiti, with James McGilvray, the CMCH seemed to be working in isolation. Nita and James were able to lend assistance by showing the CMCH how to coordinate the church-related groups.

After her second visit to Haiti, Nita visited Jamaica to see two programmes in action sponsored by the Department of Social and Preventive Medicine (S&PM) of the University of the West Indies (UWI). The first related to the training and utilisation of community health aides. These were people of minimal formal education who worked under supervision as auxiliaries on a health team with public health nurses, inspectors, midwives, and social and development workers. The programme was the brainchild of Professor K.L. (now Sir Kenneth) Standard, head of the Department of Social and Preventive Medicine (S&PM). Standard had started the programme in 1969 and had put it into action in several parts of Jamaica. Two particular areas chosen for detailed study were August Town/Hermitage, about 6 miles from Kingston, and Elderslie, a rural district.[16]

The second was the site of the so-called backyard nurseries project, which was also a project of S&PM of UWI. Here public health nurses with training in community health taught and supervised women who ran backyard nurseries where working mothers left their children during the day, since the government-sponsored day nurseries were too few for the number of children requiring accommodation.

Visiting the day nurseries and seeing the work of postnatal clinics where new mothers were being advised to breast-feed their children, Nita must have been reminded of her previous period of service in Jamaica when breast-feeding was regarded as appropriate only for the less privileged in society. Local clinics, like those in some other parts of the world were now working hard to revive the healthy practice of breast-feeding babies.

In order to emphasise the importance of breast-feeding, the CMC publication *Contact* (No. 35, 1976) was devoted entirely to the subject. Nita's paper, 'Breast Feeding – a Must or a Myth?' was the centrepiece of the issue, for not only was it timely in its attempt to stress its health importance, but the advertised benefits of milk products had recently been the subject of a legal case; it was known as the 'bottle babies' issue. Mothers in developing countries were being encouraged to replace breast-feeding by patent baby foods. The Commission on the Churches' Participation in Development (CCPD) was sued for libel by a Swiss manufacturer of milk products for publishing a reprint of an English-language article which had been highly critical of the methods of advertising and marketing and of the disadvantages associated with the use of manufactured baby foods.

The English version of the criticism was entitled '(The Product), the Baby Killer'. The non-English equivalent was apparently more severe. Judgment went against the respondent, but the court criticised the plaintiff's advertising.

In her paper Nita said that breast-feeding until the 1940s had been:

> a normal feature of daily life and as the mother went about her work, the baby was kept with her, strapped to the mother's back, slung on her side or just within easy reach, and was fed as required.

Quoting the works of pioneer paediatricians in Jamaica, Cecily D. Williams and Derrick B. Jeliffe,[17] Nita traced the shift to bottle-feeding as having been influenced by factors such as vanity, pressured advertising by baby food companies and early supplementary feeding with sweetened milk. Nita quoted from the Ugandan Okot p'Biteke, one of Africa's finest poets:

> When the baby cries,
> Let him suck milk
> From the breast
> There is no fixed time
> For breast feeding.
>
> When the baby cries
> It may be he is ill
> The first medicine for a child
> is the breast . . .

Nita thought that bottle-feeding was typical of European and North American societies during the preceding 20 years or so. It was unfortunate that people in developing countries had begun to imitate the practice. Further, Western society had convinced many women that breasts were for sexual pleasure only.

Breast-feeding a baby in public had become a novel sight, if not a spectacle. Nita highlighted a Dutch mother breast-feeding her child in an African market place as a public demonstration of some renewal of confidence in real motherhood.

> She (the Dutch mother) was soon surrounded by African women who said, 'We did not know that white women could breast-feed their babies too.' But had she done so in a European market place she would have been looked upon with suspicion if not disgust . . . The mother who successfully breast-feeds her own child becomes a help and support to others in her own community and outside it. She is the best advocate for reversal of the trend from artificial to breast-feeding.

Nita went to Brazil, in response to requests made to the CMC by some of the constituent members of the WCC. There had been requests for funding for projects as well as invitations for her to visit and advise either on new health care procedures or to revise old ones. Eileen Stark, an American nurse who had worked in Brazil for many years and was fluent in Portuguese, was assigned to Nita as field guide and interpreter.[18]

The area from Belem and Fortaleza in the north of the country to Recife and Salvador (Bahia) on the east coast was inhabited mostly by blacks and retained strong African influences. It was mainly to these areas that Africans had been brought as slaves by the Portuguese slave traders. There is much in common between the descendants of the slave populations of Brazil and of the West Indies. Nita noted that some of the ceremonies and festivals which she witnessed were similar to Shango in Trinidad and Pocamania in Jamaica, as well as, elsewhere in the Caribbean. In Belem the sight of women sitting by the roadside preparing and frying bean cakes conjured up the smells of fish being fried by Barbadian women for their late-night customers on Saturday nights at the roadside, on Baxters Road in the heart of the city of Bridgetown.

In what is virtually jungle in Belem, two female nurse trainers had set up a small health complex including a teaching clinic for training nursing auxiliaries. They had originally established a small health centre because the local people had no place near enough where they might have even the simplest of health needs met. The small establishment had in a short time become not only a health clinic but a centre where young women were taught skills which in time would make the small community less dependent on external aid for its own welfare. It was Nita's view that:

The accommodation was quite limited and the services minimal. What the trainers in nursing were really doing, although unique to the local situation, was not dissimilar from efforts elsewhere. They were teaching the local residents to use what was available and like the Aroles or Behrhorst, they did not try to impose foreign standards which would remain foreign. While offering assistance to such outposts of health teaching, we never offered criticism as a stimulus for change or improvement. If a need appeared, say, for reduction in contamination of medical dressings, we might recommend the training of an additional person to look after reducing or removing the possible sources of the contamination.

Belem was also the centre for WHO in northern Brazil. It was there too that Luke Tupper, an American physician, provided a special travelling doctor service for which he is remembered. Dr Tupper used to travel in a launch up and down the Amazon river and its tributaries which connected several villages. If someone was ill enough to require his attention, a coloured flag would be mounted near the water's edge or on the local jetty, and Dr Tupper would respond to the call.

From Belem the team visited the new settlements near the road being constructed near the Amazon. Even at the time of the visit it was clear that the new settlements would adversely affect the environment. Fifteen years later, the results are clearly visible. The indigenous Indian people are trying to stop the indiscriminate destruction of their forests by intruders, foreigner and Brazilian who want the land and its products for themselves, regardless of the rights of the indigenous people.[19]

There appeared to be little or no attempt at reafforestation, nor a plan of action by the government to protect the lives and culture of the original Indian inhabitants from the inhuman actions of uncivilised European invaders, a disregard not much unlike that which European settlers had, three centuries earlier, shown for the indigenous peoples of Hispaniola, other parts of the Caribbean and North America. That the Indians were being exploited, their way of living destroyed and their lives threatened not only by the Europeans, but also by European diseases from which they have little immunity, appeared to be of concern to very few people but the Indians themselves.

In Brasilia, the capital, and in the areas surrounding it everything appeared beautiful and clean at first sight. There were no signs of poverty, so Nita and her group wondered where the people were who provided the supporting services. They discovered later that they lived some distance from the hotel near the end of a poorly-maintained road. It seemed that they were not allowed to live near the city – shades of South Africa and apartheid.

In order to reach a clinic run by an American in the small village of Bom Jesus da Lapa, north-east of Brasilia, the visiting group travelled up the San Francisco river in a paddle steamer. The company providing the service had bought the last of the paddle steamers used on the Mississippi river. The journey took about two days.

All along the river bank were cords of wood provided by the people in the villages for fuel for the paddle steamers, as their contribution to the costs of the river passenger and general transport service. Indeed, river transport was the only reliable service, providing communication with the larger villages two or three times a week. Villagers living farther inland without easy access to the river were at an even greater disadvantage.

When Nita and her companions reached Bom Jesus, the clinic and settlement which they had come to visit were on the other side the river from the docking point of the paddle steamer. The party crossed in a small plane. The clinic was run by an American missionary nurse who taught the people basic nursing. There were even a couple of beds for the training of midwives. When she was asked if there was no other way of reaching the isolated village, the nurse replied: 'Well, if it has been discovered, no one has told us about it yet.'

Nita and her team arrived in Sao Paulo after visiting Rio de Janeiro briefly. The contrasts of extreme wealth and chronic poverty were particularly obvious around those two cities. For example, from Copacabana beach in Rio, the vacation place for the wealthy, one could see on the nearby hills the small huts of the poor people built of all sorts of material. As Nita herself observed:

> The seven-storey hotel where we were staying in Sao Paulo was situated on a corner of two streets. From the windows on one side we could see the store front of a branch of a famous chain of jewelry stores, complete with security guard. Fascinated with its appearance, I went out to window shop. Items were priced from US$3,000 to US$30,000. On returning to the hotel, I looked down from a window on another side of the hotel, I saw a woman with one child on her back and another, about two years old at her knee as she searched through the refuse from the hotel's kitchen for food for her children. Such was the contrast of Sao Paulo where millions of dollars are made daily but where there were not yet social services adequate to meet the needs of its population.

In Sao Paulo, Pastor Arturo de Mello, head of a large pentecostal church, had invited the CMC team to visit. The existing building, which seated 4,000, had become too small and a new building was being erected to accommodate more than twice that number. Several activities were in progress, at that same time, including one of worship and healing. Pastor de Mello changed into white vestments and approached a table where many of the sick prayed and sang. In her own words,

> The Pastor invited me to join him there. Assisting him was a man, who appeared to be a steward of the Church. Suddenly the 'steward' turned to me and asked: 'Are you married?' I replied that I was not. Very soon afterwards, Pastor De Mello surprised me and his hearers with the statement: 'I would like to announce the engagement of Miss Nita Barrow to (the steward).' There I stood, publicly betrothed to a gentleman I had seen for the first time 10 minutes earlier.

Asked how she had dealt with the surprise, Nita replied that she simply produced one of her amused smiles.

Pastor de Mello's church also provided formal education in a building of some 15 classrooms for school-age children from eight years old. But the pastoral care was not confined to the immediate area. Many young people migrated from the rural areas to Sao Paulo and other large cities. Some of them fell prey to unscrupulous city people who exploited their ignorance of big city life. De Mello had arranged a welfare service for these new immigrants, so that when they arrived at the main railway station, they were met and offered assistance and some protection until they found work and a place to live.

Nita found that it was the vastness of Brazil which made it both exciting and disturbing. There was much over-population caused by the migration of people to towns from the rural areas. This meant that few had opportunity to get a reasonable education and some health care. The ever-present problem for the churches was how to use their scarce resources to help the many thousands who were in need.

James McGilvray had visited Malawi when he was conducting the survey of hospitals more than a decade earlier. He had found that up to the time of independence in 1964, 29 organisations, some of which were church-based, delivering medical and health care, had their headquarters in Blantyre, the capital. But they had provided little or no health care to people in the rural districts.

After independence, the president, Hastings Banda, himself a graduate in medicine, decided to set up a coordinating council for health services to determine the health needs of the 5 million people in the country. When McGilvray met Dr Banda, he inquired why he had formed the coordinating council without involving any of the resident representatives of the medical and health agencies, including those that were church-based. President Banda replied: 'How do you talk to twenty-nine people who do not talk to each other over their own back fences?'

President Banda's observation was a well-deserved criticism and served to remind the CMC that poor communication can be destructive of the most well-meaning efforts.

McGilvray held a meeting of the representatives of the churches and explained that they were in danger of becoming obsolete if they did not find some means of coordinating their efforts to serve the whole country. Whatever method they chose should provide a mechanism for the people themselves to submit their views on their own medical and health needs. The churches acted on McGilvray's advice and the model for cooperation established in Malawi was the first of its kind, subsequently being used in some 30 other countries.

Nita's visit to Malawi to attend the annual meeting of the coordinating council in 1971 was her first to Africa after joining the staff of the CMC. On arrival by plane at the capital, Nita and Sr Dr Gilmary Simmons, the

Roman Catholic consultant to the CMC, were met at the foot of the steps of the plane by a lady carrying lengths of cloth who greeted each female passenger.

Unaccustomed to such gracious attention on arrival in a country, Nita commented to Sister Simmons: 'How kind indeed, we are being greeted with a gift of a length of African cloth.'

Nita described the occasion:

> As we were about to walk away from the plane, the length of the cloth was taken from us and gracefully wrapped around each of us and tied. We were also told that we could neither wear short dresses nor slacks while visiting Malawi. Only Muslim women, who traditionally wore trousers, were allowed to do so.
>
> We later learned that some twenty or more non-nationals, who had recently worn the then fashionable mini-skirts in Blantyre, had been deported.

What was ironic about it all was that Nita had spent a great deal of time before leaving Geneva in shortening many of her skirts.

Nita led a team, on a visit to Egypt, which included Sylvia Talbot, Moderator of the CMC and Herman Middelkoop, a CMC commissioner. The purpose was to advise working groups of member organisations on the philosophy and practice of health, healing and wholeness. The plan also included visits to projects being assisted by the CMC. One of these projects was the so-called rag pickers, families whose living quarters were set up near the city's garbage dump. The rag pickers divided themselves into groups according to the particular non-perishable items which they salvaged from the refuse. Assisted by their children, they cleaned and sold the items. Since living and working so close to the dumps was unpleasant and constituted a threat to health, especially that of the young children, the churches had become involved in trying to improve sanitation and nutrition.

The visit to the rag pickers had been arranged by Marie Assad, a Coptic Christian, who had formerly been a CMC commissioner. Nita had first met her when Marie was a trainee at the World YWCA headquarters in Geneva. On her return to Egypt Marie had continued to do social work through her church. When the opportunity arose, Nita persuaded Marie to apply for the post of assistant-secretary of the WCC where she would be responsible to the general-secretary, Dr Philip Potter, for women's affairs. Nita's involvement in Marie's selection was part of her desire to increase the number of women at the policy-making level and to reduce the male domination of the WCC.

Nita and Dr Ursula Liebrich of CMC were asked to assess two proposed projects. The first related to the provision of pharmaceutical supplies either by gifts through the existing Centre d'Approvisionnement Medical (CEPAM), or by the establishment of a manufacturing plant; the second was the provision of five clinics in Kinshasa run by the Christian Church of Zaire (ECZ).

The team recommended that the decision on the first be deferred until competent technical advice relating to drug manufacture could be obtained. The proposal for the five clinics was supported.

Together with Sr Dr Katherine Jobson, the Roman Catholic consultant to the CMC, Nita visited the English-speaking state of the Cameroon Federation.[20] They assisted the Presbyterian Church of the Cameroon (PCC) in preparing a three-year plan for providing PHC and for improving the PCC-managed hospitals. The concept of community medicine had already been grasped by some health workers and teachers, and its application as a community enterprise for development was confirmed by the visitors through workshops. One apparent hindrance to progress in PHC and related activities in health and medicine appeared to be the slow upward progress of indigenous staff members compared with that of other members of staff. Nita had seen the biased system at first hand in her own native country where the service of local staff received less recognition than that of imported, usually white, staff. She recognised the signs of frustration which ensues.

In order to promote the philosophy of PHC and its dependence for success on the involvement of communities, a series of six regional consultations were held: in the Caribbean (Port-of-Spain, Trinidad), March 1979; Central America (Omoa, Honduras), March 1979; Africa (Gaborone, Botswana), October 1979; Egypt (Alexandria), May 1980; southern Asia (New Delhi, India), August 1980; South-east Asia (Bali, Indonesia), April 1981; Pacific (Papua New Guinea), October 1981; and South America (Quito, Ecuador), June 1982.[21] The theme of the consultations was 'The Search for a Christian Understanding of Health, Healing and Wholeness'.

The African Regional Consultation was held at Gaborone, Botswana, because it was suitable politically and was convenient geographically for African participants. The interests and disciplines were represented by the 60 or more participants. In addition to the practitioners of curative medicine, there were traditional healers, health educators, pharmacists, nurses, social workers, credit union officials and church-related health workers. For many of those attending it was the first time that they had been in contact with such a variety of people sharing in the same services even though performing different functions.

The CMC was represented by Nita, then its director; Eric Ram, associate director; and Sylvia Talbot, its moderator. The two subjects, traditional healing and the christian concept of healing in an African setting, received special attention. It was recognised that the church was often lukewarm towards African traditional medicine and confused it with witchcraft, idolatry and fetishism. The consultation agreed that African Christianity should: 'find its roots in African soil . . . and embrace all that is good and wholesome in African traditional healing methods.'

The second assembly of the Caribbean Conference of Churches was held in Georgetown, Guyana, in November 1977. Nita attended the meeting with Dr Philip Potter, and while there accepted an invitation from Peter Kempadoo, Chairman of the Bantu Society, a village cooperative society in a rural district, to visit one of the society's projects. The project was being developed by women using locally grown vegetables as a way of improving the nutrition of their families and as an income-generating enterprise.

There was a need for financial support, but small projects do not easily attract funding from the usual agencies which support CMC. Writing to Nita in Geneva after her return, Kempadoo asked for US$4,000 to meet the cost of minimal shelter in the form of an old galvanised iron bond, equipment including smokeless fire places and a few items of inexpensive machinery, such as a small engine to drive an all-purpose mill. Nita was able to tell Kempadoo that the required sum of money had been secured by CMC.

Nita's Australasian experience provides one example of some desirable practices, but much of the negative was also evident.

Nita visited the medical and PHC clinics in areas including the North-West territory with its Aboriginal Women's Centre. In spite of the vast sums of money spent on the health facilities provided by the government, they were not as well utilised as those in which the aboriginal people participated in the delivery of PHC. The reason was that in the former they did not share in the responsibility for their own health welfare and where their cultural needs were ignored.

The insensitivity of government officials to the customs, culture and language of the aborigines was very real. One of the contributing factors is that the aboriginal people lacked incentive for leadership and also participation in decision making. In contrast, in New Zealand there was more involvement of the Maoris and Pacific islanders in PHC services and in community-oriented psychiatric training courses being conducted at the University of Otago in Wellington. The women of the Maori Women's Welfare League were spearheading the developmental work.

Nita continued her programme in the Pacific with a visit to Papua New Guinea,[22] where health centres constituted the major part of PHC services in the southern highlands. The standards of nursing and health personnel were maintained and unified under the General Nursing Council and the Postgraduate School of Allied Health Sciences, supported by the joint action of Christian churches and the government.

The CMC received an application from a small group of Church sisters from Australia who were conducting a PHC project in a section of the almost inaccessible highlands of Papua New Guinea. The financial aid requested was US$40,000 to purchase chain-link fencing. The German-based aid agency which the CMC had approached for that sum was quite willing to donate up to US$150,000 as a contribution to the building of a hospital, if necessary. But it could not reconcile the request for chain-link fencing with primary health care needs.

To reach the sisters, Nita had to travel by the small plane service which transported passengers, food and materials from the capital, Port Moresby, to the highlands. The plane scheduled service could not always be kept because the mist in the hills more often than not, made flying hazardous. The landing strip was really a clearing made in part of a heavily wooded area. Nita found that there were two distinct projects. One was educational, in which groups of about 40 girls were given a basic education. The other was training in nutrition, which included some agriculture and home economics. Trainees learned how to grow vegetables and how to get the best nutritional value from them. At the end of their training the girls returned to their own villages and became teachers.

A small health centre was linked to the agricultural educational programme. The machinery and tools for the project included a small tractor with attachments. The tractor, however, had proved unsuitable, because petrol and oil had to be purchased in Port Moresby and transported by plane to the site. Acting on advice, and because there was a stream of water nearby, the sisters had obtained water buffalo from the Philippines. They and their charges learnt to use the buffalo not only for ploughing and cultivating the land, but also for milk, meat and leather.

Success of the sisters' efforts had caused thievery, which put the project at risk, since not only was food grown by the trainees for everyone related to the project, but the excess was sold and the proceeds used to purchase necessary supplies. If the project was to survive, the agricultural plot would have to be fenced to keep out the thieves. Following the visit, the report and recommendation submitted by the CMC to the donors' funds were approved for the fencing.

Collaboration with the WHO had led to the CMC being invited to attend the International Conference on Primary Health Care held at Alma Ata, USSR, in September 1978. Nita, Sylvia Talbot and Stuart Kingma represented the CMC which was one of 70 NGOs and 140 governments participating.

The conference produced the Declaration of Alma Ata, a statement of ten clauses which became condensed to the slogan: 'Health for All by the Year 2000'. The declaration defined health as total well-being (Clause I) and affirmed the right of persons individually and collectively to participate in planning and implementing their own PHC (Clause IV).

Identifying the responsibility of governments for the people's health, the conference proposed that by the year 2000 a level of health should be attainable by all people to permit them to lead a socially and economically productive life through a fuller and better use of the world's resources (Clauses V and X).[23]

Simply leaving Russia is (or used to be) an undertaking requiring fortitude and patience because of the personal searches. Nita and Stuart were convinced that their Alma Ata conference badges and their Intourist escort enabled them to be exempt from the searches as they left Moscow for Istanbul. The purpose of their visit to Turkey was to make recommendations about the use of the Balikli and the Jeramya hospitals supported by the Greek orthodox church.

During their visit Nita and Stuart attended a service in the ecumenical patriarchate on the Feast Day of the Cross, seated with such visiting church dignitaries as the Anglican and Roman Catholic bishops. At lunch time, since the patriarchate was considered a monastery, Nita was not permitted to eat with the men, but was instead invited to take lunch with an archbishop in an emergency dining room.

The 230-year-old Balikli hospital had become the largest hospital in the Balkans by the end of the last century and could serve 2,000 patients, including custodial and nursing care for geriatrics. As the Greek population in Istanbul fell from about 700,000 to about 7,000 in 1978, the hospital accommodation had been reduced accordingly. The hospital provided its own milk and milk products and owned a considerable amount of real estate, mostly derived from bequests and deeds of gift, which reduced the need for external financial support.

However, the financial difficulties caused by the prohibition of sales of real estate or of public fund-raising had resulted in increasing by large annual financial deficits. The CMC recommended to donor agencies as an interim measure that they provide adequate grants for a limited period. As a basis for making long-term decisions, the CMC team also recommended that there be a cost and income analysis of each department and an assessment of need for its continuation.

The smaller 50-bed Jeremya hospital, like that at Balikli, had for more than 100 years provided curative medical care, some custodial and nursing care for a few geriatrics and an out-patient polyclinic. Income was falling and so too was the number of patients and those in custodial and nursing care. The CMC team undertook to seek some funding for the hospital for a further year or two, during which time local decisions would be made about the continued existence and role of the institution.

---

1. Discussion with Rev Dr Arne Sovik, formerly director of the World Mission of the Lutheran World Federation.
2. See *Contact*, monthly publication of the CMC, No.4, July 1951.
3. Ibid
4. An earthquake struck Guatemala in 1976 and severely damaged Chimaltenango and the project there. Buildings of adobe which housed the clinics and outpatients department were destroyed (*CMC Report*, July 1975-June 1976)
5. *Report on Activities and Concerns of the CMC*, January 1974-June 1975, 27-28.
6. *Contact*, No. 39, June 1977, 3.
7. Discussion with author, September 1994.
8. Barefoot doctors were so-called because they practised preventive and curative medicine in the rice areas of China where it was often pointless to wear shoes when attending persons working in paddy fields.

9. The Meru are an agricultural Bantu group whose main areas of habitation are the eastern and western slopes of Mount Meru near Arusha in northern Tanzania. Culturally they are related to the Chagga of Kilimanjaro. About half of them are Lutheran and the remainder adherent to traditional ethnic religion. The Meru of Tanzania are not related to the Meru of Kenya.

10. Raimo Harjula, *Mirau and His Practice, A Study of the Ethno-medicinal Repertoire of a Tanzanian Herbalist*, Tri-Med Books, London, 1980.

11. John S Mbiti in a note in *Mirau and his Practice* identifies herbalists, traditional doctors or waganga (Swahali) as the same specialists. In the book's glossary of Meru terms pp.xv, mwaanga (pl. vaanga) is defined as medicine-man, herbalist.

12. From a list prepared in November 1976 by Stuart J. Kingma, associate director of CMC.

13. *Report on Activities and Concerns of the CMC*, July 1976–December 1977, 5.

14. *Ibid.* p.8.

15. Kip later became Kenyan ambassador, first to Paris, then to London. He subsequently returned to Nairobi as Permanent Secretary in the Ministry of Foreign Affairs.

16. *Report on Seminar/Workshop on Alternative in Delivery of Health Services*, Castries, St Lucia, West Indies, November 1976, Department of Social & Preventive Medicine, UWI, 10-19.

17. Dr Cicely Williams, Jamaican, Dr Jeliffe, English, were paediatricians who had formed a pioneer team at the UWI Medical Faculty.

18. Eileen Stark was based at Belo Horizonte where she trained nurses. She was killed in an accident in 1988 when the bus in which she was travelling went over a precipice.

19. There is also concern about the murders allegedly being committed by the miners, who are intruders into the Indian living areas. At the time of writing (September 1993), the Brazilian government is investigating a massacre of some indigenous peoples. Much hope of a satisfactory result was not being placed on the result.

20. Formerly the French and British Cameroons. At independence in 1972 a federal republic of two states were formed, which in 1984 became the Republic of the Cameroon.

21. *Summary Report on the Study Programme of the CMC*, CMC/28/4, 9.

22. Formerly the island consisted of German New Guinea and Australia Papua. In 1963, after more than 40 years of international disagreement, western New Guinea became part of Indonesia and the Eastern portion independent Papua New Guinea.

23. *Contact* No. 47, 11–13

Opening of Aborigine Health Centre in Darwin, Australia, 1978

Nita with health administrators and staff of Aborigine Health Centre, 1978

Nita with Joyce Seroke, Executive Director of YWCA of South Africa

Nita with members of executive of YWCA of Philippines

Left: Nita at opening of YWCA World Council meeting in Greece, 1979

Above: Nita and four past world presidents of YWCA

Below: Nita and Errol W. Barrow

Nita as YWCA World President, with HM Queen Elizabeth II and Anne Carbury, President of YWCA (UK) at Westminster, after church service celebrating 125th anniversary

5

Advancing the Status of Women

A photograph of the late Eleanor Roosevelt, standing in profile, holding a copy of the Universal Declaration of Human Rights was eloquent for two reasons. First, the copy of the document, shown face on, is held by the left hand which is level with the top of Mrs Roosevelt's head. She holds the bottom with her right hand well below waist level. The physical size of the copy of the photograph displayed appeared to convey the magnitude of the social impact which the original document has had on the world for more than 40 years.[1]

The second reason is that Mrs Roosevelt, one of the twentieth century's greatest female leaders, indeed agitators, for what is now termed gender equality, was the chairman of the United Nations (UN) commission on women which produced the draft document. In 1948, when the declaration was first prepared, accepted and published, the term feminist had not yet become a real word in the English language, so that its connotations had not had any impact. Soon came the word 'discrimination' used as a verbal weapon. That uncomfortable word with its synonym prejudice, had previously only been associated with the denial of opportunity or of rights of one racial group by another. Seldom had it been used to convey the denial of women's rights. The word 'rights' was creeping with a new meaning into lexicons since in earlier times it had seldom been applied to the status of women. Male dominance in the work place, in the home and in all places of human activity had become, especially in the West, a subject not only of women's discontent but also of agitation.

In some earlier civilisations, women's legal position was effectively one of equality with men. In ancient Egypt, besides the practice of monogamy, which clearly related to security for women and the family, marriage contracts provided for the wife's ownership of property. In the Aegean (around 1200 BC) women participated in religious ceremonies. In Islamic countries, however a man's responsibility for the honour of the female members of his household resulted in male dominance. In certain countries in medieval Europe, a wife retained ownership of property although her husband administered it.

From early in the current century women have been agitating for a change in their status. So important was the demand of women for the improvement in their status that within two years of the establishment of the UN itself, that body set up the UN Commission on Women's Rights.

The decision to declare a 'Decade of Women' was made at a meeting of the participant governments of the UN at a conference held in Mexico City in 1975,

At that meeting it was also agreed that in 1980 a mid-term conference of Non Governmental Organisations (NGOs) would be held to review the progress made during the first five years. A final, end of Decade Conference would be held in 1985 to consider what might be done to maintain or increase improvements gained.

It is unlikely that the institution of a Decade of Women would have been proposed by the UN of its own volition. It had resulted from the pressures which women through NGOs had exerted within the UN as well as through their own activities throughout the world. Women's desire for greater recognition of their work and services had become urgent and pressure from women was being put on governments especially in assemblies where governments were represented. The UN Commission on the Status of Women had the task of trying to coordinate those groups and individuals representing the interests of women.

Since the UN had agreed to pursue the matter of improvement in the status of women and to discuss and evaluate progress by means of conferences, women's organisations would also hold their own NGO conferences in the same countries and at the same times when the Official UN Conferences were being held. Three such conferences were held: in Mexico City in 1975, in Copenhagen in 1980 and in Nairobi in 1985. For the End of Decade Conference and for the preceding two as well, UN womens' committees were established with headquarters at the Geneva base of the UN, which met annually to conduct a review of all aspects of the work related to the progress of women since 1975.

Member states, through their governmental representatives, discussed policies and arrived at consensus whenever possible.

Conferences of NGOs are not constrained by governmental policies. Consequently the members tend, more often than not, to speak freely within the conventions of polite language, and occasionally somewhat provocatively when expressing views which would have no place in diplomatic assemblies. In this way NGOs have the advantage of being able to reveal issues which are explosive, irritating or controversial.

The 1975 conference of NGOs in Mexico was therefore the first opportunity that women from almost every country had to meet and discuss their problems, both common as well as those related to special areas of the world. The 1975 conference included, for example, women from the South Pacific who had never previously left that region; women from the Caribbean and Africa who had never been involved in international discussions; women from South Africa suffering from the insults of apartheid; women from Asia whose lives had been disrupted by the Vietnam war; women from Israel and Palestine who were strongly antagonistic to each other.

Some strong differences which led to confrontation, were much in evidence at the 1975 Mexico conference and had made it a somewhat painful experience as the women began to talk to one another. Nevertheless, there was the feeling of a developing sisterhood. It was hoped, therefore, that the decision to establish the Decade of Women would ensure that the delicate but cohesive bonds established among the women would strengthen noticeably in the years following.

The mid-term 1980 conference would review the progress and the final conference, held in 1985, would identify the changes, if any, which had been effected and point the way forward for women to achieve their proper place in the modern world.

At the 1980 NGO conference in Copenhagen, the women talked freely about issues such as female circumcision which could never be discussed at a governmental conference. The 1980 conference did have its moments of difficulty when for example the national Israel/Palestine confrontation was more acute than it had been at the time of the Mexico meeting.

The information derived during the period 1975–80 clearly manifested the true economic status of women and the effect which that status had in rural and urban areas as well as the increasing burden of poverty, which had become more dehumanising as the poor of the world became poorer. It indicated that the new international economic order bore no promise of change in the unequal status of women. This was an important issue for discussion. The proposed order appeared to be dependent upon global resources which were being exploited by the nations of the north. There would be great difficulty in ensuring that third world women obtained a fair share of the resources to enable them to improve health, education and nutrition.

At the Nairobi conference (1985) where feelings ran high, fired by the strong female instincts for survival, Nita became an oasis of sanity. She insisted on maintaining links of communication between the NGO conference and the inter-governmental conference, through which the latter was kept informed of the status of issues which the NGOs were discussing, and where possible, of the level of feeling associated with those discussions.

In 1983 Nita had just completed her second term as president of the World YWCA and had also retired from the WCC as one of its Presidents. In that same year she was invited to be the coordinator of the 1985 NGO conference, Forum '85, nominated by the president of Zaire, who was president of the International Organisation Co-ordinating Non-governmental Organisations at the time.

Dame Nita's development as a leader in the NGO world began at the Uppsala meeting of the WCC in 1968, which covered many fields from theology to health. The council got into the heat of worldwide criticism when it turned out to be a strong supporter of independence for all nations. The Uppsala meeting also gave an impetus to Dame Nita's interest in health care. The meeting recognised that the traditional hospitals only reach a few and the concept of primary health care was born, Until then, traditional medicine had been largely ignored, even despised. After Uppsala, interest in it grew and it was recognised that health depends on food, water and sanitation.

> 'You don't have to wait till you are ill before you go to the doctor,' says Dame Nita, 'You should take care of the positive aspects of the family's health, which means, of course, looking after the women of the family.'

Nita had been looking forward to going home to Barbados, but nevertheless accepted the post. So instead of going home she found herself living in New York almost continuously for the next two years, so as to be near the UN where the facilities and contacts were. She set up a planning committee for Forum '85. Since none of the NGOs received funds from the UN, Nita's first major task was to raise funds for the conference, the planning committee consisted of women from organisations with official status at the UN including the World YWCA and the United Methodist Women. It was to the latter organisation that Nita turned for help initially. The United Methodist Women provided the Forum '85 planning committee, not only with a floor in its building but also with much of the office furniture and secretarial help.

With her well developed human skills Nita succeeded in welding the Forum '85 staff members into a cooperative team of workers. Such a description of the support and administrative staff involved in the preparation of the 1985 conference does not indicate the volume of work and level of commitment required of them nor of Nita. For example, simply to state that Nita made what was effectively a successful world tour partly as a public relations effort in support of the forum gives no indication of, nor makes any reference to, the discussions held with the many women's groups which she met during her travels. One purpose of each such meeting was to advise the participants about the special qualities which they might use in presenting their views at the forum in order to achieve success, those of empathy and cooperation rather than argument and confrontation.

With so much goodwill for a beginning, Nita and her committee launched their fund-raising appeal which would and did benefit from Nita's tour. The appeal was not easy because the official conference, which would also be held in Nairobi, was itself so badly in need of financial assistance that its organisers were approaching many of the same potential donors as was the Forum '85 planning committee. Many of the governments that supported the planning committee were generous in their donations; among these were Canada, the UK, Australia, New Zealand and many in Europe, especially Germany and Scandinavia.

The planning committee also made use of contacts, mainly ambassadors, at the UN. As the chairman of the planning committee, Nita had not only to initiate action but meet potential donors and representatives of governments who required explanations. Such visits also included those arranged by the several women's organisations in many of the countries. For this purpose Nita visited Finland, Sweden, Canada, the UK and indeed wherever the women's organisations thought that they needed her injection of dynamic enthusiasm.

Other supporting groups also met at the annual reviews of the planning committee. Nita and her colleagues invited to those meetings representatives of organisations whose presence was not really required but who would observe the kind of effort which preparation and planning required. Some of those women came from organisations in the Caribbean, Africa, Asia, parts of Latin America and Europe. Others were not necessarily members of organisations, but were working with women's groups. For example, one such person was a Vincentian woman who was the leader of a successful community group in the Rose Hall area. Another woman, a trade unionist, who had successfully organised domestic workers, was brought from Trinidad. When Nita suggested that hard-earned funds be used to bring the Trinidadian to Geneva, she was challenged on the grounds that the woman was not known, or had not been heard of before, Nita replied: 'When a woman can organise domestic workers and get them to have so much clout that the government and many others regard her as a threat, she deserves to be looked at.'

The responsibility of being coordinator of Forum '85 became a major test for Nita, for she clearly drew on the enormous prestige which she had already gained through her services to the YWCA, the WCC, the International Council for Adult Education (ICAE) and through other contacts which she had made over the years. Early in 1985 when Nita had just returned to New York from a WCC meeting in Geneva, she received a message from Kenya that President Moi had said that there would be no Forum '85, and for good reason. The reason was that the president had recently heard, quite correctly, that at the conference held in Copenhagen in 1980 there had been much social disruption, including a public demonstration of militant women marching and displaying behaviour which would be quite unacceptable to the people of Kenya and would be an assault on the sensitivities of the community.

Nita called Bethuel Kiplagat, Kip, on the telephone from New York and learned that the message was correct. She indicated to Kip the embarrassment which would result from the cancellation of the forum, especially since substantial financial contributions had already been received in its support by numerous governments. The only word which Kip said on the phone was: 'Come.'

Nita caught the next plane out of New York, that same night. When she arrived in Nairobi she found that the planning committee for the official conference was meeting. She had also heard that there were some members of that committee who felt that Forum '85 would get too much publicity thereby overshadowing the official conference. One of these was thought to be a former associate of Nita's in the YWCA hierarchy. Nita recalling the difficult situation said:

> On arrival, I found that the Official Committee was meeting. Every access to the President was blocked. However, through the interest of Kip and of the Foreign Minister, especially the influence of the latter, we suddenly found ourselves invited to a tea party being given for the Women of the Official Committee. To our delight, President Moi was present. I therefore was given the opportunity of speaking with him.
>
> To the President I repeated that funds in support of the Forum had already been received and indicated the embarrassment which his decision to cancel the Forum would cause. On the matter of the disturbances in Copenhagen in 1980, I personally guaranteed that there would be no street demonstrations as there had been in Copenhagen and that there would be no attempt to shock the citizens of the host country.

President Moi accepted Nita's assurances and honoured the responsibility of his government to provide housing for the expected 10,000. So enthusiastic a supporter of the Forum '85 did the president become that he arranged for 2,000 women from the rural districts of Kenya to attend the conference.

The 1985 Nairobi conference was supposed to comprise about 10,000 women (the actual official count was 17,500) compared with 5,000 at the 1980 meeting in Copenhagen. The Copenhagen community was committed to feminism and the NGOs were virtually able to take over the country for two weeks. But similar sympathies did not exist in Kenya and so no excessive displays of feminism could be paraded, and most certainly not with nearly such emotion as in Copenhagen. Indeed, the Kenyan government, following the discussions with Nita established clear guidelines. There would be no feminist demonstrations of solidarity nor protests as there had been in Copenhagen. This was because of the extreme cultural differences between Denmark and Kenya and respect had to be shown for the long-established culture of the host community.

It was also Nita's responsibility to ensure that political opinions which might arise at the NGO conference were kept within bounds. Apart from the national political issues which would adversely affect relationships during the conference, there were issues of women's organisations claiming precedence of representation. Nita had to use her sense of fair play and firm discipline to maintain order. One of those issues based on strong national feelings was the Iran-Iraq confrontation.

At the previous conference, when Iran had been one of the leading activist nations in the UN Princess Ashra, sister of the Shah of Iran, had been an international leader pressing for women's rights. The Khomini revolution had taken place in Iran and women had lost all the ground which they had gained in their fight to remove their inequalities. Iraq was also one of the nations with one of the most active women organisations. It would be a herculean task for Nita and her helpers to maintain a working atmosphere at any meeting during the Forum where Iran and Iraq both were represented.

There were other world issues likely to inflame tempers at the conference. Among them were the Israel-Palestine issue and the Nicaraguan and Central American conflicts with the USA. Both of these impinged on the rights of women and their status, since they were world-peace threatening issues, and would appear on the agenda. Nita had to find ways and means of ensuring that the conference would result in discussions which would build solidarity among women rather than intensify existing divisions.

Time and again during the conference Nita drew on her prestige within the WCC and on her deep religious faith and established credibility. Jewish representatives could sit and talk with her freely and she could empathise with them and give assurances that the conference would not be hostile to Israeli and Zionist aspirations. Women from third-world countries felt free to discuss with her the degrading situations within their communities. All sought guidance on how such issues might be discussed without appearing to betray the mores of their individual societies whilst giving voice to their yearnings for the removal of the yoke of second-class citizenship.

The necessity to have a firm hand but a delicate touch was uppermost in Nita's mind from the first day of the conference. She also lost no time in signalling to the members the need to be sensitive to the customs of the host country as well as to the opinions of the national groups at the international conference.

In her opening address on 10 July 1985 Nita stressed that:

> The climate in Nairobi is different from that in Copenhagen. In 1980 the international political climate was much less reactionary and confrontational than it is today, We know much has been made of what did not happen at Copenhagen. The press reported on the lack of consensus, but a consensus about what? What happened was unfortunately not in the press, but you are the living examples that if it did not happen you would not be here today.[2]

Nita began her speech describing a dream which she had of the end of the Forum '85 some 10 days later. She 'saw' a stage of a theatrical happening which took hours to unfold as women from all the continents and of all ethnic groups

> told their sisters in song and dance and words and music the story of Everywoman. The night's performance transcending all barriers of class, colour, ideology, captured the essence of hopes and dreams of the last ten years and the

centuries of patriarchal rule before 1975.
The affair would end with day breaking when thousands of women would rise to their feet singing . . . knowing that . . .
'Woman time a come, A new day dawning, Yes, Woman time a come. A new day dawning.'

Addressing an estimated 10,000 women, Nita acknowledged the financial support given to the forum to permit the attendance of so great a number of women, especially those from third-world countries, Nita reviewed the two preceding meetings of women held during the decade, Mexico 1975 and Copenhagen 1980. Forum '85 unlike those two, was being held in a third-world country, with all the varying interpretations of the term.

> For this reason I believe that the physical location of the Forum will influence the attitudes which women bring to the meeting. We all know the line-up: the visitor, eager but fearful; the native, proud and anxious. Kenya is not just a safari, it is a country like any other with problems and pluralities that cannot be denied or quarantined.

Nairobi would assume great importance as the meeting place, for it would be there that women would devise ways of harnessing TV power to advance their purpose. 'Consensus might not be possible, but understanding is.' After paying due appreciation to the convenors and administrators of Mexico '75 and Copenhagen '80, Nita noted that gains had been made by women during the 'Decade'. The problems which still existed were caused by economic depression, poverty and failed political solutions; but that concomitantly resourcefulness and determination to survive had become part of the force of life and of the source of empowerment.

> in spite of the fact that we shake our heads and rue the elusiveness of freedom and equality, we have caught a glimpse of the word 'possible' and we know that we feel different, that we are different women from the women we were ten years ago. Not just older; Stronger, Bolder, Surer.

The conference had its own daily paper, Forum '85 produced by the planning committee. It was staffed by an international team of journalists based at the University of Nairobi.

Under the headline of 'Strong Leader, Mild Touch', a commentator wrote, in the issue of *Forum '85* 11 July 1985 of Nita:

> She is strong as an ox yet mild as a dove at the same time. She is Nita Barrow, whose title, Dame, makes her sound like a demure, tea-drinking lady, but whether or not she drinks tea as Convener of the Planning Committee for the NGO Forum, she is also a powerful manager who has all the combative spirit of a freedom fighter. Now she has put all her tremendous energy into the task of 'nursing' 10,000 women through the crowded days of the Forum.
>
> By profession, Dame Nita is a nurse with an international reputation. For the past 40 years she has been a vibrant contributor to the fields of education

and health care both in the Caribbean, where she comes from and all over the world, working for the World Health Organisation and the World Council of Churches. She is currently President of the International Council for Adult Education.

During the busy days of the Forum, the University of Nairobi will be her 'Church' and Dame Nita's only concern will be to care for the 10,000 souls trying to find their identity as they search for the future. 'Be prepared mentally first of all,' she advises, 'You have to know what your preferences are. Believe me, when you know what you want and who you are, you also need to find out where to go, but that does not mean confrontation.'

'Not even with men?'

'Don't get me into that.' was her reply, 'Some form of oppression exists, but it is not the same all over the world. In some countries men are oppressed. If all people are oppressed the women can't claim that they are the only ones to be interested in liberation. It is up to women to decide what are their goals. I don't think women can say that they don't have the chance. We have the vote, we have the rights. But there has been a whole period where there little development for women has taken place, Politically women have not taken many positions of power.'

'In my thirties I was director of a major hospital and was one of the first principal nursing officers of the Commonwealth. Many doctors were male, certainly those who were my colleagues, but I always felt on an equal footing with them. There was no problem being a girl in my family. There was no question of girls being treated differently from the boys. From my mother's side we have a tradition of girls being educated. We were three girls and two boys in the family in Barbados. My grandmother insisted that we should have equal education. I have always felt liberated.'

'But what about girls where there is no family tradition of educating girls, the ones who perhaps live in remote areas with few resources?'

'I will never define for other women their needs. I can suggest some principles; one person should not choose priorities for others. We can find groups of women with common priorities. Others may go along with them. But other people have to know where their objectives lie. Every woman has to know her own priorities. The mistake is to place the responsibility on other people.'

Perhaps Dame Nita takes on too much responsibility herself. The organisation of the Forum was mainly her responsibility, although there was a hard-working crew of the Kenyan NGO committee and her own staff from the NGO planning committee in New York, Geneva, Vienna and Paris who worked hard to bring women from all over the world together.

What are Dame Nita's hopes for the Forum and the UN Conference?

'I have said in other places and I say it here: I have no expectations. What we are hoping for is to create a climate, listen and hear as well as speak. I will not presume to predict what will happen at the UN Conference.'

In the course of her career Dame Nita has visited 80 countries and each one has offered something unique, she says, not for her as a tourist but as a worker. The dimension of women was added to her travels through her involvement with the World YWCA, an organisation with members in more than 70 countries and of which she was president for eight years.

There are many facts to be written about Dame Nita's life but you will have problems trying to draw a map of her soul. However, we know that her interests include reading and writing, even cooking (and she willingly provides a meal for a worn-out fellow worker). So we will present something she has written, a folk song from Rajasthan in India. In choosing this folk song, she has shown a deep understanding for women, and the song is perhaps a contrast to her strong demand that women are to shape their own future:

> Send me not in marriage,
> Father, to Bikanen.
> Let not my father-in-law's house
> Be there, eh boy.
> It is hard to fetch water in
> Bikanen . . .
> In fetching water, the soles of
> daughter's feet are worn out
>
> The soles of her feet, eh boy.
> The daughter's head has become bald.
> Eh boy . . .

During one of the brain-storming sessions of the planning committee of the conference in Geneva (actually held on International Women's Day, 8 March 1984), some of the opportunities for friction during the forum had been discussed. The problem was not only to avoid the disagreements which would occur when so many people with limited freedoms, real and imagined, met. The challenge to the planners was how to make each incident an isolated one, and not one of many eruptions or blemishes on the body forum which might lead to major illness and the possible death of the purpose of the conference. The solution was found in the concept of a peace tent, a place where no animosities would be permitted, where occupants would be committed to seeking peaceful solutions to the most agonising problems, a place where it would be almost sacrilegious to sustain an argument in the face of the common cause of feminism.

Nadia Hijab,[3] a journalist attending Forum '85 described the peace tent as an attractive innovation:

> set up as a large tent by the side of the Education Building (of the University of Nairobi, the site of the Forum) . . . The blue-and-white peace tent is the result of six months work by some 40 women from 15 different countries, . . . The women . . . took the opportunity to propose a 'feminist alternative to men's conflict and war'.

By the time that the peace tent became a reality, it was more than a reservation for temporary co-existence; it was rather a sanctuary, smelling of new wood, where although there was not enough space to walk about, there was not enough atmosphere in which to recreate oneself – and enough panelling for personal and conference notices. One notice, pathos-tinged but rich in hope and confident of triumph, hid its vulnerability and touch of humour in embroidery: 'This house is a nuclear free zone.'

Nita's leadership and diplomacy and the role of the peace tent probably met their greatest test simultaneously. The censorship board had approved for showing at the National Film Centre a film entitled 'Laila and the Wolves – the Hidden History of Women in Palestine and Lebanon', made by a Lebanese film-maker Heiny Srour. The film was advertised to be shown at a fixed time on the day before the end of the conference. The would-be audience included a group of international film-makers. Much to the disappointment of the women and the frustration of Heiny Srour and her peers, the showing of the film had been cancelled by the local authorities.

The not unreasonable anger first showed in an impromptu press conference in the conference grounds and then threatened to erupt into a public demonstration. One of Nita's 'fire wardens' summoned her to the scene. With her proverbial Job-like patience and the diplomacy worthy of a UN chief, Nita managed to get the complainants into the peace tent.

> She headed towards the peace tent, asking only Forum women delegates to follow her. There she made sure the tent was cleared of 'all men'. She said she didn't want 'gentleman of the Press, security or snoops'. Dame Nita said, 'I do not like to bring security in because I feel I can reason with women.'
>
> She then told the women they were free to hold a march if they wished, but she would ask them to hand in their Forum badges,[4] i.e. their identification tags issued by the Kenyan government, on the way out of the university, to protect the interests of the other women at the conference. Nothing would come of such a march, she said, but something might come of her efforts to negotiate an acceptable solution.

Heiny Srour addressed the women present, citing bias on the part of the authorities. She did not understand how a film could be withdrawn once it had been passed by the censorship board. A feature film on Israeli women had been shown earlier in the week with no problem, so there should be no problem about a film on Arab women.

Nita declared her respect for Ms Srour as a film-maker. She had no doubt that a genuine mistake had been made or that Ms Srour was the innocent victim of a kind of backlash. A Lebanese film-maker had shown a film earlier during the conference which turned out to be different from what had been described in the documentation attached to it. Nita felt that no one else should be made to suffer for that incident; if, however, the women would agree that she try to solve the problem, she would work through the night to ensure that the film would be shown.

The women agreed. All that need be recorded now is that after discussion with appropriate persons, Nita was assured that the film would be shown before 5.00 p.m. the following day.

Nita described the organisation of the conference in these words.

> The organising of so many women was no mean undertaking. Conference material had been prepared for about 10,000 persons. Suddenly to be told on the second day that all the material, including badges, had run out was nothing less than a nightmare. Those without registration material were not those who had registered. Virtual panic ensued. Instructions concerning procedure for registration were ignored. It was a case of emergency . . .
>
> Many of the people whom I knew from my association with the ICAE, YWCA, WCC, attended as representatives of those organisations. They pitched in and set up emergency registration. Those women coped. The final count was 17,500. One of the most important items which every participant should have was the badge, that passport to free movement and protective emblem. Two young women, one the wife of the present Peruvian Ambassador to the UN, the other Toolin Akin, now Van Poulin, were in charge of the issuing of much of the material. These two women overcame the difficulties so that there were few who felt that their needs were not satisfied.

Of Toolin, and the results of her work and that of her assistants, Nita stated:

> I have never seen a young woman do such a magnificent job. Her ability to get on with people was extraordinary, the demands on her in Nairobi were extreme. She and her assistants worked every night up to 2.00 a.m. We got all the material we could from the women's groups, when required. We also managed to get enough of the programmes. There was almost chaos since nearly everyone who attended wanted to participate in a workshop.
>
> Certain of the women who had come to the official meeting visited the Forum site and spent much of their time with us. They felt that the Official Conference was a talk shop. Their special badges permitted them to move freely between the two conferences.

The Kenyan organising committee which acted as local agents for the planning committee had been able to mobilise the Kenyan women and catch their imagination, making them realise that they were participating in and hosting an event which would be momentous in the history of liberation of women of the world. In spite of the activity of the local committee members, it was still necessary for the planning committee to meet three times a day. Its members also acted as advisers to all the other sub-committees and working groups.

The government of Kenya had assumed responsibility for the housing of all delegates. It was understood that all that needed to be done in that respect was to state that accommodation was required for a certain number of people. However, no one could have anticipated the large number of late registrations, which brought the final count to 17,500 women. Based at the campus of the University of Nairobi, the Committee asked that two of the halls of residence be provided as part of the accommodation, because many of the delegates from third world countries would not be able to afford to stay in hotels. In the end, many of those with hotel rooms shared their accommodation with some of those whose accommodation was precarious.

Nita recalls overhearing a question put to one of the delegates from the third world:

'How did we manage?' 'Women know how to ease over.'

The University dining halls could accommodate 2,000, so its facilities were stretched to the limit and the efforts of the staff matched those of everyone else who were part of the Forum and of the supporting services. But the women of Nairobi, in anticipation of the need for greater cooking and eating facilities, set up stalls at strategic points on the campus, where meals were prepared and eaten. There was no shortage of food.

After the first day or two, everyone who experienced inconveniences of any kind seemed to accept them in good spirit. Although the pressures were constant and varied there were few that were unsurmountable. Throughout the whole two weeks of meetings there were only two cases of illness reported among the 17,500 women.

Early in the planning stage for Forum '85, one of Nita's friends in New York, Inga Gibel, the women's representative on the American Jewish Committee telephoned Nita and told her that the Jewish women were going to have nothing to do with Forum '85 because their representatives had been badly treated at the Copenhagen conference. Inga invited Nita to visit and speak to the Jewish community representatives.

Nita knew that the problems at the Copenhagen meeting were related to long-existing animosities and could not be blamed solely on the Jews or on the Palestinians. Part of Nita's persuasive strategy was her direct though discreet reference to occasions at the Copenhagen meeting when Palestinians were interrupted in their presentations.

After hearing the views of the representatives, Nita promised that if the Jewish women agreed to attend the forum they would be given the same hearing during the conference as anyone else provided that they agreed to work under the rules of the planning committee, one of which was the right to be heard.

Speaking after the forum, Nita commented with evident satisfaction:

> We built up a good relationship with the group long before registration time. I was overwhelmed by the response. When the time came for registration the Jewish women registered for workshops in which Palestinian women were also participating. It was always in the workshops that we got the problems. The Forum managers were watchful that explosive situations did not develop. They did their best not to put Jewish women and Palestinian women in workshops in the same room or to have either one of those national groups occupying a room immediately after the other. Despite all that care, a problem did arise when someone inadvertently arranged for a Palestinian workshop before an

> Israeli one or the reverse. One group would not leave the room at the end of the allotted period in order to accommodate the other. There was no other room available at the time . . .

Once again one of Nita's "fire wardens" in haste sought her out and reported. Nita went to the room and sent all those present to the peace tent to sort out their differences. She guaranteed the victims of the supposed inequality of treatment that a room of equal size with equal facilities would be provided.

By the end of the conference, the two groups of women had established personal contacts which they promised to maintain afterwards. Nita believed in 1992 that there was still a joint committee.[5]

In reply to a question put to her about her own memories of the more stimulating moments of the forum, Nita did not hesitate in her response.

> We sponsored 83 women from the Pacific region and we brought together 2,000 women from areas outside Nairobi . . . one woman made a speech I will never forget. She had come from one of the warmer villages far from Nairobi, and had visited the city for the first time in her life. She wore a sweater pinned around her, one which had been offered by another woman from Europe or USA, which did not fit and had to be secured by safety pins. It was on the last morning of the Forum when many were stating what their future expectations were. This woman rose and in Swahili said that she never thought that in her life she would be in a university. She grew bananas and she sold bananas to support her five children. All that she wanted to say was that she was going back home and grow more bananas. The President (of Kenya) would have to find markets for her bananas so that her children would be able to go to the University and get what she had not got.

This was spoken by a woman who, when she had first arrived at the forum had spoken to no one and had been uncomfortable. In Nita's view that incident exemplified what had been a guiding theme: that the opportunity had been provided for women, for the Kenyan villager, to state their needs, unwittingly speaking for millions of other women, however inadequately, and stating that they now all had an identity.

Inga Gibel should have the final word. Identifying herself as a Jew, a Zionist and a feminist, she labelled the final document prepared by Forum '85, as a victory for truth, justice and the possibility of consensus – which the UN had recently been unable to achieve. Taking her cue from Rosario Manalo, a Filipino delegate quoted by the *Times*, Gibel confirmed that the women of the world had won, that even the UN in spite of itself had also won. It had taken the women and the two preceding conferences to do it: to come to the realisation that neither the Jews nor the Palestinians were the centre of the universe. Gibel summarised the cruelties which had been the expressed collective concern of the thousands of women at the forum; the increasing number of refugees resulting from the selfish power play of neighbouring nations, the inhumanities of apartheid.

At the very base of the column of despair were the poor, black women of South Africa, Uganda and Ethiopia, where the only future foreseeable was pain, death, the misery of watching one's children die and the death of hope itself.

The forum's success in uniting many of the women of the world was in large part attributable to Nita:

> another factor in the success of Forum '85 . . . was the convener, Dame Nita Barrow of Barbados. Dame Nita, a warm, motherly, gentle yet very tough administrator, ... spent the months before Nairobi making it clear that she would not tolerate a repetition of the past . . . Dame Nita had also expressed the hope that the attendees had learned that the issues were health, development, peace, education, employment and equality which affect all women, and that women need to discuss how they were affected by them, not argue about them.

On a note of satisfaction and mild exhilaration, Gibel emphasised how many third world women who had arrived at the forum with their own agendas, were led away from them towards a global sisterhood and a hope for the future.

The end of Forum '85 became, in the opinion of many women's organisations local, national and international, a beginning of another responsibility for Nita. The new responsibility was that of favoured champion of and speaker on the Rights of Women and the Status of more than half of the people of the World.

Her new responsibilities began within months of her successfully concluding her task of Convenor of Forum '85. Accepting an invitation to address the UN Department of Public Information on the occasion of the 40th birthday of the UN on 4 September 1985, Nita began by saying:

> Those of us who have been associated in one way or another with the UN know about the old cliché about the organisation: 'If there was not an UN we would have created one.' We also know that it was created a male organisation in 1945; by 1947, the Status of Women Commission became an established entity.
>
> But the analogy does not begin and end there the analogy can sustain all sorts of nuances, for example most women (so I am told) go through a traumatic period as they approach their 40th birthday. In fact the trauma begins at the age of 30 and reaches crisis proportions around 40. Why? Because the prevailing culture this modern western culture that we have all adopted sends women the message they are beginning to show the signs of old age, and in this culture looking old is certainly worse than eating forbidden fruit. Fortunately it doesn't take too long for the woman who really is serious about her own development to realise that the truth is 'that life begins at 40 . . .'
>
> We all know, in the past decade, the United Nations has been seized with that most political of all issues – the ISSUE OF WOMEN. Yes . . . I know there were other issues of great significance, apartheid, the middle east, the new

international economic order, global and regional war and peace, the list is long . . . When the UN declared 1976 – 1985 the Decade of Women, little did we all realise that it was facilitating the coming together of all the major political issues that face the international community today. What is more, the women of the world demonstrated in July 1985 on the Great Court of the University of Nairobi, for all the world to see that all concerns are women's concerns although battling and disagreeing on issues they demonstrate the ability to cut through futilities and rhetoric and recognise essentials and miracle of miracles, consensus was reached in the women's just as NGO animated and facilitated the process which led to the birth of the UN in 1945 so that NGOs nurture and facilitate the process which led to the culmination of UN's Decade for Women and the coming of age, in Nairobi, of the International Women's Movement. In Nairobi the issues for WOMEN (women's equality role, her responsibilities for personal, national and international development (all for the maintenance of peace) were clearly demonstrated.

She referred to the themes of the forum 'Equality, Development and Peace':

Nearly 20,000 women at Nairobi articulated attainable objectives and these they saw would only be obtained through their own efforts – the women took the problem seriously and have gone back home to address them but as we celebrate today with the UN we ask the UN to look within its own house for a new order.

Referring to a speech made earlier in the day she continued:

You will forgive me that as a woman having worked with the UN and observed it from an NGO viewpoint, I say that no where has there been more evidence in the area of women's issues of a spectacular example of inequality of employment for women than in the UN. As we look at it we perhaps excuse it by saying it is representatives of the governments of the world, and as governments often lag behind the perceptions of people, maybe this chequered achievement is understandable. It is particularly difficult for the UN organisation or any other big one to be bold in the face of constraints. imposed on an international organisation by its member states.

If we refer it to the challenge which the UN organisation is given for the next 40 years nothing can be done in the immediate future but that is what they should consider. Nairobi was one of the first occasions when the complete agenda of the UN was debated realistically although there was often agreement to disagree between the women, nevertheless there was a remarkable degree of consensus on many issues. This was a way of work which allowed a unique opportunity to answer the challenges of Nairobi. 'Some 150 resolutions from a conference will come the new Assembly of the UN in the Fall surely there should be an earnest attempt and a way to move forward positively with new approaches to the old agenda, particularly in the area of women. So that the 21st century will be different and the year 2025 sees much more positive achievements. It is not I but 20,000 women who represented women of the world at Nairobi who challenged the UN to deal with the issue of women as a main agenda item for the 15 years that separate us from the year 2000. That alone will be a formidable task and therefore I need not look further for other agenda items.

Six months later, during the first two weeks of March 1987, in San Francisco, California, Nita was found participating in the first Eleanor Roosevelt International Caucus on Women Political Leaders sponsored by the National Democratic Institute for International Affairs. By that time she had also become Barbados' ambassador to the United Nations and permanent representative. Among the 62 women leaders from 38 nations were included three Barbadians: Dame Nita Barrow, Mrs Maisie Barker-Welch, Ministry of Development, Labour Relations and Community Development, Miss Billie Miller, Former Minister of Education.

The Caucus showed that in spite of the varying backgrounds of the participants, the women had experienced similar difficulties: Advancing in politics while balancing a career with family duties; the near trauma of having to face an electorate more than once or twice before being elected; receiving press attention similar to that of their male colleagues but with somewhat more scrutiny of their private lives. The major recommendation in which Nita also concurred was that an international institute of women's participation in politics should be created which would among other things, monitor women's progress in politics and act as a clearing house of strategies and practical political tactics.

By September of the same year, 1987, Nita's message to The United Nations Development Fund for Women (UNIFEM) on occasion of its Official Tenth Anniversary was one from 17 world leaders which were published[6].

In her message Nita, after indicating the support of Barbados for the UNIFEM, she identified the need for increase in contributions of Member States to the fund:

> We welcome the progress made in the preparation of regional priorities strategies and support the recommendation of the Consultative Committee to establish a UNIFEM presence at the sub-regional level.
> We believe that this approach will help in effecting the Fund's mandate and facilitate the implementation of projects from Member States.

Nita's call for increased support of UNIFEM had been made earlier at the Third Committee of the UN General Assembly on 30 October 1986, Her statement on the Status of Women was from one who was an acknowledged proponent and champion of women's rights and who had within the preceding two years been at the head of Forum '85 and was the only female member of the Eminent Persons Group (EPG) which had seen real evidence of degradation and deprivation of women of the rights of companionship and of the lives of their children.

Addressing the Third Committee Nita pointed to the End of Decade

Nairobi Conference and the Forward-Looking Strategies (FLS) as an achievement for all women. The current session of the General Assembly of the UN in supporting women must demonstrate its commitment by placing women in important positions in the UN itself. The Commission on the Status of Women established in 1947 should be required to study the FLS and give thought to projects to ensure progress. Referring to the reservations which some Member States had of some of the matters related to the FLS, Nita advised caution so that resolution might be reached which would be acceptable to all.

At the end of March Nita was Guest Speaker at the 10th anniversary dinner of the 'Women's and Foundation/Corporate Philanthropy' in Atlanta. The theme of the anniversary Celebrations was 'New Ways to Lead':

> So far mention has been made of only one challenge of Nita to any of the UN Standing Committees or to the General Assembly itself. Perhaps one of the most useful important was that in her address of 14 July 1988 made in her Statement to the UN Second Regular Session of the Economic and Social Council under the heading: 'Some Aspects of Women in Development'.

In her statement Nita reminded the Council that in a recent address she had said that during any economic crisis and any period of structural adjustment, women were among the first to suffer. Too often, she argued, the contribution which women made to economic activity was underestimated. The reason for that was two-fold: their contribution generally did not attract analysis and the analytical tools used were inadequate for the purpose. More up-to-date information on the role of women in development was required for initiating action for enhancing the status of women in economic development. The availability of such information was identified by UN member states in the Nairobi Forward-Looking Strategies for the Advancement of Women.

Thanking the Secretariat for the annexure to the World Economic Survey of 1988 which was being discussed, and drawing attention to an aspect which related to education, Nita stated as the view of the Barbados delegation that if women's economic activity was to be enhanced, then they must be equipped with the required skills. In the provision of services, women continued to occupy the lowest levels. Such extended stratification was undesirable. The situation was common to both industrialised and developing countries. The remedy lay in providing educational opportunity, which in turn would require some change in the attitude which prohibited access of women to higher levels of education, It was also the view of Barbados that women must be involved in the preparation, design and implementation of policies which will effect improvement in their status.

The occasion of the International Day of Solidarity with the Struggle of Women in South Africa and Namibia, 9 August 1989, Even though Nita like her colleagues at the UN knew that elections would take place in Namibia in November of the same year, she nevertheless made a statement as Barbados' Representative to the UN on 9 August, International Day of Solidarity with the Struggle of Women in South Africa and Namibia.

Identifying with her brothers and sisters in South Africa and Namibia, Nita commented on the apparent lack of enthusiasm of some of her colleagues for the occasion. Intending to stimulate her hearers, Nita referred to her recent meeting with a group of South African women who stated that the so-called major reforms publicised by Pretoria had the effect of being 'one step forward and two steps backward'. Such was the continued treatment of South Africans whose women had to bear possibly the larger share of deprivation and denigration. They not only performed the greater share of agricultural tasks and sold the excess produce, but some as wives of miners were deprived of the company and support of their husbands who were forced to live in separation for extended periods in all-male camps near the mines. The ultimate cruelty to the women was the abduction or abuse of their children.

---

1. *Women, Challenges to the Year 2000*, UN Department of Public Information, DP 1134.
2. Ruth Seligman, Extract from *Forum '85* issue of 11 July 1985.
3. *Forum '85* issue of 10 July 1985.
4. Each delegate was provided with a badge which not only gave her the right of entry to meetings, conference rooms and open areas, but also provided a form of protection when visiting off-conference sites, the city included.
5. Discussion with author in 1992.

[1] UNIFEM bi-annual publication 'Development Review' October 1987,

6

International Council of Adult Education (ICAE)

Any discussion of the ICAE would be incomplete without reference to the life and work of Roby Kidd, who went out of his way to involve Nita in its work. Professor J. Robbins Kidd, who was Canadian, was appointed assistant director of the Canadian Association of Adult Education (CAAE) in 1947 and later became its director. His work throughout Canada and much of the developed and developing world became more widely known after the UNESCO conference on adult education in Montreal in 1960. His work in adult education is associated with his chairmanship, beginning in 1966, of the Department of Adult Education of the Ontario Institute for Studies in Education in Ontario. He held this post, subsequently serving as professor, until 1982 when he died.[1] To mention that he was involved with 15 other world organisations dedicated to adult education would barely indicate the level of his service to many thousands of less privileged peoples.

In 1979 the 7th Annual General Meeting of the ICAE was held in Finland. One of its seminars, attended by representatives of 37 countries, was on the topic of 'Adult Education and the Future'. Out of that came an agreement on the priorities of adult education, which would promote economic and social justice and world peace.[2] After the seminar Roby visited Nita in Geneva, where he also had other educational matters to attend to. He tried to involve her in ICAE's work, especially in its expansion programme to Communist countries, mainly the Soviet Union, China and Vietnam. Since Roby foresaw that primary health care (PHC) education would be a part of any such undertaking, he realized that Nita, one of the international proponents of PHC, would be more than an experienced supporter of the project, which would later require visits of ICAE teams to China.

In view of what happened, it would not be unreasonable to assume that Roby also had Nita in mind as a possible successor to Robert Gardner as president of the ICAE at the end of his three-year term in 1982. Roby discussed with Nita the work of the then six-year-old association in some detail, together with the events which had led to its formation after the Tokyo Conference on Adult Education in 1972.

The establishment of the International Council of Adult Education (ICAE) had been a dream of Roby's for some time. As a Canadian delegate to the UNESCO World Conference on Adult Education in Tokyo in 1972, attended by prominent national adult educators, Roby saw how he might gain the support of the international community for the formation of the ICAE. At Tokyo Roby therefore called together some 50 of those who had shown interest in forming such an international organisation. It was agreed at the meeting that an ICAE was needed and that Roby should take the idea forward, either by a feasibility study or through an experimental period. Rejecting both, Roby proceeded directly to establish the ICAE, naming many of those who attended the first meeting as founding members and himself as its first secretary-general.[3] The new association adopted a ready-made multilingual journal, *Convergence*, which had been founded in Canada in 1968 and was dedicated to spreading the word on adult education.[4]

When Roby suggested to Nita that she not only might consider being involved with the ICAE, but indeed might become a member of its executive committee, Nita told him that she had never been involved in an adult education programme and was ignorant of the discipline. Roby assured her that all her adult life she had been doing nothing else but adult education. Having won her over, Roby arranged with his successor, Budd Hall, to invite her to the next annual meeting of the ICAE to be held at Marly-le-Roi, Paris, France, in 1982. In any case, Nita might have attended the meeting representing another NGO, the World YWCA, since she was its president. Unfortunately, Roby died a few months before the conference and did not see the ICAE achieve the high level of international acceptance for which he had worked so hard.

For the first time, an ICAE annual conference was opened by a head of state, President Francois Mitterrand. President Mitterrand was accompanied by five of his ministers, one of whom, Andre Henri, participated in the conference for a period, indicating by his presence his country's appreciation of the work of the association. Mexico too was represented at a level, most flattering to the ICAE executive, by Luis Echeverra, a former president.

Nita made it clear when she accepted the invitation to the conference that she would be signalling that women, who had been doing a considerable part of the work of the ICAE, should be more visible. Referring further to the absence of women at the decision-making level of the association, Nita gave as her opinion:

> Although women were the ones doing very much of the work in adult education, they had not been considered in the overall structure. Margaret Gayfer,

> the editor of 'Convergence', had taken it as her special responsibility to encourage women to attend the conference. I had been asked to assist with the women's programme and to address and lead the seminar on the role of women within the context of the theme of the conference 'Towards an authentic Development: The Role of Adult Education.'
>
> From my early arrival at the conference I was approached from time to time and asked if I would consider succeeding Robert Gardner as President. I was at the time still World President of the YWCA and Director of CMC, . . . On the day of the elections I was sitting next to Miles Horton, founder of the Highlander Centre[3] in the USA, who was to be honoured for his 50 years of service. Having noted the large and obvious male leadership, I said to Miles that I did not think that I wanted to be part of the system. Something was going on at the time to which I was not paying much attention. It was in fact the election of the President. Since there was only one name submitted, the election was very brief. Miles turned with a broad smile on his face and said to me: 'You are part of it now.'

Nita took her place among the 23 men on the dais. The only other woman there was Margaret Kidd, Roby's widow, who received a posthumous award on his behalf. Nita was apparently unaware that the microphone in front of her was active. What was meant by Nita to be a comment, *sotto voce*, to Margaret about the presence of so many men on the dais was heard all over the room. Nita's voice was clear as she said, 'This has got to change.' This statement of concern and intent were the first words of the president-elect and was greeted by a roomful of laughter, mostly male guffaws. Change there has been indeed, for by the end of her second and final term as president in 1990, there were four women vice-presidents.

The secondary role of women, which persisted in the ICAE, had not gone unnoticed by Margaret Gayfer. In her effort, which proved successful, to increase the attendance of women at the Paris conference, Margaret managed to secure funds from donors to pay the passages of some of those who needed such help. In the end 140 women attended. To all, or nearly all of the women, it appeared that the men, well-meaning in their efforts to improve the education of women, were not involving them in the decisions which affected their welfare. In order to send the message clearly and dramatically to the men, a group from the 140 women got together and wrote a song, 'Women Hold up More Than Half the Sky':

> We want you to understand
> It's because you are men
> We bring this message to you
> Some of our sisters are not here
> But they were, they were
> And the message is long overdue

> You said 'man' and 'he'
> Where were we
> Women hold up half the sky
> You said 'man' and 'he'
> But where were we
>
> We were invisible
> We were unheard
> And we know why.

The secretary-general, Budd Hall, gave a brief summary of adult education in the world context in his report to the Paris general assembly. Referring to a 1928 Adult Education Commission which brought together people from North American and European countries and Japan, Hall said that it was 'important as the first concrete expression of adult education of an international nature'. The next meeting of a similar kind was in 1949, at Elsinore (Helsinger), Denmark when the importance of inter-governmental structures as contributors to the maintenance of peace was stressed. Some 85 nations were represented.

An important international statement was made at Montreal in 1960 when representatives of some 60 countries formed the International Congress of University Adult Education. But it was a further 13 years before the ICAE was launched. Budd Hall mentioned the interest of President Julius Nyerere of Tanzania in the efforts of the ICAE to promote adult education worldwide, which he displayed at the Dar es Salaam Conference in 1976, the theme of which was 'Education and Development'.

Hall listed the several professional groups present and specially noted the increase in the number of women attending, and also that they had come from 35 countries. As if to emphasise the known purpose of the increase in the number of women present, Budd Hall quoted a past president of the ICAE, Malcolm Adiseshiah:

> the 'New International Human encounter' . . . showed the strength and knowledge of this no longer 'invisible constituency' . . . It resulted in a sharp critique of the opening session . . . that ignored 'she' and referred mainly to 'man' and 'he' rather than 'we' . . .

Nita's observation about the absence of women on the executive of the ICAE presaged one of her objectives during her Presidency. Her aim was not merely to seek a higher place for women in the ICAE pyramid, but to bring women from all parts of the world closer together and reorganise the management system of the ICAE, which until then had been managed almost entirely, and understandably so because of the ICAE's origin, from Toronto. In addition, the male-centred power structure was quite evident at headquarters: the men were the professionals and the women were mainly support staff who did not feel that they were actively involved in a great creative endeavour. There was also a need for greater interaction among the staff so as to remove feelings of inadequacy which seemed to exist among the less senior members. The subtleties associated with status, real or imagined, had invaded the work-place and had done nothing to change those feelings.

Pat Rodney[6] was asked if she could provide any additional details of the action which Nita had taken early in her presidency to improve female staff morale at the Toronto office. She said that soon after she joined the ICAE staff she had heard that Nita had travelled to Toronto from New York for the sole purpose of speaking to each member of staff in order to find out what problems existed. Following her visit, Nita had quietly made the council more conscious of the need to change its approach to female staff.

Pat Ellis[7] felt that Nita was good for women's morale especially at meetings of the council where men were in the majority and tended to dominate discussion. Pat particularly remembered one occasion at the ICAE general assembly at Buenos Aires in 1985. There were two men, senior representatives, who were always among the first to speak on any subject. Having decided to end their assumed monopoly, Nita informed them: 'You have had your time for talking . . . I am not listening to you . . . I am looking at the time and if there is a minute or two near the end I shall hear you . . .'

Another of the new administration's early initiatives was the formation of a programme advisory committee, the purpose of which was to provide opportunities for wider participation in the decision-making. This new activity got off the ground at a week-end at Nita's residence in New York. The new structure consisted of simple changes to accommodate the decentralisation of the ICAE, made more effective by the adoption of six regional associations of the ICAE. These were:

AALAE	– African Association for Literacy and Adult Education
ALECSO	– Arab League Educational Cultural and Scientific Organisation
ASPBAE	– Asian-South Pacific Bureau of Adult Education
CEAAL	– Concejo de Educacion de Adulturos de America Latina
CARCAE	– Caribbean Regional Council for Adult Education
EBAE	– European Bureau for Adult Education

Other decentralisation followed. In order to relieve the pressures of administering all major functions from the Toronto headquarters, some administrative responsibilities were distributed to associations where there was known expertise available. St Lucia became the base for International Literacy; Learning for Environmental Action was sited in Brazil; the Women's Programme was managed from Senegal and Peace and Human Rights established its headquarters in Finland.

Arthur Stock's[8] comments on Nita having been easily accepted as a leader of the ICAE was that the ICAE at that time needed strong leadership in order to continue along its high moral plateau. Nita, he thought, had arrived when Roby's influence was waning, since he had given up the post of secretary-general. When Roby died soon afterwards, the ICAE looked to Nita, who provided the firmness of a leader and the companionship of co-worker.

The international thrust which the ICAE had been given by Roby Kidd and which had been maintained by his successor, Budd Hall, might be exemplified by a project whose report seems to have received its name from the song written by the women at the Paris conference, 'Women Hold up More than Half the Sky'.[9] The project was concerned with a workshop held in Rajasthan, India, in 1981.[10] The tour included visits by an ICAE team of 16 women. All but the two leaders were from the third world countries of Kenya, Nigeria, Malaysia, Philippines, St Lucia, Barbados, Sri Lanka, Nepal, Iraq, Venezuela, Brazil, Fiji and Tonga. The visitors gained an introduction into local history and culture, and formed an agreement with their hosts that the term 'non-formal' education was to be preferred because it connoted community participation; further, that in promoting changes between women and their communities, every attempt should be made to ensure that the purpose of improving the status of women was not to make them more effective tools in serving the needs of other sectors and groups. The idea that women of third world countries were the ones most in need of non-formal education had a sudden demise at the ICAE executive meeting of November-December 1983 held in Baghdad, Iraq, during the Iran-Iraq war,[11] when some of the industrialised countries had to acknowledge that there were quite a number of people in their own countries who were illiterate and showed what action they were taking to create functional literacy and numeracy.

Because of the importance of adult education in Iraq, it had been agreed that a seminar on that subject should be held there, followed by the two-day ICAE annual executive committee meeting. The meeting place and accommodation were on an island in the Tigris river. Because of the hostilities, the host country provided a level of security which was unusual. The perimeter of the residential and working area was surrounded by 104mm anti-aircraft guns. In addition, the expected and ubiquitous military personnel were quite visible and took great care that none of the guests of their government strayed out of sight. If anyone walked too far away from the centre, for example while taking a stroll, an army officer would politely suggest that such an excursion was unwise. However, there was no sense of unease among the visitors; everyone appreciated the care exercised by the Iraqi government, but some felt it a little confining. Both Nita and Arthur Stock found a degree of bizarre irony in the whole situation, since one of the subsidiary subjects of the seminar was 'Education for Peace'.

The successful seminar and the executive meeting were not held without one or two problems for Nita, a female president of the ICAE visiting a Muslim country. Nita related two incidents with much amusement:

> The meeting place and accommodation for the participants consisted of a virtual village of beautiful bungalows. I arrived rather late in the evening, about 11.00 p.m., from Geneva. I was told by one of the assistant hosts: 'Your husband has arrived and he is in the bungalow.' With some amusement rather than trepidation, I was ushered into the bungalow provided for the President and the Treasurer. It consisted of three large bedrooms, really suites, one of which had been converted into an office for the President, one for the Treasurer and the other for the President and his wife! In the President's bedroom I found Paul Belanger, a member of the ICAE executive, comfortably installed. The hosts must have assumed that there was some mistake in communication which indicated that a woman was President. What is more, since the only surnames of guests beginning with 'B' were Paul's and mine, then most certainly as far as the management was concerned, there had indeed been a spelling or other error and I would have to be Mrs. Belanger![12]
>
> That night Paul slept in the living room on the sofa with a blanket for warmth. Paul who now lives in Germany, still signs his letters to me as 'your husband'.

But Nita was reminded once more that in Muslim countries until quite recently it was rare to find women in leadership positions. Custom was such that women were seldom seen in public places and therefore not often heard. On the last evening of the conference there was a public lecture attended by a few women. The minister had arranged to present parting gifts to all members of the ICAE executive committee on behalf of the government. Each member received a leather wallet containing a clock and a man's shaving kit decorated with silver. As Nita took her leave, she thanked the minister for the gift.

> Thank you very much for your beautiful gift, but I have no husband and no current boy-friend to whom I might give these. It was very thoughtful of you just the same . . . The next morning while we were awaiting the plane, the Minister himself came with much haste and presented me with a black chador, gold embroidered. Accompanying him were two young ladies who demonstrated the accessory's beauty and stylish elegance.

The general assembly agreed to meet every four years instead of every three since the period between one assembly and the next was too short. Presidential elections take place at meetings of the general assembly so that a consequence of this decision was a one-year extension of Nita's second term, to which she was elected. The executive committee met annually and were so arranged as to follow seminars or studies which gave the leaders and other persons or groups in the host country opportunities to discuss what they were doing about adult education and to learn new approaches. Perhaps one of the most extensive studies took place during Nita's second year as president when the ICAE undertook to honour its commitment to:

a three-year programme with the People's Republic of China, designed to study and report on adult and non-formal education experiences in China. Phase one of the programme consisted of visits to China of two small study groups, and the preparation and dissemination of materials for use both within China and abroad.[13]

The programme was negotiated by Christopher Duke, who was at that time director of the Department of Continuing Education at Australia National University and a Hong Kong colleague. The preliminary visit was of senior officers of the ICAE in 1981, which Nita attended at Roby's invitation. The second was in late 1983, led by Nita as president of the ICAE.

Learning about the system of education in China was a new and stimulating experience for the visitors. Chairman Mao's philosophy of education was based on his view that:

> not to have a political point of view is like having no soul . . . Our educational policy must enable every one who gets an education to develop morally, intellectually and physically and become a cultured, literate socialist oriented worker.

The cultural revolution of the mid-1960s was damaging to development and progress in China, except possibly in the field of PHC. Some of the work undertaken to reduce illiteracy and improve other aspects of basic non-formal education had, in effect, ended. What therefore existed in the early 1980s was the effects of concerted post-cultural revolution, national efforts to revise programmes in adult education, and revive and expand others as far and as quickly as possible in order to gain lost ground.

The first ICAE group in 1981 visited 12 provinces, among them Beijing, Shanghai, Chang-sha and Shen-yang. Nita noted that film and TV were widely used to give nurses and doctors short-term courses in PHC and to supplement training in the treatment of diseases, such as diabetes, and in teaching patients to look after themselves after discharge from hospitals or treatment at clinics. That nurses as a body of professionals were independent of doctors gladdened Nita's heart and reminded her of her own successful thrust many years earlier in Jamaica for similar recognition of nurses. The Shanghai branch of the Nurses Association, a professional body and a trades union, had a membership of 20,000 directed by a board of 93 nurses.

A visit to Chengdu provided opportunity for the ICAE group to study a more common means of improving literacy. Short-term regular classes were well established to support the needs of basic education. In addition, for training the already literate and employees in factories and similar institutions, the municipality itself maintained a spare-time university with eight faculties, including engineering, chemistry, computer studies and business management, reinforced by a research group. An important principle which supported the entire effort of basic education, work-oriented studies and educational advancement, including research, was that all participants were paid during the hours when they attended the university. This practice appeared to be of general application.

The Municipal Shanghai Part-time University, with branches conveniently placed in neighbourhoods, employed a staff of 440 professors and 302 lecturers. Some of the students of this institution had invented new industrial techniques in spinning, and had applied computer technology to preparing mechanical drawings and improving defence systems.

It was common for workers to be in the workplace for half a day and to study for half a day. For those in the rural areas there were correspondence courses available, together with TV assisted instruction to supplement other forms of instruction.

Nita summarised her observations of the system:

> With the assistance of our China-based Vice-President, we worked closely with local educators on widening the participants' experience which was in some ways unique. It was a case of education on the job. In factories there were four groups of workers in the rota system. At any given time during the day one group would be in the classroom and one on work shift. What we witnessed was education rather than training. We were uncertain about the arrangement of the system, or what a Westerner might call the approach. Employees were not given the choice of deciding whether they attended classes or not, continuing education was one of their conditions of employment. Factories were built in the rural areas so as to discourage migration to the cities and its well known ill effects on family and community life.
>
> In many factories there were not only nursery schools but nurseries where women left their children and where they went to breast-feed infants when the need arose. It seemed to us that the Chinese had much to teach the Western peoples about making provision for the needs of women in the work-place. We discovered that the idea that women in China were not valued was partly myth. We also discovered that there was room for women in the hierarchy.

On the second visit to China in late 1983, Nita headed a large group representing most of the member countries of the ICAE. During the first week visits were made to educational institutions in Shanghai province followed by a scientific seminar which lasted five days. Nita as co-chairman in her opening speech set the objectives which were geared to the needs and interests of their Chinese colleagues. What contributed to the success of the visit and the almost total absence of abrasive comment was Nita's presence. Even though the ICAE delegation was made up of professional adult educators, most of them enthusiastic and militant servants of adult education throughout the world, nevertheless there were times when politics or differences of ideology might have led to difficult and contentious situations. Sensitive to the relationship between China and the Soviet Union, Nita took pains to ensure that she was seen to be without any political bias or party to any conspiracy to impose new and damaging theories on the unwary. She was seen as a trustworthy person of great eminence.[14]

One of the moral imperatives which the ICAE was well placed to support and act upon was the full emancipation of women. Nita's inception as president was well-timed and coincided with the new thinking. As noted earlier, she made it clear that equality for women was one of her objectives. Nita ideally epitomised the type of woman who all people hoped would evolve from what would be for many women a struggle. She was emphatic, clear and unequivocal in her statements on what should be accorded to women. It was done in a way which made most people listen and find her views reasonable and acceptable; she could express them openly even in Arab countries and people would respect her for them.

In China Nita found that many women had been provided with the opportunity for professional advancement and liberation, especially since the end of the cultural revolution. One such was Madame Lilli, Director of Workers' Education in Shanghai and Co-chair with Nita of the scientific seminar; another was Madame Cora Deng, vice-president of the powerful China's Women's Federation and general secretary of the National YWCA of China for more than 30 years, who was at the time nearly 90 years old. There was also Madame Phoebe Siu, a deputy president of the YWCA. Nita had met Phoebe during her 1981 visit. For some years during the cultural revolution Cora Deng was confined to the top story of the YWCA building which during the difficult years had been taken over by the government and used as a hostel and restaurant. During that period there was no functioning YWCA; there were no churches, only certain houses where people met at their own risk to worship together. During the 1982-84 period, and later, with greater liberalisation and contact with the West, institutions, including Christian churches which had gone underground, reappeared. Nita counted nine churches open in Shanghai in one of which, she attended divine worship one Sunday.

The YWCA building had been returned completely refurbished to its previous owners. Restitution in the form of rental was paid to the YWCA for the period during which the association had been compulsorily, though temporarily, deprived of the use of its own building.

The ICAE had made its contribution to the growth of what was fast becoming a worldwide interest in literacy as a means of liberating the human spirit and developing a true sense of self-worth. The Labat method of 'each one teach one' had not been embraced by the ICAE. However, there was another method tried and proven from about 1960 in Jamaica in its literacy programme (JAMAL) where teaching materials were used which related directly to the lives of the adult people in the programme. Under the direction of Joyce Robinson, O.J. items associated with the participants' daily occupations were used as aids to learning. If therefore farmers were the students, they might be taught to read through their need to read labels and directions on bottles of herbicides. Their arithmetic would be learnt through the necessity to weigh and measure quantities of fertiliser, say, or measure an area of land for a specific crop.

In Iraq Nita saw the Federation of Women increase the literacy of women in some areas by some 80 per cent. No bells were rung and no speeches were made about that kind of community service, but when the Iran-Iraq war ended in 1988, the women were ready for new responsibilities.

In 1989, at the annual executive meeting of the ICAE, an International Task Force on Literacy was set up following a conference on the subject. Lalita Ramdass, the newly elected ICAE president (in September 1994) identified the main issues in her report on the 'Discussions and Outcomes of the Conference':

(a) The link between illiteracy and poverty and marginalisation. Most visible in developing societies but equally a factor in industrialised nations.
(b) social and cultural factors, e.g. bias in favour of sons against daughters, child marriage and dowry, feudal and orthodox attitudes . . .
(c) Ideology behind economic policy and planning. Government statistics show that over one third of all households are headed by women as primary earners.
(d) Resource support through teaching/learning materials, training and personnel required to reflect the needs and voices of women.

As a result of the conference which coincided with the ICAE annual conference in 1990, Pat Rodney was put in charge of the ICAE programme for the International Year of Literacy (IYL). In order to secure reasonable unity throughout the ICAE, some 40 representatives of the six ICAE regional associations met in Namibia later in the year. From that meeting each regional association indicated the methods which it would use in implementing the programme for the year.

The International Year of Literacy was launched at Bangkok, Thailand, in February 1990. Nita managed to secure funds to assist some of the representatives to attend. One of these was Joyce Robinson, whose experience Nita thought should be available to as many persons selected to lead the literacy campaign as possible. Although Joyce's commitments elsewhere were equally demanding, Nita managed to persuade her to go to Bangkok. The theme of the meeting was 'Education for All'.[15] Joyce said that Nita had insisted that some of the graduates of the ICAE and other literacy programmes throughout the world be present. The meeting was in fact Nita's final one before she gave up office. Nita identified the more satisfying moments of that conference.

The 'New Literates' were encouraged to discuss their experiences. Many of them responded, one being a woman from the island of Dominica who had attended a literacy programme partly assisted by a Miss Campbell of JAMAL. The Dominican said that she was the mother of eight children, some of whom had grown up and emigrated to other countries. Until she had become literate she had to find someone who would read her children's letters to her. She had suddenly realised that she had no way of knowing if what she heard was what was written. She could now read for herself. She could also now write to her children and tell them about other members of the family and how she had spent what money they sent to her.

One young West Indian man of about 20 years of age said that he had attended school as a youngster but had never learnt to read or write. He had been able to cover up his illiteracy until he emigrated to the USA where he realised that he could get no promotion where he worked, nor elsewhere, if he remained illiterate.

A couple from the USA neither of whom one would think was a 'New Literate' had a story similar to that told by the West Indian young man, except that the careers of both had been under threat through illiteracy.

The launching of the IYL was marked by the voyage around the world, not of a person, but of a book called 'Words are What I've Got', compiled by the International Task Force on Literacy, in which there are 141 original pieces of prose or signatures written by some of the new literates from all over the world. Pat Rodney, the coordinator, ensured that the book reached Barbados, so that Nita, who had by then become the governor-general, could share in the symbol of triumph of a worldwide unity in action to defeat worldwide deficiency and degradation of the human spirit.

Part of the preface of the book was written by Budd Hall, former secretary-general of the ICAE, and is given below:

> Words are magical creatures, symbols on paper. When viewed by another it images feelings, ideas even, hope perhaps . . . They exist in our heads through thousands of languages . . . they can be used to keep us from achieving what is our right. They can also be used to pull back the curtains of confusion, to give meaning to a loved one's thoughts many miles away. . . . The funny markings which we see on paper are not the signs of wisdom, or depth of feeling, The real words are those inside each of us.

The book was presented to the UN secretary-general to mark the official end of the IYL, an ICAE initiative to which other NGOs contributed. However, this did not also mark the end of Nita's association with the ICAE nor the end of the association's links with her.

At the suggestion of Budd Hall, ICAE raised $30,000, the income of which will provide funds for an annual award, 'the Dame Nita Barrow Award' to recognise and support regional and national adult education organisations which have made a significant contribution towards the empowerment of women in the adult education movement.

Two other awards made annually at meetings of the executive committee are the J. Roby Kidd Award, in memory of the first secretary-general and founder of the ICAE, and the Nabila Brier Award in support of women's educational programmes in Palestine.

---

1. Nancy J. Cockrane and Associates, J.R. Kidd, *An international Legacy of Learning*, Centre of Continuing Studies, UBC Vancouver, BC, Canada, 72.
2. *Ibid.*, 109.
3. Discussion with Professor Arthur Stock, a founding member of the ICAE and a former director of the National Institute of Adult Continuing Education in England and Wales.
4. See note 1 above, 77–80.
5. Highlander Institute is the organisation which initiated work in adult education with the poor people of the Appalachian mountains in the USA. Miles Horton, its founder, recently died.
6. Pat Rodney is a member of staff of ICAE and was the co-ordinator of the International Literacy Year (1990). She is the widow of Professor Walter Rodney of Guyana whose assassination took place in Guyana during the dictatorship of President Forbes Burnham.
7. Pat Ellis is a member of the ICAE executive.
8. See note 3 above.
9. The report (April 1983) of a project and workshop of the ICAE was by Anne Bernard and Margaret Gayfer, staff members.
10. It is unlikely that Rajasthan was chosen by chance. During 1964–1968 the universities of Columbia and Rajasthan had collaborated in a joint project of 'continuous learning' and the role of universities in such an exercise, (J. R. Kidd, *An International Legacy of Learning*, 167 *et seq.*; see note 1 above).
11. The Iran-Iraq war (1980–88) began with Iraq's invasion of Iran following the overthrow of the Shah in 1979. Loss of life and damage to the economies of other countries were extensive.
12. Paul Belanger was then secretary-general of the Institut Canadien d'Education des Adultes, the French-Canadian equivalent of the Canadian Association of Adult Education (CAAE).
13. See S.C. Dutta, *An International Legacy of Learning*, Chap.7, 109 (see note 1 above).
14. Discussion with Arthur Stock, member of the delegation.
15. Joyce Robinson, in discussion with the author.

Nita as ambassador, attending meeting of Nonaligned Group of Nations, Yugoslavia

Nita being greeted by President Mandela of South Africa in Pretoria, May 1994, at the time of the presidential inauguration

Nita as President in Bangkok, Thailand, in 1990 launching International Year of Literacy (IYL), with (left to right, standing) Sybil Barrow (sister), Claudette McConney, Pat Rodney, Joyce Robinson

The Barbados official delegation of Dame Nita and Philip Greaves at the inauguration of President Mandela, with Sir Shridath Ramphal and Mrs Leah Tutu, 1994

Nita with Archbishop Desmond Tutu and Sir Shridath Ramphal in Pretoria, May 1994

Nita with Rev and Mrs Alvin Scantlebury at Smith College after receiving an honorary LLD degree

Left to right: Mercy Oduweye, WCC Deputy Secretary-General, the Greek Orthodox Representative, Brigalia Bam, Sir Shridath Ramphal and the Anglican Primate of Canada, Edward Scott

7

South African Mission and Later

The Foreword of *Mission to South Africa, the Commonwealth Report* (1986) begins:

> Over the last six months a remarkable thing happened in one of the saddest corners of our small world. A group of seven people from five continents, black and white and brown, gave everything they had to offer – integrity, humanity, compassion, understanding and wide experience – to holding back a darkening storm. It was remarkable most of all because, against the odds, the Commonwealth Group of Eminent persons (a title each of them eschewed) showed, by the quality of their efforts for peaceful change in South Africa, that both change and peace are within the grasp of its people. For a brief moment, the world – and pre-eminently, South Africans of all races – glimpsed a path of negotiation to a more worthy future.[1]

The Eminent Persons Group (EPG) had been set up by the Commonwealth heads of government at the meeting in October 1985 in Nassau, Bahamas. At an earlier meeting in New Dehli they had stated:

> only the eradication of apartheid and the establishment of majority rule on the basis of free and fair exercise of universal adult suffrage for all people in a united and non-fragmented South Africa can lead to a just and lasting solution of the explosive situation prevailing in Southern Africa.[2]

The document of the Commonwealth heads, *The Accord*, gave support to the arms embargo against South Africa established under United Nations Security Council Resolutions 418 and 558; affirmed the Gleneagles Declaration of 1977, which requested Commonwealth members to discourage sporting contacts with South Africa; and recommended to the members of the Commonwealth the adoption of further economic measures against South Africa, indicating clearly that if adequate progress was not made within a reasonable period of six months, some of the members of the Commonwealth would institute more severe economic and other strictures.

The heads of government felt that punitive measures could not be the sole concern of the EPG in its mission to lead a former Commonwealth member towards a mode of national life acceptable, not only to other members of the Commonwealth, but to the world as a whole: that all men, regardless of colour, race, creed or religion are entitled to certain basic freedoms. The heads of commonwealth governments recorded in the *Accord* their belief:

> that we must do all we can to assist the process while recognising forms of political settlement in South Africa are for the people of that country – all people – to determine. To this end we have decided to establish a small group of eminent commonwealth persons to encourage through all practicable ways the evolution of that necessary process of political dialogue . . .[3]

The *Accord* listed five steps for the dismantling of apartheid and for avoiding greater tragedy. These steps were to be taken by the authorities in Pretoria as a matter of urgency. In summary they were:

> Declaring that apartheid will be dismantled and real action taken to do so;
> Ending the state of emergency;
> Releasing immediately and unconditionally Nelson Mandela and other opponents of apartheid who were also in detention;
> Establishing political freedom and unbanning political parties including the African National Congress;
> Initiating discussion with relevant groups and persons for the purpose of establishing non-racial and representative government.

The EPG was given no terms of reference, since these might formalise their work, reduce its human face and give it a resemblance to a quasi-legal commission of enquiry. The mandate given to the EPG is summed up in the extract from Annex 1 of the *Accord* quoted above.

The members of the EPG, whether they were deliberately chosen to be or not, were representative of the major races of the Commonwealth were: Malcolm Fraser (Co-chairman) a former prime minister of Australia; General Olusegun Obasanjo (Co-chairman), head of the federal military government in Nigeria in 1976–79; Lord Barber of Wentbridge, UK, a former chancellor of the exchequer; Dame Nita Barrow of Barbados, president of the World YWCA and a co-president of the World Council of Churches; John Malecela, former foreign minister of Tanzania; Sardar Swaran Singh, a former minister of external affairs and a former minister of defence of India; and the Most Rev. Edward Walter Scott, primate of the Anglican Church of Canada, who had been Moderator of the World Council of Churches 1975–83.

Before leaving for South Africa the members of the EPG underwent two days of intense briefing. During that period there was much diplomatic activity, including convincing the government of South Africa that the members of the EPG should be granted visas. Nita never inquired, but she felt certain that somewhere in the arrangement was the possibility that some of the members, including herself, might be offered the unacceptable designation of 'Honorary White'. Nita believes that the visas to facilitate their visit were granted because the government of South Africa was anxious to establish that things in South Africa were better than they were. The sanctions, in spite of reported violations, were having some effect but the government was not prepared to admit it.

Members of the EPG visited South Africa three times. The first occasion was a preliminary visit in February 1986 by the co-chairmen, Malcolm Fraser, General Obasanjo and Dame Nita. The second and third visits of 2–13 March 1986 and 13–19 May 1986 were made by all the members.

That the EPG did not consider its effort a success; that the members were themselves disappointed; that their individual sensitivities had been badly violated; and, that like the rest of the civilised world, they did not wish to anticipate the results of the stubbornness and continuing inhumanity of the South African government, are probably best deduced from the EPG's letter which accompanied their report.

> If we are sad that our efforts to achieve those objectives (see extract of Accord above) in South Africa have been unavailing, it is not so much out of a sense of disappointment at the personal level, but acute consciousness and concern at the consequences of our failure for the future of that country.[4]

If the main purpose of the EPG mission was to be fulfilled, then the South African government and the representative organisations of blacks, including the ANC, would have to end the violence practised by both sides and approach the negotiation table, the proper place where a reasonable future for all residents of South Africa might find the beginning of peaceful living and a civilised life. The EPG found the intransigence of the South African government incomprehensible. In the course of carrying out their mandate, the members of the EPG, not only met with government ministers, but with groups and individuals representing religious denominations, social organisations, business and commercial interests and members of anti-apartheid movements.

Indeed, it is still incredible that, as late as 1992 reports were being received from usually reliable sources that while the De Klerk government was negotiating with Nelson Mandela and the ANC, it was clandestinely and simultaneously supporting violence between the ANC and Inkatha. If such reports were accurate, it meant that the government was effectively, albeit by remote control, promoting loss of life by exploiting rivalry between Africans. The objective was obvious: the more that the black Africans could be encouraged to kill one another, the fewer would be left to create difficulties for the white Afrikaners. In addition, the unnecessary strife between the black Africans would prolong and undermine the negotiations.

That the government of South Africa had no intention of accepting the EPG's proposals and the conditions associated with them was forcibly demonstrated with arrogance and insensitivity. Early in the morning on the day of the last scheduled meeting with the 'Constitutional Commission', which included many of the cabinet ministers with whom the EPG had met individually, the South African security forces launched simultaneous raids on Gaborone in Botswana, Lusaka in Zambia and Harare in Zimbabwe. It was claimed that these were ANC bases. This seemed a clear indication that the government was not prepared to negotiate. That inference was based on two assumptions: that the government felt that it could successfully control the internal unrest and that it could limit and cope with the impact of sanctions and other forms of external pressure. Within three years it became clear that the government was wrong on both counts. The internal unrest increased and could not be satisfactorily contained, and the external pressure for fundamental change continued to increase. These realities led to a steady decline of the South African economy.

The voracious appetite of European countries for the lands and wealth, mineral and other, of the peoples of Africa was at the root of violence in South Africa. It had begun before the eighteenth century with the founding of the Dutch East India Company, its station at the Cape of Good Hope and its expansion into the neighbouring Bantu lands. The Dutch systematically killed off the Khoikhoi (Hottentots) and the San (Bushmen), with their superior weapons or by forcibly removing them from their traditional grazing lands, and with European diseases, among them smallpox against which they had no natural resistance. The arrival of the British after the Napoleonic wars soon led to the supremacy of the new arrivals over the earlier exploiters.[5]

The discovery of gold and diamonds in South Africa in the late nineteenth century gave some of the poor farmers of Dutch descent and some of the blacks, hopes of improving their lot by leaving the unproductive lands and migrating to the new areas of wealth. In the eyes of the first-class citizens (the British), the Afrikaners were second-class citizens in South Africa and the blacks were non-citizens in their own country. To both the Anglo-Saxons and the Afrikaners, the native African was at best merely a source of manual labour. As the mines were developed at the expense of compulsory black labour and from capital investment and private enterprise interests originating from Britain, more British families emigrated to South Africa, mainly to the Cape Colony area which had been annexed by the British in 1798 and had become a prosperous colony. Further migration from Britain continued over the years (as many as 5,000 in the early 1820s). As development accelerated in the cities to the benefit of the British and to the exclusion of all other comers, the blacks became less and less a people in their own country. The British in the nineteenth century broke the power of the native kingdoms and chiefdoms of the indigenous peoples of South Africa, including the Zulus, thus introducing disorder into the social structure of the newly semi-enslaved Africans.

After the Boer War of 1899–1902, the Afrikaners found themselves impoverished farmers. There seemed to be no solution but to emigrate to the cities in search of work. There they found themselves in competition with blacks and many became the employees of prosperous Indians. Such adversity contributed to the progressive hardening of their attitudes towards all other races. The combination of difficulties led to the development of a strong sense of Afrikaner nationalism, greater even than that which existed among their forebears, who had bequeathed to them not simply a sense of racial superiority innate to the European, but a disregard for the lives of non-white people.

The Act which united the British Cape Colony and Natal with the two Boer republics as the Union of South Africa was passed in the British parliament in 1910. It included provision for equality of the two white races, while completely ignoring the civil rights of the blacks and the browns by whom they were vastly outnumbered.

The Afrikaners, copying the unconcern of the British government for the civil rights of Africans, demonstrated their contempt for them, initially, by the Act of 1910, denying them parliamentary representation. The Land Act of 1913, one of the first acts of the independent Union of South Africa, was also the first legal step taken to denationalise the non-whites and keep them as a source of cheap labour to provide power for the prosperous machine of the whites. (It is useful to remember, however, that at this time the vast majority of blacks and browns in other parts of the British empire did not have the franchise either.) Other laws subsequently enacted, including the Group Areas Act and the pass laws, were logical extensions of the dehumanising process of the system of apartheid. Appeals from black representative groups against progressive phases of apartheid were ignored by the countries of the Western world separately and collectively within the League of Nations.

As president of the World YWCA, Nita had come into contact with the apartheid system. There had existed in South Africa two branches of the YWCA, one in which black and brown women were members and which was affiliated to the world organisation, and the other, for whites only, but which was isolated from the world body. When Nita was the director of the CMC, she had been unable to visit South Africa where the need for primary health care was indeed great. It had not been possible for her to do so because the Dutch Reform Church of South Africa was not a member of the WCC, which the South African authorities had dismissed as 'Communist'. The charge of being Communist, or Communist-affiliated, savoured of more than a touch of the African equivalent of McCarthyism in the USA.

The Dutch Reform Church, with its Calvinist doctrine, had experienced no difficulties in convincing its members that they were the chosen people. They were the modern equivalent of the Jewish remnant, endowed with Mosaic leadership and predestined to inherit the earth. To the Boers of the Great Trek, the modern Canaan waiting to be inherited was all of the land occupied by Bantu, Xhosa and other nations of Southern Africa. The deliberate programme of expropriation, expulsion and genocide thus had both an economic and a religious foundation. The prime minister, Daniel Malan, himself a former Dutch Reform Church preacher, was one of the chief architects of apartheid. He used carefully selected biblical texts as the spiritual and theological platform on which to build the evil philosophy of racial oppression.

The South African National Party, which formed the government of that unhappy country since 1948, probably forgot that its formation in 1913 was indeed the beginning of a revolution as violent as that in Russia of 1917 and with similar objectives of social nationalism:

> in perhaps the greatest of all South African ironies, the National party first came to power in a coalition of the labour party and with the support of Communists, who raised the stunning slogan, 'Workers of the world unite for a white South Africa!' Afrikaner members of the Mine Workers Union mounted a revolt in 1922 . . . when four of the strike leaders were sentenced to death, they went to the gallows singing 'The Red Flag.'[6]

Nita's presence as one of the EPG was important and morale-building for the blacks and browns of South Africa, restoring to those groups, at least for a brief period, some confidence in the human race. Many Africans saw Nita for what she was: a black woman recognised by the world as a member of the intelligentsia and one of that rare group best identified as world citizens. Describing the importance of Nita's visit to South Africa as the only female – and black – member of the EPG, Brigalia Bam, a black South African member of the YWCA branch affiliated to the world body and executive director of the South African Council of Churches, recalled Nita's visit:

> There were three important things about Nita's visit. She had earlier been the first black World President of the YWCA. For us the YWCA was the one movement for women that made it possible for us in South Africa to have links with the world. Many of our Non-governmental Organisations (NGOs) in South Africa had been forced to break the links with parent associations outside of the country.
>
> While in South Africa as a member of the EPG, Nita visited what is known as the World Affiliated YWCA and met some of the members, among them the director, Mrs Joyce Seroke; Mrs Virginia Gcabashe and Mrs Mbkanyane, members of the executive; Mrs Ellen Kuzwayo, treasurer of the Transvaal YWCA and former staff member of the World YWCA; Mrs Mhlambi, now (1991) president of our Association. Nita provided the strongest link for the South African women with the rest of the world. She came to us as our heroine, as our greatest female model.

The second point is that related to the fact that we are living in a country where we are continually being told that we, blacks, are not people, that we cannot lead, that we do not have the competence to do so. Suddenly, there is in our country, visiting, this warm and humble person, one of us, designated by the leaders of the Commonwealth: an Eminent Person. This person is one who had made it clear long before she set out as part of the EPG that she proposed to visit women's groups, church-affiliated and secular.

The third is that Nita, a woman, had made it to the top in the world of men. In a world where men dominate politics, an important national activity from which we black South Africans are excluded. It was stimulating to what little pride had been left to us, to see a woman participating as a member of the EPG, a group which would play an important role influencing the future and change in South Africa. For ambitious black women in South Africa, there were only three professions open to them: nursing, teaching, and social work. Nita, the distinguished world citizen, honoured by the Queen with the title of Dame, was herself a nurse. The pride of us women was not better expressed than by my eldest sister Jean, herself a nurse. 'We have made it!' she said in her moment of exuberance. Similar pride in Nita's profession was specially noted by other women as they met her formally.

The provisions of the Bantu Education Act of 1953, which was one of the repressive legislative measures initiated in 1948 by the Malan government of the National Party, enacted that the language of instruction in African secondary schools would be Afrikaans. While this measure was totally in keeping with resurgent Afrikaner nationalism, it was correctly seen by those to whom it applied as part of a continuing process to legalise a system of education for black children grossly inferior to that provided for white children. The Act embodied Dr Verwoerd's infamous statement: 'There is no room for the Bantu in the European Community, above the level of certain forms of labour.'[7] The objective was to stifle ambition and train blacks to be a working class only. Black boys or girls were required to attend schools in dilapidated buildings with filthy and inadequate toilet facilities, broken windows, few desks, not enough books, with classes of a hundred or more. The teachers would most likely have little more than an elementary education and would be tired and uninspired by the hopeless task. The school might have police and soldiers on the premises to keep an eye on the students and spot 'agitators.'

In mid-June 1976 some of the students of a secondary school, not having learnt enough Afrikaans to pass the matriculation exams, feared that they would fail. In desperation they decided that they would boycott school until Afrikaans was removed from the curriculum and English or Zulu restored. A rally was called and the Black Women's Association and the Black Parents Association supported the children's protest. The security forces panicked and fired live ammunition into the rally of children. The world was shocked by pictures of the South African 1976 version of the Massacre of the Innocents, in particular, the photograph of the newly dead body of 11-year-old Hector Peterson being carried in the arms of an older child, whose face was a picture of heart-rending misery and distress, while Hector's sister ran alongside, her face evincing bewilderment, pain and sorrow.[8]

Death, if it did not result from beatings by the police, might nevertheless be delivered more efficiently, directly and indeed wholesale by the agents of the government. So it was for 69 blacks in the Sharpeville massacre of March 1960, when the victims were shot in the back as they attempted to run away from a scene of protest with their non-weapons of stones. Death was also handed out by hanging after trial in which the process of justice was questionable, or in detention after police torture, as to Ngudle (1963), S. Moipane (1969), Steve Biko (1977) and about 50 others.[9] The shooting down of defenceless blacks was a deliberate policy of the South African government. Patrick Duncan[10] reported that the minister of defence had told army officers in 1959 that they were not arming to fight an external enemy, but to shoot down the black masses. As a trial run for the Sharpeville massacre, the Windhoek police killed 14 people who resisted being transported to Bantustans (homelands).[11]

The young people too learnt that life for them had little value and nothing to offer in the foreseeable future. Their inborn sense of self-preservation was violated to the point where many saw violent death as their only prospect and were not afraid because they had become accustomed to violent death as part of their daily existence, violent death as a consequence of protest against the dehumanisation and degradation meted out to them and their relatives by the Afrikaners. They were not afraid to die in defence of the humanity of their people.

Nita, was asked to identify in the *Report* of the EPG what she thought summarised the views of the group on the subject of brutality and violence suggested:

> We were left with the impression of a divided government. Yet even the more enlightened ministers whom we met seemed to be out of touch with the mood in the black townships, the rising tide of anger, the impatience within them and the extent of black mobilisation. So, of course, were the majority of the white South Africans –only some ten per cent of whom, we are told, have ever seen conditions in the townships.
>
> Put in the most simple way, the blacks have had enough of apartheid. They are no longer prepared to submit to its oppression, discrimination, and exploitation. They can no longer stomach being treated as aliens in their own country. They have confidence not merely in the justice of their cause, but in the inevitability of their victory. Unlike earlier periods of unrest and the government's attempt to stamp out the protest, there has been during the last eighteen months no outflow of blacks from South Africa. The strength of black conviction is now matched by a readiness to die for those convictions. They will, therefore, sustain their struggle whatever the cost.

Three members of the EPG – Nita, Malcolm Fraser and General Obasanjo together with Emeka Anyoka, secretary to the commission – set out early one morning to visit the township of Alexandra. Nita dressed like a local woman in her desire to identify more directly with her hosts-to-be. So successful was her effort that on appearing in the hotel foyer, Obasanjo and others of the group did not at first recognise her.

The four visitors travelled to Alexandra in a car driven by an employee of the South African Christian Council, rather than in the more visible Mercedes Benz provided for their use. Nita said that she would enter the township alone since she would not be noticed. Fraser wished to go and felt that he might escape detection if he curled up in the back seat with Obasanjo and Anyoka. But his hopes were ill-founded. Nita, the pseudo-resident, occupied the front passenger seat with Winston, the driver. In order to enter the township, the car had first to pass one Casspir armoured car which was patrolling the township even though it was not under emergency regulations that day. As the car with its driver and four passengers was about to enter the township another Casspir advanced towards the car. A white soldier left the Casspir, approached the visitors' car and inquired the nature of the business of the occupants. Anyoka explained, but the group was nevertheless escorted to the nearby police station. At the police station Nita was assumed to be a local black and was ignored. She remained seated in the car with the driver enjoying 'Life Savers' sweets while Fraser, Obasanjo and Anyoka were taken into the guard house or station and questioned. After about half an hour, they returned to the car, infuriated. Fraser and Anyoka were ordered to leave the township immediately, having been refused permission to visit under a law which forbade blacks and whites to travel together as passengers in the same vehicle. All the way back to the hotel the humiliated and disappointed three members of the EPG gave vent to their anger. On returning to their five-star hotel, Fraser, Obasanjo and Anyoka immediately got out. Before leaving the car, Nita said almost in a whisper to Winston, the driver: 'You wait for me, I am going back to the township.'

In order to avoid being seen by the others who had been denied permission to visit the township, Nita used a side exit of the hotel to sneak out and join Winston. In the role of joint conspirator, Winston drove behind a bus to the entrance. Another car, an official one, was later sent to the Roman Catholic presbytery, just outside the township, to await Nita. The Roman Catholic priests were white and therefore were not allowed under the Group Areas Act to live inside the township. To enter Alexandra unobserved, Nita mingled with the some of passengers as they alighted from the bus. She was soon joined by two youngsters of around 16 years old who worked with the South African Christian Council (SACC). Their job was to keep an eye on the other youths of the township and try to head off any trouble. For the duration of the visit to

Alexandra their special job was to act as guides to Nita. In order to do so effectively, they pretended to be her nephews.

Our partially frustrated visit was made at a time when some residents of the township were trying to hold a funeral for six or seven people who had been killed in the continuing violence. The customary wake which precedes a funeral had been interrupted and permission had been refused by the Afrikaner authorities for its continuation. Anglican Bishop (now Archbishop) Desmond Tutu; Rev. Dennis Shorey, a Methodist Minister; and Rev. Dr Alan Boesak of the Dutch Reform Church had gone to Capetown that day to plead with the government to allow them to bury the dead with the customary ceremonies.

I visited the home of one of the senior resident leaders. I was taken to a not unattractive stone bungalow. The road leading to it was rough, with open sewers on both sides. The house had eight or nine rooms and apparently was occupied by an equal number of families. I entered by the back door leading to two rooms, one of them was a bedroom with one bed, neatly made, one chair and an old fashioned Dover stove. The two rooms together virtually formed the luxury apartment of the building. There was no running water in the house nor in the yard. The only running water available to the occupants of the house was about half a mile away. It was supposed to serve the occupants of some 42 households.

I asked to see the bathing facilities. The lady of the house said: 'I am too ashamed to show you. I shall let one of the young men do that.'

I was shown into the yard where some children were playing and was shown a block of three 'privies' served by buckets. In one of the 'privies' the capacity of the bucket had been exceeded. None of the three doors could be fastened to provide privacy. There was nothing resembling a water toilet.

We returned to the house. The women who had been invited to meet me were beginning to arrive. As we awaited the remainder, the lady of the home and I chatted about the social life of the community. I learnt that there was segregation in all areas. Even Rev. Dr Alan Boesak, one of the founding members and a former President of the United Democratic Front, himself a brown man, had been prohibited from preaching in any Church for blacks because he was of mixed race, a brown man.

In Alexandra, a small corner of South Africa, itself a land of wealth and of plenty, almost one million people were forced to live in squalor and on the border of starvation. Many of them would not survive were there not a strong community spirit. Everything was shared. I noted that the whole story of unnecessary misery had been related without any anger though without acceptance. I was speechless in wonder at the personal dignity which existed in spite of the rulers' attempts to dehumanise 75% of the population of the country. That the attempt had so far failed presaged a long and bitter struggle. It reminded me of the reason for the presence in South Africa of six other persons and myself.

Nita was invited to take a walk around part of the nearby area. She saw a standpipe and found its surroundings indescribable. Because of her experience in health care, she knew that insanitary conditions near a public standpipe, especially where there is no concrete base, promoted the spread of disease. At the standpipe there was a long line of adults and children, all malnourished. Some of the children had glaucoma and other eye diseases. In speaking with some of them Nita learnt that there were no regular clinics. The residents of the township had never experienced the luxury of a visiting physician, far less a resident one.

The nearest hospital was the Baragwanath Hospital, where Winnie Mandela had worked as the first social worker until 1958 when she joined women protesting against the pass laws which had been extended to include women. Winnie, then expecting her first child, was among the more than 2,000 women who were arrested and thrown into jail without trial. That incarceration was the first of the government's persecutions of Winnie as a member of the ANC and as the wife of Nelson Mandela. Winnie's persecution subsequently included the loss of her job, a series of detentions totalling 491 days, banishment and imprisonment for six months.

During this unauthorised visit to Akexandra, Nita wished to remain to attend the meeting due to be held later in the evening when Bishop Tutu, Rev. Boesak and Rev. Shorey would report to the residents the result of their representation to the government for the resumption of traditional funeral ceremonies for those killed in recent confrontation with the security forces. As the thousands of residents assembled, Nita's hosts did more than suggest that she should not stay within or near the assembly.

> No, they said, we cannot allow you to attend. You never know when the police will attack such meetings. They are totally irresponsible. They use blacks against blacks. There is always the possibility of a stray bullet. Your welfare is for us too great a responsibility.

Nita, though disappointed, ended her visit but consoled herself with the company of her two young companions who had been her guides during her visit. She invited them to travel with her in the car. The youngsters, delighted with the experience of travelling in a Mercedes, tried out every gadget much to the silent concern of the driver. 'We have never driven in a car like this before, Ma'am,' said Barney, one of the youngsters. 'We only wish our friends could see us now. They will never believe us when we tell them that we had a drive in a Mercedes'. Nita recalls:

> I was learning so much about the youngsters. They had not been to school because they had rebelled against Bantu Education. When we reached the hotel, I invited them to my room. 'Are you hungry?' I asked, 'Oh yes, Ma'am.' As if one should ask growing boys such a question! For Barney and his friend, I ordered hamburgers, hot dogs, french fries and Coca Cola for four. Just watching them enjoy themselves was the event of the day!

> . . . they told me what they would do when they grew up and got into power. They described how they would revenge themselves on those who had brutalised them and their people.
>
> I said, 'But you would not be doing any different from them (their oppressors) because you will kill people . . .' 'Ah yes Miss, we know the bad ones and we know the people who are good; we going to take care of all the bad ones . . .'
>
> 'This means that you might answer with your lives.' I said. It is their answer which has remained with me. One of them replied: 'I don't have any education, so I have no choice. I have no job, so I can't do anything with my life. The job I have now is just because of the Church's help. I have no country. I have no vote and without a vote and a country I am not even a human being.'
>
> How do you talk philosophically to despairing youngsters? . . .You show them that a better day is coming, that they should be ready. You say all the things you do not believe yourself, but you still have to say them. . . .

But Nita's story of her visit to Alexandra and her enjoyment of the company of Barney and his friend did not end with her encouraging words to the adolescent youngsters. Less than one year later in August 1987, she attended a World YWCA Council Meeting in Phoenix, Arizona. The South African representatives included, Joyce Seroke who mentioned that she had brought to the meeting a film called 'Mama, I am Crying'. She wished members of the Council to see it. It was about the life of African people in South Africa and had been produced by a white South African friend, Betty Wolpert of the Maggie Magaba Trust[12] who had earlier produced a film on the ANC.

Joyce Seroke explained how the film got its title. Betty, wishing to film part of Joyce's day-to-day activities, visited Joyce in Soweto and in doing so, Betty became an illegal guest, according to the law, a sort of guest-in-hiding. In the late afternoon of the day of Betty's visit, they were both in the garden near the road when two youngsters, both not older than 17 years, passed by and cried shame on Joyce for associating with a 'honky'. Joyce explained to the youngsters why Betty was her guest and that the film she was going to produce would be shown outside South Africa so that others would learn about the kind of life the government of South Africa had forced on blacks in their own country. Somewhat blasé, the youngster had replied to Joyce's explanation: 'Mama I am crying, Mama I am crying . . . I will never see that film.'

One youngster in the film, Benjamin Oliphant, explained that he felt so strongly about the police brutality and their killings of his own people that even if his life was threatened he would speak out for his people. Within a short time after the completion of the filming, he was found shot dead.

On seeing the film Nita was sure that Benjamin, whose nickname or shorted name was probably Barney or sounded like Barney was one of the two youngsters who had been her guides, companions and guests at the hotel room hot dog late luncheon.

Arrangements were made through the South African Council of Churches (SACC) for Nita to meet as many women's groups as possible. The meetings took place at the offices of the SACC. Nita related:

> I had two informal meetings with YWCA groups in other places. One of the meetings was held in Johannesburg with a group which represented a cross-section of women in the community. It was at this meeting that I met Helen Joseph, an Englishwoman and a member of the ANC. She had been charged with treason together with Nelson Mandela, Chief Albert Luthuli, President General of the ANC; Walter Susulu, Secretary-General of the ANC, and fifty eight others. She had also been placed under house arrest for her membership in the Free Mandela Committee and for refusing to give evidence against Winnie Mandela. It is believed that she was responsible for arranging to have the children of Nelson Mandela educated outside of South Africa, and that for their own safety.

At those meetings the women told the most moving stories of their sufferings, including those caused by the dislocation of family life where their men were forced to live in camps in the cities for long periods while they and their children remained in Bantustans living in squalor far removed from the view of whites and visitors from the Western world.

At the time of her visit to one of the groups, three young men were on trial for their lives. As the meeting was about to end the front door was suddenly opened and two young men came in and said that the mothers of the young men who were on trial were outside of the meeting place. They had just left the courts with the mothers and thought that they should bring them to the meeting. The women entered, very dignified in their head-ties and looking very solemn. They began to tell their tale. It was yet another tale of victims of apartheid.

The mood in the room changed. Before they came, everyone had been rather militant, but when they heard from one woman speaking for the other two without hysteria, they became solemn and very sad. She stated that the death sentence had been passed on the three youths.

Recounting the experience, Nita said:

> I was moved to tears . . . someone put a headkerchief on the floor and without any prompting everybody present put in money. . . . A young woman who turned out to be a Methodist local preacher spontaneously stood up and for about 5 or 10 minutes said one of the most suppliant prayers I have ever heard. When she finished speaking nearly everyone present was in tears. It is difficult to convey the atmosphere in the room. Besides sorrow, there was anger. The women in that room were angry; but, too, they were determined to change their conditions. They were not women with power or money, but felt strongly that they wanted something better for their children . . . and then to have the three women come in and say, in effect, that their children would not be there when the changes came.

The event most anticipated by Nita during the mission was meeting

Nelson Mandela for the first time. As a member of the EPG group she had already met Winnie Mandela.

> The members of the EPG were amazed that she (Winnie) had retained her sense of humour, that she had the ability to smile, to smile in the photographs with us . . . She was very dignified and pleasant. When she began to speak about the 'struggle' as she called it, her personality changed completely. The anger, controlled anger, at what her people, Nelson, her children and herself were experiencing, although it was controlled anger, it was expressed in terms indicative of her commitment to change without any desire for revenge, expressed or implied, on the perpetrators of the crimes against black South Africans.

Nelson Mandela is a Tembu, one of the largest ethnic groups in the Transkei. He was educated at a mission school and at Fort Harare University from which he was expelled in 1940 along with Oliver Tambo, but he was able later to complete his studies in law at Witwatersrand University. Tambo and he opened a law practice in Johannesburg in 1952.

In 1944 Walter Sisulu, Tambo and Mandela formed the Youth League of the ANC, which became the radical section of the ANC. Mandela was the leader in June 1952 of a joint group of the ANC and the Indian Congress which defied the unjust laws. Mandela was arrested and charged under the Suppression of Communism Act.

Together with Chief Albert Luthuli, president of the ANC, and several others, he was banned. Mandela was banned again in 1956 when he was one of more than 100 persons charged with treason. In a trial lasting six years the government lost its case, but by that time, because of the requirement to attend court for the period of the trial, Mandela had also lost his livelihood as a lawyer.

After the Sharpeville massacre of 1960, Mandela established the Umkhonto we Sizwe (The Spear of the Nation), as the agent to force change through acts of sabotage. In 1961, having evaded arrest for some time, Mandela escaped from South Africa and undertook an eight-month tour of many African countries, including Ethiopia, during which he met heads of state and of governments who gave, or promised to give support for the struggle of the ANC. He also visited the UK. Returning to South Africa, Mandela continued to be elusive, but was finally caught by the police, having been betrayed by some one supposedly in their pay. He was arraigned on charges of conspiracy to overthrow the government by violent means and was sentenced to jail for life.

On a particular day, by appointment, the members of the EPG had a meeting with the minister of justice who lectured the group on the importance of ignoring the false information which had reached the rest of the world about the evils of apartheid. Nita found this affront to the group's intelligence pitiable, if not insulting. Just before the meeting ended Pik Botha, the Minister of Foreign Affairs, entered and quietly told the Co-chairman of the EPG, Lord Barber, that the group was being taken to meet Mandela. From the experience of the previous two days Nita was not surprised that the members of the EPG had not been given any earlier notice by a minister or anyone else of the visit to Mandela. Indeed, no atmosphere of confidence had been created which led any member to believe that the EPG would be permitted to meet Mandela at all.

Nita described this special and memorable occasion:

> having walked down to the basement of the very expansive block of buildings where the offices of the ministers were situated. We were quickly taken away in cars driven by well-dressed men, who were clearly security officers. We were very excited.
>
> When we arrived at the entrance to Pollsmoor prison where Mandela was being held we were met by the Governor of the prison, a most affable person who preceded us into his quarters. We entered the Governor's office where we were accommodated in upholstered chairs and a settee. The Governor excused himself and left the room. Within a minute or two he returned accompanied by Nelson Mandela. I have never got over the first sight of Nelson. I had thought that we would meet a dejected old man, in poor health and poorly dressed. The man, Nelson Mandela, who entered the room was dressed in a beige open-necked shirt, his well-tailored brown trousers, which had knife-edged creases, were held at the waist by a belt in the red, green and gold colours of the ANC, with an engraved and gorgeous copper buckle which I later discovered was a gift from Zambia.
>
> Nelson Mandela's elegant six-foot-plus figure was topped by a head of well groomed greying hair of the proverbial pepper and salt shade. It was fascinating to see how well he had withstood the isolation of more than twenty years from the members of his family, from his friends, from his world. It was a heady experience to meet the man who had become the symbol of freedom for his people, the man who had refused release from prison if only he would deny armed struggle as a means of obtaining freedom for his people.[13]

During their meeting with Nelson he was able to tell his visitors where they had been, whom they had seen and interviewed. He seemed well-informed of their activities to date. He sought their impressions about some of the persons whom they had met. The co-chairman of the group, Barber, could not contain his curiosity about the source of Mandela's information.

He said, 'Excuse me, Mr. Mandela, you know everything that is happening. How do you manage it?'

Mandela smiled: 'Well, I am allowed my papers, I have a small radio and sometimes when it is convenient,' he looked directly at the governor, 'they even take me driving . . .'

> Nita said, 'All I did was spend my time gawking!'
>
> When we had earlier met his wife, Winnie, in Johannesburg and discussed certain aspects of our visit with her, she had said to me that her husband feared that he might not be allowed to meet the members of the EPG.

'Since it is possible that he might not see you', she said, 'he has asked for a photograph of the only female member of the group'.

While sitting with Nelson, I remembered what Winnie had said about his wish. I took from my purse a passport-size photo of myself which had been taken earlier in the year, scribbled a souvenir type note across the back, and passed it to Nelson.

Acknowledging the gift, Nelson said, 'I am glad to see you in person, you are even better looking than your picture.'

Of course, that compliment with all the graciousness of a ladies' man, made my day.

We discussed many matters related to our mission with Nelson. We had met Chief Buthelezi the previous day and having noted, with much concern, his opposition to Mandela and the ANC, we were anxious to hear Mandela's point of view. In his reply, to our request for his opinion of Buthelezi and his stance, Mandela stressed that Buthelezi, as the leader of a substantial number of indigenous peoples, would have to be part of any group which negotiated with the South African government. Mandela displayed no animosity towards Buthelezi in spite of the many incidents of physical conflict between members of the Inkatha and adherents of the ANC.[14]

The whole manner in which Mandela spoke of Buthelezi was conciliatory.[15] He had no wish to denigrate any person or group because he did not believe in their ideology. Clearly, Mandela was totally committed to democracy.

At the risk of making too great a digression, a vignette of Chief Buthelezi might serve some purpose if only of providing background against which the conflict between the ANC and the Inkhata group might be viewed.

Chief Gatsha Mangosuthu Buthelezi is chief minister of the KwaZulu, and president of the Inkatha. The organisation (Inkatha Ye Siswe, 'For the freedom of the Nation') was formed by Buthelezi's uncle in 1912 as a means of preserving the Zulu heritage and culture and part of its former greatness which existed in the nineteenth century under the imperialist, expansionist and formidable Chief Shaka, who in less than 20 years converted his small Zulu chieftaincy into the most powerful African kingdom of some 2 million subjects. Shaka was a military strategist and defeated the Boers as well as crack regiments of the British invader. His power was only broken by the technology of the propelled bullet and the mass-destructive cannon in much the same way as European peoples took North America from the Indians.

Before 1962, when the ANC became more resistant to oppression, Mandela and Buthelezi became close friends. The two young men were youth leaders and would in different ways lead their people as heads of states and revolutionaries.[15] After 1962 when Mandela, Susuli and other leaders of the ANC were jailed and the ANC almost destroyed by the government, Chief Buthelezi and Inkatha helped to fill the void.

Buthelezi became head of the KwaZulu, thus preventing anyone weaker being installed as a puppet of the South African government. Buthelezi rejected for his people the so-called independence offered by the government and accepted by others. He was therefore the only person besides members of the liberal party who, until 1973 when the black consciousness movement arose, voiced their opposition to the Verwoerd government.[16]

From the mid-1970s Chief Buthelezi became a controversial figure when his ambition for the Zulu nation conflicted with the ANC's quest for unity of blacks and browns. This conflict was exploited by the government as late as 1993, even when it appeared that prime minister F.W. de Klerk was leading his party towards reconciliation and towards a New South Africa, Buthelezi showed little enthusiasm. However, when the final test of unity of the indigenous peoples of South Africa came in April 1994, Buthelezi was able at the eleventh hour to place the future of a New South Africa above his ambitions for the Zulu nation.

When asked for her opinion of Mandela, Nita was quick to respond. She said that she could not do better than give the unanimous opinion of the members of the EPG who after meeting with him found his character easily definable. An extract from the report of the EPG on the meeting with Mandella illustrates him as a man who, after more than 27 years in prison, would not accept freedom for himself at the expense of the principles of the ANC. He was the man who would not be free when the ideals of his people and the ANC itself were banned, he would not be free without the release from prison of other political prisoners, nor would he purchase his freedom by forswearing violence, the only means left to the blacks to gain their own freedom.

> He reiterated his belief that violence could be controlled. The government knew of his commitment to help in that. But his release would not be enough – prior understanding as envisaged in the concept between the ANC and the government on the steps to be taken, including the withdrawal of security forces from the townships would be essential. It would be necessary to ensure that he and his colleagues could move freely around the country using their persuasive powers to create a condition of calm in which the agreed process could begin . . .[17]
>
> Our mandate was to foster a process of negotiation across the lines of colour, politics and religion, with a view to establishing a non-racial and representative government. It is our considered view that despite appearances and statements to the contrary, the South African government is not yet ready to negotiate such a future – except on its own terms. Those terms both in regard to objectives and modalities, fall far short of reasonable black expectations and well accepted democratic norms and principles . . ..
>
> Any reservations by the government about dismantling apartheid would inevitably and understandably be viewed by the vast majority as a ploy for perpetuating white power in a new guise, a willingness to change its form but not abandon its substance. . . .[18]

The government faces difficult choices. Its obduracy and intransigence wrecked the Commonwealth initiative, but the issues themselves will not go away, nor can they be bombed out of existence. It is not sanctions which will destroy the country, but the persistence of apartheid and the government's failure to engage in fundamental political reform.[19]

The Commonwealth governments and also the UN through a resolution did encourage its members to impose greater sanctions on South Africa. South Africa indicated that if greater sanctions were instituted it would in turn retaliate by imposing sanctions on the landlocked black neighbouring countries of Botswana, Lesotho and Swaziland, a threat which had been anticipated. The idea was immature, for as one of its own journalists, John D'Oliveire in the *Argus Africa News Service* issue of 2 July 1986, wrote, 'If further international sanctions provoke the South African government into taking punitive measures against its neighbours, the ultimate loser could be South Africa itself.'

Nelson Mandela was released from prison in February 1990. The South African government under F.W. De Klerk began soon afterwards to dismantle apartheid. Mandela succeeded Oliver Tambo as the head of the ANC and led negotiations with de Klerk. Those negotiations were not always smooth but by the end of the first quarter of 1994 everyone was beginning to see some light. Although Buthelezi remained aloof for some time, he did in the end enter his Inkatha party as a party contesting the first free elections in South Africa, and like de Klerk and his party accepted the 60 per cent vote of the people for the ANC party and the presidency of Mandela.

The new South African government is seeking ways and means to make those blacks who were displaced from their traditional lands possessors once again. Other tasks remain, including that of providing education for a free people who will share their native country's wealth with the descendants of those who would not see what the pendulum of human cruelty has always taught. Fortunately for South Africa and for the world, one of the greatest miracles of the twentieth century has occurred in South Africa, a miracle of forgiveness and of understanding and one of brotherhood led by Nelson Mandela and F.W. De Klerk.

When asked about the greeting which she received from President Mandela when she returned home in May 1994 after attending his inauguration ceremony, with a twinkle in her eye and a smile Nita quietly said: 'Nelson did not forget the disappointment of the members of our (EPG) group in 1986. . . . He said, "remember that you and your colleagues started all this . . ."'

Nita returned from South Africa in May 1986. Within five months she had been appointed Barbados' ambassador to the UN and permanent representative. Since she was then resident in New York she became easily accessible to many groups and organisations which had interest in the difficulties which South Africa and its people were experiencing and wished to hear from someone who had seen the suffering.

One of the first invitations came in February from Bishop Trevor Huddleston who invited her to take part in an International Conference on 'Children Repression and the Law in Apartheid South Africa' to be held in Harare, Zimbabwe in April 1987. Nita was forced to decline because of prior commitment.

In March 1987 however Nita was able to join as one of a panel of six persons in the Eighth Annual Hope College (Michigan) 'Critical Issues' Symposium. Dale Dieleman of the *Grand Rapid Press* Newspaper on 9 March wrote under the headline 'Visit to South Africa bares horror of Apartheid, UN delegate says . . .'

> (Dame) Barrow said 'only after seeing the system at work can people begin to understand that apartheid means that three-fourths of that population are not considered human beings' . . . They (the EPG) found Pretoria government officials saying 'It is time for apartheid to be over, it is time to negotiate', but also heard anti-apartheid organisation leaders caution, 'We are afraid the president promises but does not deliver.'

Dieleman recorded Nita's comments on the more than 100 laws supporting apartheid, on the minimal value of reforms, on the views of Mandela, Bishop Tutu and Boesak, on the quiet dignity of the enslaved blacks and on the calumny of pitting blacks against blacks.

> Blacks, especially the youth, have nothing to lose. It will be a struggle to the end, (Dame) Barrow feared, They (youth) say: 'So what? We have no jobs, no vote, no country.'

During her service to Barbados as its Ambassador to the UN Nita has addressed the various committees of that organisation on many issues outlining the policy of her country. None, she believes, affected her emotions more than that delivered at a meeting of the Special Committee Against Apartheid on 18 July 1988 on the occasion of the 70th anniversary of Nelson Mandela's birthday.

Nita began her address by mentioning the sorrow, the profound regret associated with the harsh reality of Mandela spending his golden years incarcerated by a despised and universally denounced apartheid regime.

After reviewing the life of struggle of Mandela and his entry into the battle for the rights of his people and his sharing the leadership of the struggle against the evils of apartheid, Nita voiced the feelings of Barbadians, which were the same as those of other democratic nations. In doing so Nita said:

> With the firm conviction that Mandela will be freed eventually and full democracy and freedom will come to his beloved South Africa, Barbados joins with

all freedom loving people the world over in calling for the immediate and unconditional release of Nelson Mandela.

In February of the following year, 1989, the British Council of Churches held a conference on the subject of 'Britain and Southern Africa'. The speakers were: Rev Maxwell Craig, moderator of the Church of Scotland; Rev. Dr Alan Boesak, president of the World Alliance of Reformed Churches; Rev. Jose Chipenda, general-secretary of the All Africa Conference of Churches; Rev Robert Runcie, Archbishop of Canterbury; Rev. Bernard Thorogood, general-secretary of the United Reformed Church, Lynda Chalker MP, Minister of State, Foreign and Commonwealth Office; Dr Jurgen Schmude, president of the Synod of the German Protestant Church and Rev Simon Barrington Ward, bishop of Coventry.

In his letter to Nita inviting her to participate, Rev Brian Brown stated that there were clear and important differences between the British government and the churches in the UK and in South Africa. The purpose of the conference was to present those differences to the government as convincingly as possible.

The differences to which Rev Brown referred were those relating to the imposition of sanctions on South Africa. Resulting from the report (1986) of the EPG on the intransigence of the South African government, many Western nations increased the sanctions on South Africa, knowing that such action would result in a downturn of the economy of that country which would result in bringing the government to its senses.

Although Lord Barber, the co-chairman of the EPG, had been Prime Minister Thatcher's nominee, her government, indeed Mrs Thatcher, to put it mildly, was not convinced that sanctions would effect the desired change of heart of the South African government. She was certain, so she stated, that the very people who were the victims of apartheid would suffer more as a result of sanctions. She seemed to have managed not to notice that the acknowledged leaders of the black South Africans had openly supported the imposition of sanctions. The British churches did not agree with the Thatcher government view on the matter and therefore called the conference.

To end this chapter an incident associated with apartheid occurred in 1989 which brought out the true character of Nita as a formidable opponent of such injustices.

Beginning the second week of May 1989, Rev Frank Chipenda, general-secretary of the South African Council of Churches (SACC), together with Archbishop Desmond Tutu, Rev Dr Allan Boesak and Rev Dr Beyers Naude, former SACC executive member set out to visit special groups, including the World Conference on Mission and Evangelism of the WCC, other persons and President Bush.

While in Wisconsin, Chipenda was hospitalised with a sudden and mysterious life-threatening illness which turned out to be related to the possible skin absorption of organophosphates from his clothing which contamination was traced to his baggage.

So shocking was the situation that news conferences were called simultaneously in Madison, Wisconsin and at the USA office of the WCC in New York. Nita speaking not as a representative of her government but as one of the presidents of the WCC, issued the press statement.

Having defined the chemical found in Chipenda's clothing as mysterious, Nita stated:

> It is tragic evidence of the demonic forces present in the apartheid system. We are grateful that Chipenda's doctor has been able to save his life and we pray for his total recovery.

Clearly in anger, but with suitable restraint in expression, Nita then stated:

> We appeal to the white population of South Africa to condemn this vicious and cowardly act, no longer to remain silent because these deeds are done in their name, on their behalf and in defence of their privileges.

---

1. *Mission to South Africa, The Commonwealth Report*, Penguin, 1986, 13.
2. Ibid., 142.
3. Ibid., 143.
4. Ibid., 16
5. Allister Sparks, *The Mind of South Africa*, Knopf, New York, 10, 83-84.
6. Ibid., 125
7. Helen Joseph, *Side by Side, Autobiography*, Zed Books, London, 49.
8. Photo from Fatima Meer, *Mandela*, Madiba Publishers, Durban, 1988, 313.
9. Donald Woods, *Biko*, Holt & Co, New York, vi, vii.
10. Patrick Duncan was the son of a former governor-general of South Africa. He was a founding member of the Congress of Democrats and of the Liberal Party.
11. *Higher Than Hope*, 135.
12. The Maggie Magaba Trust is a South African based organisation committed to developing self-help and providing training and relief for the less priviledged persons in the community.
13. Early in 1985, Mandela was offered conditional release from prison. He had refused it. At a rally of some 15,000 members of the United Democratic Front, held in Soweto on 10 February 1985, his daughter Zinzi read her father's declaration rejecting the prime minister's offer.
14. Fatima Meer, writing that the relationship between Nelson and Buthelezi began when the former was the general-secretary of the ANC Youth League 1944 or later, believed that '. . . they formed a friendship that survives to this day'. *Higher than Hope*, Penguin, 1990, 37.
15. *Higher than Hope*, 37-38.
16. *The Mind of South Africa*, 271 (see note 5 above).
17. *Mission to South Africa*, 112.
18. Ibid., 131.
19. Ibid., 137.

8
Service with the YWCA

Nita's initial contact with the YWCA was in the 1940s in her first period of service. Her responsibilities and commitment had increased by representing the YWCA of Jamaica at the meeting of the Council of World Body in Lebanon in 1952. At the next council meeting of the world council, which was held in the UK in 1955, Nita was elected to the executive committee of the World YWCA. She continued to serve until 1967 as one the 25 members chosen from YWCA national affiliates all over the world. Among those elected at the same time as Nita, were Ghanaian, Annie Jaigge (who became a high court judge in her own country), Brazilian, Marly de Barros, Phoebe Shukri of Egypt and Leonor Stok de Llovet of Argentina. Until the 1955 meeting the membership of the committee had tended to be more representative of the associations of the northern hemisphere because (though never stated) members were expected to be able to meet the cost of their travel and accommodation when attending meetings. In order to remove this limitation, the world executive raised funds in 1955 to facilitate the attendance of some of the representatives of those associations who would not otherwise have been able to attend.

The membership of the outgoing executive committee in 1955 included Mrs Lilace Barnes, an heiress to a company in the USA and the Hon. Isabel Catto, daughter of Lord Catto of the UK, then president of the Bank of England, who later became president of the World YWCA. The young and energetic general-secretary was Elizabeth Palmer who was later to have a great deal of influence on Nita's career in the YWCA.

The 1950s was the immediate postwar period when the wind of change was blowing throughout the third world. In Africa, the Gold Coast gained its independence and became Ghana; Nigeria joined the Commonwealth as an independent country, and New Guinea and Togo also gained independence. There were political crises throughout the African continent, mostly caused by challenges from the indigenous peoples of Africa, who were dissatisfied with their continued exploitation by European invaders and with their enforced second-class world citizenship. Such difficulties existed from Suez in the north to southern Africa where there was oppression in the name of apartheid, supported by the Dutch Reform church. Asia, too, was undergoing change. Cambodia, Laos and Malaysia became independent. In the Caribbean, the English-speaking islands from Jamaica in the north-west to Trinidad and Tobago in the south entered a Federation which failed within four years.

It was at this time that Nita was given major responsibility within the YWCA in the Caribbean. A survey undertaken in 1951 by Eleanor French on behalf of the World YWCA had shown that some island associations which had been started mainly by expatriate women had subsequently become dormant or defunct possibly when their leaders returned to their native countries. An example was the Barbados association. Eleanor French's inquiry into existing status of the YWCAs had provided some stimulation to the weak YWCAs of the region. But other support and encouragement were given by people like the Canadian, Emma Kaufmann, also of the World YWCA. Emma had supported the start of the YWCA in Japan and some years later, having taken a particular interest in the Caribbean, she had also assisted in establishing the YWCA in British Guiana (now Guyana). In 1957 the Caribbean Area Committee of the YWCA was formed with Marion Foster as area secretary, succeeded by Carmen Lusan of Jamaica. Nita was the first chairman, holding that post until 1970 when she took up residence in Geneva. The membership of that first committee included Phyllis Mordecai (later Lady Mordecai) of Jamaica, May Roderiques of Guyana, Phyllis Osborne, Grenada and Barbadian, Betty Bourne (now Holland), representing Trinidad and Tobago. The area committee was supported through the Mutual Service Programme of the World YWCA and the YWCA of Canada, which also provided the services of trained persons, among them Jean Campbell, Phyllis Haslam, Marion Foster and Marguerite Hart. Nita was well placed to be president of the area committee of the West Indies' YWCA. She was a council member of the World YWCA. Her post as project officer to WHO/PAHO required her to travel not only in the Caribbean where she was based, but to other parts of the world where as a member of the World YWCA executive her duties took her. When asked how she made it possible to serve the YWCA when she was with PAHO/WHO and later when she was with CMC, Nita replied:

> Before travelling to a country where there was a YWCA, I would make contact with the Executive of that association as early as possible. Whether my stay was short or extended, I would make it possible some evenings, after having completed my official duties, to visit and/or work with the local association.

This method of ensuring her involvement with YWCAs wherever she went was used to great effect as the years passed. One example of the opportunities which the arrangement provided for Nita to learn more about the countries she visited than she might otherwise have, was that her contact with the YWCA of Uganda in 1972. Nita was visiting Uganda as director of the CMC of the WCC during the period of Idi Amin's presidency. Nita arrived in Uganda soon after President Amin had expelled some 50,000 Asians.[1] The Asians had more or less monopolised the commercial enterprises of the country and their sudden exodus had severely affected the economy to the point where imported items were extremely scarce. Nita's story of how she saw dressmaking being taught is an example of the YWCA members adaptation to change.

> When I arrived on a visit to the YWCA local branch, I found a class in dressmaking in progress. The teaching material being used was paper; made-to-fit paper patterns were first prepared so that errors were not unduly costly. There was just no cloth available for teaching. The building used by the association was in poor condition and small, therefore some classes were held under trees.

The general-secretary of the YWCA of Uganda, Joyce Mungherera, though quite young, was responsible for the development of the association in Uganda. Joyce had succeeded an American who had been seconded by the Mutual Service Committee of the World YWCA and by whom she had been trained. The success of the YWCA lay partly in its refusal to be drawn into any religious conflict. Muslims and Christians worked harmoniously together in the YWCA.

Indeed, at one time Joyce was faced with a difficulty which, but for her courage, could have limited or ended the existence of the national YWCA. President Amin had ordered that all women's organisations be brought under the control of one of the government departments. To Joyce this meant that external funding, then being received for the support of the YWCA, would also come under government control and might be appropriated for other uses. Joyce refused to comply, stating that the local association was a part of a worldwide non-governmental organisation and could not therefore become part of a government department. Her refusal resulted in an order to close the association. The Muslim women marched in protest. President Amin, being also a Muslim, found himself in some difficulty with people of his own religious persuasion and withdrew the order.

A YWCA World president is elected every four years by the Council. In 1975 the World Council met in Vancouver, Canada, not only to elect a new president and executive committee, but to receive reports from its various subcommittees and to plan for the next four-year period. At that meeting, which ran for two weeks in July, Nita was elected president in succession to Mrs Athena Athenassiou by the 450 representatives of some 70 of the 80 national associations affiliated to the world organisation. Nita's election was an indication that the ability and service of all members of the executive committee would receive due recognition and reward. Mrs Joyce Scroxton, who was one of the UK delegates elected to the executive at the same meeting, thought:

> The outgoing President was a brilliant Greek. Nita was elected because people knew about her and her ability to communicate. They knew that she was committed to improving the quality of life for women worldwide. At her election I saw no face which was not lit up. It was a joyful occasion, the Africans were ecstatic, Nita was the first black woman to be elected to the post.

The council meeting was also the last which Elizabeth Palmer attended as general secretary. She had served the YWCA for 25 years and had been a very energetic and far-sighted general-secretary, who had largely been responsible for changing the image of the World YWCA guiding others towards recognizing the need for the leadership of the World YWCA to reflect more clearly, by representation, the membership of its affiliates.

The procedures for the election of Elizabeth's successor, Joyce felt, were not the best possible, nor was Nita satisfied with the result – such understatement gives no indication of the racism associated with the selection contrary to the association's professed Christian principles and the affirmation that 'racism must be eliminated by whatever means', as the YWCA of the USA stated. The nominations committee came up with four candidates, one each from the UK, Finland, New Zealand and South Africa. The first two were eliminated, leaving Erica Brodie of New Zealand and Brigalia Bam a black South African.[2] Brigalia was clearly the most competent and experienced, being a YWCA leader in South Africa and also the director of the women's section of the WCC. Besides some questionable methods used in campaigning, there were some surprising tactics at the actual election and embarrassing discussion bordering on the acrimonious. Eventually Erica Brodie was elected by a slim majority. After the meeting one of the Asian members of the executive committee approached Nita offering her apology for not having supported Brigalia, confessing that her reason for not doing so was that she could not return to her native association and tell the members that the World YWCA had not only a black world president but a black general-secretary as well.

Before the end of Nita's first term as president, Erica was replaced by Ruth Sovik, the wife of Arne Sovik, who is best known for his work as a distinguished theologian of the Lutheran Church. Both Ruth and Arne have served as missionaries in many parts of the world, including China. Arne was one of the strongest supporters of the formation of the CMC of the WCC. Before becoming general-secretary of the World YWCA, Ruth had served in the secretariat of the WCC.

When Nita became world president of the YWCA, she had already been an associate director of the CMC for nearly five years. During that time the donor agencies had learnt to identify her and the CMC team with the selection of projects which were real in their effect on social and economic development, whether or not the projects for which their support were concerned with public health care. When the same agencies were approached by Nita as world president of the YWCA, seeking assistance for a local or a national project, there were few questions asked relating to the integrity of the proposal or its feasibility.

One example was the YWCA affiliate in Nairobi, Kenya, which in the 1970s was undertaking projects which would provide a steady income. Nita visited the association while she was on official duty travel for the CMC. She found the members busy with a building programme which included a hostel for the accommodation of young working girls with small incomes, and blocks of flats, near the Uhuru parks though not on the same site as the hostel, built to attract some of the more prosperous young women and visitors. The YWCA of Kenya became the centre for training for neighbouring states, including Zimbabwe.[3]

It is at Executive Committee meetings of organisations that major decisions are made pending subsequent concurrence or otherwise of the wider membership. Such practice was normal for the World YWCA. The executive committee meeting in June 1977 was reminded that the Soweto massacre of 67 protesters by agents of the South African government had taken place one year previously. That perhaps as much time and discussion had not been given to considering the massacre was due to the absence of a representative knowledgeable about the deep animosities of the races in that country. Normally, the general-secretary of the South African YWCA, Mrs Joyce Seroke, would have urgently presented the issues involved. But Joyce was a black South African whose affiliation to the world body was well known. Cruelty, like its parent, evil, dislikes exposure, so Joyce was refused a passport by the South African government.

The concern of the World YWCA, not only for Joyce Seroke but also for the welfare of the president, Jane Phakathi[4], was such that Heather Crosby, a member of the executive who was scheduled to visit the YWCAs in Southern Rhodesia was asked to visit also the associations in South Africa to learn at first hand about the conditions of Joyce Seroke and Jane Phakathi; as well as others who were reportedly being maltreated. On her return Heather reported that the solidarity shown by the World YWCA by her official visit, as well as action taken earlier by the world president, Nita, and Elizabeth Palmer, the general-secretary, had given some encouragement to the victims of apartheid. In Southern Rhodesia Heather visited some of the YWCAs in the rural districts and learnt of the bad effects which the guerrilla warfare being waged against the Ian Smith government was having on the people's lives.

Nita was first exposed to the work of the World YWCA when she attended the YWCA council meeting in 1951, where she learnt that the YWCA was among the first organisations to respond to the need of Middle East refugees in 1948 and also participated in the decision that the World YWCA could not regard its involvement in the suffering of refugees as temporary. Refugees therefore became a major concern of the World YWCA, which created the post of secretary for refugees in order to direct its efforts and be better informed on the continuing human tragedy, particularly as it affected women and children. The post appears to have been temporary.

The executive committee spent a considerable amount of time and resources on refugees. Barbara Gibaut, the member of the YWCA staff responsible, reported that young people 13 or 14 years old were leaving South Africa and fleeing to Botswana and other neighbouring countries. In an attempt to alleviate some of the suffering of the young refugees, the World YWCA rented two buildings during 1976, one to act as living quarters for some 15 girls and the other to accommodate classes for teaching marketable skills. Below are summaries of some of the reports on the work done with refugees in other parts of the world.

Dora Audeh, executive director of the YWCA of Beirut, Lebanon reported that more than 100,000 Palestinians[5] had taken refuge in Beirut in 1948. Still more had been arriving since 1967 and the seven local associations had been actively helping the refugees, but with continued fighting in and near the area, they were forced to curtail their efforts. With much determination the associations at Tyre, Sidon and Hadath had concentrated on the care and teaching of the very young. The associations at Rumieh, Tripoli, Boucherieh and greater Beirut worked with adolescent girls and conducted a vocational programme.

Priscilla Padolina, a staff member of the World YWCA who was working with refugees in Thailand where there were many refugees from Cambodia, felt that more could be done if the local people participated in greater numbers. Reporting also on the YWCA in Bangladesh, members learnt from Priscilla that besides conducting classes in management, the YWCA was also active in family planning and in outreach programmes in literacy, nutrition and vocational subjects.[6]

At the Committee meeting the following year, Nita and the other members in a special session led by Ruud van Hoogevest, Co-ordinator of Refugee Services of the WCC, expressed their alarm at the rapid increase in the number of the world's homeless people. The continuing political upheavals in Cyprus and in the Middle East, the civil wars in Ethiopia and Somalia and the then recent exodus from Burma had added another 200,000. The migration of young people from South Africa and Rhodesia had continued. The Vietnamese 'boat people', fleeing in small boats to places as far away as Hong Kong and Australia had become one of the most distressing human situations. The refugee women suffered most, trying to bring up families without money or hope. Cut off by language, culture and fear, their desperation became greater as the men and the children adjusted to the new circumstances by mixing with others at work and at school. The women were left at home alone and despondent.

The committee was also reminded that although the United Nations

High Commission for Refugees (UNHCR) was active in most matters affecting refugees, the NGOs and voluntary agencies such as the YWCA had to provide the kind of assistance which was outside the UNHCR mandate.

The YWCA had some time earlier established five major subjects for its continuing attention: environment and energy, health, human rights, peace education and refugees. There is no evidence that health received special attention because Nita was also the director of the CMC, which had in 1978 embraced the WHO/UNICEF sponsored Alma-Ata objective of 'Health for all by the Year 2000'. There is no doubt, however, that it did excite her interest and attract much of her personal attention. The executive committee meeting received a report in which Nita joined with Thelma de Santamaria, a vice-president of the YWCA and Angelica Saez, a staff member, to emphasise the urgency of 'health for all'. That catchphrase, familiar to those associated with other NGOs, such as the WCC and WHO, had not been copied from any of those organisations, but had become identified with the YWCA as one of its five major objectives and primary health care (PHC) would be the most suitable vehicle for the purpose. Furthermore, a suitably qualified person would be required to oversee the implementation of the project, which would embrace Asia, Africa, Latin America and the Caribbean. Through her continued interest in the Caribbean and her intimate knowledge of the region, Nita was able to help find the right person, Doreen Boyd, a Jamaican nurse trained in Canada and at UWI in social sciences. After being based in Barbados for a period, Doreen was invited by Ruth Sovik, then general-secretary of the YWCA, to undertake full responsibility for the international programme based in Geneva.

Nita was re-elected for a second term as world president at the council meeting held in Athens in 1979. The re-election was not unusual, since three of her predecessors, Lilace Barnes, Hon. Elizabeth Catto and Athena Athanassiou had also been elected twice. Soon after her re-election Nita sent Joyce Croxton of the UK, one of the vice-presidents, to Kenya to visit a group of women who had set up a project with the technical assistance of an engineer. The women had themselves harnessed water from a waterfall for an agricultural enterprise. They had also built a dispensary and a church and were erecting a school building. The World YWCA was helping them set up a poultry project to provide protein for themselves and their children as well as income. Joyce's report ensured the donors' continued aid.

In February 1980 Nita as world president led a delegation of officers and members of the World YWCA to join the president and members of the YWCA of Great Britain (GB) in celebrating the 125th anniversary of the National YWCA of Great Britain. The highlight of the celebration was the service of thanksgiving held at Westminster Abbey on 15 February 1980 where the Queen joined in the service.

Dame Nita, resplendent in her doctoral robes of the UWI, delivered the address based on the motto of the association, 'By Love Serve One Another'. The address was also in part a brief history of the YWCA movement and especially of the YWCA of Britain. The beginning of what would later become the association was based on the existence of two groups of women. One was a prayer group led by Emma Roberts, formed in 1855, and the other worked to provide shelter for some of the less fortunate. This second group established its first hostel for Florence Nightingale nurses travelling to the Crimea. The two groups merged in 1877 and took the name of Young Women's Christian Association. The movement spread through Europe and the USA. A kind of a union was formed first by the associations of Great Britain, Sweden, Norway and Switzerland, and it later included those of other countries. By 1898 the first world conference of the YWCA was held in London when 22 countries were represented.

Placing some emphasis on the expansion and role of the YWCA, Nita reviewed the past and suggested that in spite of past achievements, 'the sort of imagination which brings success is one that sees a distant summit, a general route to it, and specifically where to put the feet for the "next ten steps"'[7]

> ... but the will to take the next ten steps remains. And you are not alone. You are surrounded by the witnesses from your own past ... from a sisterhood around the world of some 84 different national associations ... you are part of the re-affirmation stated in the World YWCA Council meeting in Athens in September 1979 that, as long as there is injustice, racial prejudice, poverty and unnecessary suffering in the world, there can be no acceptance of things as they are by a Christian organisation ...

Having completed her duties associated with celebrations in England, Nita accepted an invitation to give the address at St David's Cathedral in Wales.

During 1982 the concern of the World YWCA and its affiliated associations about female refugees throughout the world and especially in the Middle East became more acute. The executive committee acted in response to an invitation from the YWCAs of Lebanon and Jordan and agreed to send a special delegation led by Nita to visit and report on affiliated YWCAs and on the status of refugees, especially the women. The group included some 19 persons from 14 countries who represented the diversity of the world movement; they had special qualifications and experience, having studied the region and its tragic history.[8]

In 1983 the delegation, led by Nita, who was then near the end of her second term as world president, set out for the Middle East on what was designated the 'World YWCA's Middle East Encounter – In Search of Peace and Justice'. The non-resident delegates included Margaret Mugo of Kenya, Ann Northcote of Canada, Joyce Scroxton of the UK, Ivy Khan, general-secretary of the YWCA of India, Virginia Chaplin and Mary

Wolfe of the USA, Taufa Vakatale of Fiji and Sheila Moyes of Scotland, the general-secretary, Ruth Sovik, and Genevive Camus-Jacques, both senior staff members. The resident members were Samua Khoury, president, and Doris Salah, secretary, of the YWCA in Jerusalem.

The visit took place soon after the Israelis had bombed Beirut and the Lebanese had massacred some 300 Palestinians in two camps outside Beirut.[9] Arriving in Beirut less than 24 hours after the destruction of the US Embassy there by a bomb, the delegation found the situation very unsettling. The members of the delegation did, however, not only visit refugee camps, but spent a portion of the three weeks visiting the YWCAs of Beirut in Ashrafieh and Haddath. They were unable to leave the city since the outlying areas were, in effect, occupied by Israeli forces.

Joyce Scroxton[10] spoke of her moral cowardice, as she called it, and said:

> Nita kept us all together in great harmony. We had one problem at Immigration because our Fijian colleague who was with us was not permitted into Lebanon because Fijians had been part of the UN Peace-keeping Force when one of them had killed a Lebanese. Our Fijian colleague had to fly back to London and out again to meet us in Jordan.

The Lebanon YWCA conducted training courses for young girls and ran nursery schools; especially for children who no longer had parents. In Jordan the delegation met many of the intelligentsia of Palestine, including the Bishop of Jerusalem, the Vice-Chancellor of Bierzat (Palestinian) University and two mayors, one of whom had lost both his legs. Doris Salah, who was herself really a refugee had, together with her family, been driven out of their home in Lebanonn. Many persons had been similarly treated. Their homes and property had been appropriated by the Israeli authorities or by their agents.

The Crown Prince of Jordan, Prince Hassan, spent a morning briefing the delegation, which included one American and one Canadian Jewess, on the work done by the YWCA, especially its contribution to the development of Jordan. The prince made farewell gifts to the delegation of books written by him, one of which would cause much trouble later during travel in the region.

The presence of the delegation in Amman, Jordan, provided considerable moral support for the remnant of YWCAs outside Jordan and demonstrated the concern of the World YWCA for them. In relating their distress, the refugees and the nationals living in Jordan and the West Bank pleaded with the members of the delegation to educate Western people to understand that the Balfour Declaration had been abrogated. Although it had supported the right of the Jews to have a home, it had also stated that the people living in the lands which they would occupy should not be molested nor displaced. To assure her hosts of the purpose of her visit, Nita said:

'We hope to be part of the peace process because the only way to ensure peace is to have people understand what has made for the lack of peace.'

It was the delegation's role:

> to spread at first hand the knowledge which we have received, because the press does not always give a proper picture of a situation . . . the delegation's first step on its return will be to report to the World-YWCA executive meeting, to be held in May (1983) in Geneva, on those parts of the Middle East which we have visited. Our second step will be that of reporting to the world-YWCA council meeting in October (1983) in Singapore, whose delegates are drawn from 80 countries . . . we hope for peace and justice for all people in the region and want UN Resolution 242 to form the basis for treatment of the Palestinian problem.[11]

The 1983 visit to Lebanon was Nita's fourth. The first was in 1951 when she had represented the Jamaica YWCA at the council meeting. The shelters in the refugee camps in Jordan at that time were mainly tents and were supposed to provide temporary shelter only. Nita's subsequent two visits had left her as depressed as the first because in spite of the assistance provided by UNHCR, the women's despair was very real and the drabness and subhuman standard of living in tents as dwelling places had become permanent. On this occasion Nita met some of the grandchildren of the 1951 Palestinian refugees, still living in camps, dispirited and unhappy even though tents had been replaced by more permanent structures.

Although the YWCA in Israel hardly existed anymore, there were small groups of former members living in Jericho and in Jerusalem who wanted to become affiliated to the Palestine Association. A meeting of the interested parties was held in Jordan. The representatives living in Palestine had to cross the Allenby Bridge[12] between Jordan and Jerusalem in order to attend. Entering Jordan was a traumatic experience for two members of the delegation and for Ivy Khan it was her second, since the first time she had been excluded from Lebanon because she was Indian and when she attempted to cross the bridge she was detained for want of a visa. The Israeli officers at the border were not amused. Nita remained at the border with Ivy while the other members of the delegation passed through. Relating the incident, Nita said: 'To this day I do not know what Ivy said to the officer at the border, but whatever it was, he became confused and let her through as he mumbled something about some kind of a nut.' The other difficulty was experienced by Virginia Chaplin who had placed Prince Hassan's book inside one of her bags, which was seen when the bag was opened for inspection. The Israeli officers at the border were very thorough in their search of personal effects and baggage. The prince's book was regarded in Israel as subversive literature and when a copy was discovered in Virginia's baggage she was immediately taken away. When she rejoined the other members, she was very upset at the indignities to which she had been subjected, especially since she was a national of a country friendly to, if not supportive of, the Israelis. Samia Khoury, national president of the YWCA of Jordan, was directed to another customs area. She too was subjected to search without dignity.

The discussion of the report at the World YWCA council meeting in Singapore in 1983 precipitated the following comment from Samia Khoury: 'You came and shared our agony, you saw our plight and heard our cries. You gave us moral support, hope.' Sheila Moyes of the UK also reported positively on the statements which the YWCA had brought to the churches and to the British government. Mary Wolfe of the USA said: 'We Jews and Arabs do not need one more enemy. We need a common friend. If you cannot be one, please do not say anything.' But Nita had the last word on the subject: 'We can see that a seed has been sown. Go and tell those who are now partners in the enterprise.'[13] The delegation was regarded by some as having had Arab sympathies, but such a view was not unexpected from the British Board of Deputies of the Jewish community. The report was also sent to the British Refugee Council and was probably the first of its kind which the Refugee Council had ever received about the effects of long-term camp-life conditions upon women.

It is quite difficult for a person who has never been subjected to humiliation founded on racism or other bias to understand the feeling of devaluation of spirit and denigration of one's self-worth as a victim. It appears that as associations and groups condemned practices which in the extreme were exemplified by apartheid in South Africa, the worse the situation world wide became, or perhaps publicity made it seem so. The World YWCA through its executive committee had been forced to deny affiliation to an all-white association in Durban because of its racial policy. The association to which non-whites could belong in Soweto was therefore isolated and entirely dependent upon leadership and training from the more privileged blacks, some of whom had been forcibly removed from their former homes in places like Sophiatown and placed in the township. One such couple was Dr and Mrs Xuma. Mrs Xuma became president of the YWCA in the township. Her husband was one of the founders of the African National Council. By coincidence Mrs Xuma was elected to membership of the executive committee of the World YWCA at the same time as Nita and served for the very same period of 12 years. It was from Mrs Xuma that Nita first began to learn about the evils of apartheid.

During their periods as world presidents of the YWCA, Lilace Barnes (1947–55) and Elizabeth Catto (1955–63) had both reported that when they visited South Africa, they were not allowed to drive up to their hotel in the same car with the black president of the local association. Nita experienced similar restrictions during a brief stopover visit on her way to South Africa. When Nita went to South Africa in 1986 as a member of the EPG, she had already had first-hand experience apartheid. Her close friend and former colleague at CMC and YWCA in Geneva was Brigalia Bam. With Brigalia's connivance Nita would slip away in the evenings and visit YWCAs in the township. Indeed she acted so confidently that she was able to go to the farm of the Bam family in the Transkei to visit Brigalia's mother on her eightieth birthday.

In discussion with Archbishop Ted Scott of Canada, a member of the EPG, the subject of Nita's extensive travels and worldwide friendships came up. He said:

> When we stopped at any city in our journeys to the front line states and other places, the first thing Nita did was to take out her address book, one about three inches thick. She would go to the nearest available phone and call persons whom she knew personally.
>
> Because of her work with the WCC and the YWCA she knew women everywhere. Her contacts became useful, indeed essential. In South Africa, the women had been carrying much of the load in the struggle but they had not received the recognition due to them. Nita symbolises that new breed of women, who are informed, intellectual and analytical, women who understand issues at a deeper level but also with sensitivity to people.

Whether devising means of bypassing an unjust system or supporting other women in reaching, if not extending, their own potential, or indeed celebrating their achievements, however small, Nita seemed to have not only an inexhaustible source of energy and exuberance of spirit, but a sense of fitness of things.

The 1983 council meeting in Singapore marked the end of Nita's eight-year, two-term period of office as world president. To leave such a gathering of women leaders simply by indicating the end of a council meeting would give no sense of atmosphere other than that of the business of individuals and groups undertaking a task in a world which seems to care little about, but depends much on, its women with social consciences and deep commitment to the equality of rights for all.

Imagine the late nights of women meeting to draft and re-draft summaries and resolutions,

> sandals falling apart, bodies falling apart clothes looked exhausted by the erratic care caused by cavalier labelling on detergents at the . . . general store. Once my underwear was subjected to dandruff shampoo, on another occasion I found it standing at attention, rigid with starch. The bathrooms had become the centre for high level conferences. While struggling with the . . . plumbing . . .
>
> The Council was proof that woman's work is never done – not even that of our President. Murielle Joye, our Treasurer-elect heard a slight rustling outside her window late at night. Looking out she saw under the moonlit trees a figure in a bathrobe, leaning down to haul her laundry out of a plastic bucket . . . our President, Dame Nita. There are no privileges of rank here, we are all peasants.[14]

Nita agreed to hold the next council meeting (1987) in Phoenix, Arizona, USA, and then performed her final act as world president. On handing over the responsibility to her successor, Ann Northcote of Canada, Nita said:

> You are going forward into the future, hopefully . . . renewed by the vigorous and increasing input of younger women; as a movement which does not cling to tradition . . . if we differ, let us hope that we have now attained the maturity that we can differ with each other in love . . .

Although demitting office as YWCA world president relieved Nita of her formal responsibility of leading the organisation, she nevertheless continued to perform duties for the World YWCA not only as immediate past president, but also as field agent for the YWCA. One of these was the result of her visit to South Africa as the only female member of the Commonwealth Eminent Persons Group (EPG) mission to South Africa in 1986.

In 1987 the YWCA council meeting was held in Phoenix, Arizona. A seminar, 'Development with Justice', would form part of the self-training for the 500 or more members who would attend. There was a mishap in the preparations and it suddenly looked as if there would be no guest speaker. An urgent appeal was made to Nita to address the three-day seminar. Nita accepted, arrived at the appropriate time, delivered the address and prepared to leave on the next plane for the Bahamas, much to the disappointment of the members of the council who had looked forward to having her spend the remaining period of the council meeting with them.

Nita was forced to decline the invitation. She was committed to attend the 50th anniversary of the YWCA of the Bahamas as the guest of honour. The Bahamas YWCA had for a brief period been in need of stimulation and rejuvenation. With the approach of 50 years of service to the community, the members agreed to mark the occasion with suitable celebrations. While worrying about the problem, the president of the local association saw a television interview with Nita who was visiting the Bahamas on business associated with the UN. She contacted Nita the next day and gained a commitment from her to attend the celebrations as guest speaker. As a result, the YWCA prepared a programme which had the desired effect, that of revival of the YWCA.

---

1. Uganda was a part of British East Africa until 1920 when it became a protectorate. In 1962 it became independent.

2. Brigalia Bam is one of a well-educated family of black South African patriots. She has been a member of the YWCA since about 1966. Hers was one of the 'front-line' families. Her brother Fikile, an attorney-at-law as a member of the National Liberation Committee was imprisoned with 10 others on Robbens Island, supposedly for sabotage, at the same time when Nelson Mandela was incarcerated

there and were subject to the most unusual indecencies. For instance Prison officer Van Rensburg in a display of uncivilised baseness would violate ordinary sanitation codes at the prisoners' 'food table'. He also openly told lies about his chosen victims. Fatima Meer (revised edn), *Nelson Mandela*, 267.

3. Originally Southern Rhodesia. In 1953, together with Northern Rhodesia and Nyasaland, a federation was formed, which lasted about ten years. UDI, the tenet of an oppressive non-democratic state, was declared by the Ian Smith regime. In 1980, however, Robert Mugabe, following internal upheavals, headed the new independent state of Zimbabwe.

4. Jane Phakati and Joyce Seroke, together with 17 other heads of black organisations, including the Black Parents Organisation and members of the Black Women's Federation, were arrested for participating in a public protest in support of the black students who refused to learn Afrikaans.

5. In 1917, the British foreign minister, Arthur Balfour confirmed British support for the creation of a Jewish state in Palestine provided that there was no interference of the civil and religious life of other peoples living there. The League of Nations in 1920 gave the mandate for Palestine to Britain.

Britain's attempt to slow the rate of Jewish immigration to the new state resulted in conflict during which nearly 100 British people were killed in an explosion. After the Second World War and armed conflict between the Jews and the Palestinians, Ben Gurion in 1948 declared the State of Israel, the borders of which were later defined by agreement with neighbouring Arab countries. Further conflict involving Israel's neighbours was severe and led to Israeli occupation of portions of Egypt, Jordan and Syria.

The Palestinian Liberation Organisation (PLO), formed in 1964 and led by Yasser Arafat, continued to fight to retain or regain the independence of Palestinians. Finally, in September 1993 in Washington, an historic foundation document for peace was signed by the antagonists. Part extracted from Cook & Stevenson, *Longmans Handbook of World History*, Longmans, 1991.

6. Minutes of executive committee of the World YWCA, July 1977.

7. Nita quoted from Simms writing in 'The YWCA – An Unfolding Purpose', the extract having been taken from Charles Horton Cooley.

8. Report of the world council meeting of the YWCA 1-14 November 1983, YWCA, Geneva, 39.

9. Itzhak Kahan, an Israeli judge, conducted an enquiry into the massacre. His report caused a political uproar in Israel and resulted in the resignation of Menachem Begin as prime minister. Keatings Historical Notes, 29954.

10. Vice president of the World YWCA, interviewed January 1993.

11. *Jordan Times*, 4 April 1983.

12. Named after the British general who captured Damascus and Jerusalem from the Turks in 1917.

13. Report of the world council meeting of the YWCA, November 1983, 39.

14. Report of the World YWCA council meeting, Singapore, 1–14 November 1983, Nancy Boyd Sokloff, 41.

9

Resident Representative to the UN

When the UN General Assembly opened its session in mid-September 1986 two women joined Ms Edmonde Dever of Belgium as the only women ambassadors of the 159 permanent representatives of countries: Mrs Nora Astorga, the Sandinista revolutionary of Nicaragua, and Dame Nita Barrow of Barbados. The North American press, according to Michele Lansberg of the *Globe & Mail*,[1] considered Mrs Astorga a 'Latin Mata Hari', a designation which was not popular with her. In an inspired assessment of the women Lansberg commented:

> The two women though utterly dissimilar, stirred a ripple of excitement on their arrival. Both are vitally involved with the most dramatic issues facing the world forum . . . Dame Nita and Nora have enough energy to refloat the tired old ark on the Hudson. The betting here is that the 200 per cent increase in female representation will have a 1000 per cent more impact than many routine appointments. Just think what another 50 such women might do.

The two new arrivals at the UN would soon find common cause in their respective countries, opposition to the politics of self-interest masquerading as 'collective self-defence' practised by the USA under the Reagan administration.[2] Within one year of Nita's and Nora's assumption of duty, the International Court of Justice at The Hague had rejected the USA's attempt to justify its military and paramilitary activities against Nicaragua. The court also required that reparations be paid to Nicaragua. When the USA indicated that it need not recognize the International Court's decision, Nicaragua took the matter to the UN General Assembly in the form of a resolution urging the USA to adhere to the ruling of the International Court. When the resolution was put to the vote, Guyana, Trinidad and Tobago and Barbados, the last through Nita as its permanent representative, were the only English-speaking Caribbean countries among the 94 countries which supported the resolution. In her address Nita noted:

the Nicaraguan resolution had brought into question the very concept of international law. . . . Barbados is deeply concerned about the maintenance of peace in the region and, therefore, finds it difficult to countenance any activity which, in the judgement of the Government, may endanger the chances for peaceful settlement of disputes.[3]

Not long after the passing of the UN resolution, in a report of the US State Department to Congress on voting practices in the UN, Barbados was listed as having voted only 20.3 per cent of the time with the USA. This, together with apparently similar figures for other countries, evoked from Senator R. Kaasten Jr and former US ambassador, Jeane Kirkpatrick, in the *Washington Post* strong comments about 'friends' who fail to support the USA at the UN. Barbados' ambassador to Washington, Peter Laurie, in a reasoned 'Open Letter' in the October 1986 issue of *American Politics*, found the charge flawed. Indeed using the same instrument of measurement employed by the critics, Laurie showed that:

> one of the ten issues identified by the State Department as 'key' to the US interests at the last General Assembly – the 1986-87 biennium budget – the most consistent supporter and therefore, supposedly best 'Friend' of the US was the Soviet Union.

The ability to represent one's country and make statements especially in disagreement with majority opinion within a given forum requires not only a facility of language and mastery of the art of understatement, but it also demands a skill of virtually hearing what is not being said and understanding the difference between what is desirable and what is expedient. This is especially so where the business of ordinary human existence and simply staying alive is the business of the day. Although wealthy nations seem able to pay greater attention to the power they wield and their status on the world stage, all at the expense of the welfare of its ordinary citizens, so-called third-world countries are often forced by their more powerful non-neighbours to make survival in its literal sense the main business of everyday.

During Nita's residency the problems of southern Africa were often before the UN. It was clearly not easy to relate the apparent lip-service of some of the African front-line states to the thrust against apartheid. Such vacillation presented no difficulty to Nita who had visited Botswana, Zaire and Zimbabwe either as a member of the Eminent Persons Group (EPG) of the Commonwealth or as director of the Christian Medical Commission (CMC) of the World Council of Churches (WCC). She understood clearly and sympathised with the difficult real-life policies those countries had to pursue as neighbours of South Africa. Nita stated:

> The situation of Botswana, for example, had to be fully understood. That country could never state publicly nor act decisively against the illegalities of the

South African government. To understand it one had to visit and see. The week before the EPG visited Botswana in 1986, 400 tons of animal carcasses eventually destined for South African dinner tables had gone to waste because the South African consignees had not sent their refrigerated trucks for the perishable cargo as was the practice. It was assumed that the nation of Botswana, through its animal farmers, the vendors, was being punished because it had agreed to a visit from the EPG. Indeed a delegation headed by Pik Botha was arriving in Botswana as we were leaving. The object of their visit was to ensure that agreements formerly made with Botswana were kept.

Lesotho had suffered similar economic arm-twisting a fortnight before the EPG members arrived for their visit. What South Africa did was to suspend shipments of gasoline there for two weeks. It might be more diplomatic not to do more than state that South African foreign policy towards the African front-line states was lacking in humanity. By using intimidatory methods South Africa was able to keep their landlocked neighbours 'in line'.

Nita could appreciate the problems of countries like Lesotho and Botswana, which in principle abhorred the practice of apartheid but because of their dependency on South Africa even for access to sea ports were unable to express their views openly. Indeed, such countries were forced to trade with South Africa in order to survive. As if that were not enough of an indignity, there was the added charge of hypocrisy made against those countries by people who effected not to understand when trading with South Africa conflicted with their position on apartheid.

When Nita arrived at the UN in 1986 as Barbados' Permanent Representative preparatory work was being done on a parent resolution for the international conference on drug abuse and illicit drug trafficking scheduled to take place in Vienna in 1987. Barbados was very active among the group of countries trying to reduce the growth of the narcotics trade. There was, however, difference of opinion among the representatives about the method of dealing with the problem. Some thought that it would be better to suppress the traffic while others thought that restraining the demand for drugs would be more effective. At least one large country preferred to concentrate on stopping the cultivation of the narcotic-yielding plants. Certain Latin American countries reminded the meeting that it was the poor peasants in the Latin American countries who, because of the market for drugs, were able to cultivate the plants and thereby provide a reasonable standard of living for their families. Nita, representing Barbados, subscribed to both views. In addition, if the combined approach was to be successful, it would be necessary that some alternative means of making a living be found for those presently cultivating narcotic-yielding plants, such as replacing the highly profitable crop by another. Because of the convention that one nation avoids commenting on matters internal to another, it is doubtful whether any representative was indiscreet enough in such a diplomatic forum to suggest that there might also be some real attempts at promoting land reform for the benefit of the dispossessed indigenous peoples.

Early in 1990 during a seven- or eight-week period of preparation for the UN conference on the environment to be held in 1992 in Brazil, a stage was reached when certain difficulties appeared insoluble at the administrative staff level. At that point the problems were referred to a group of Permanent Representatives, including those from Malaysia, Jamaica, Singapore, Vanuatu and Barbados. When discussion again approached deadlock, Nita reminded them that since the conference would be held in 1992 there was no need to delay completing the resolution because of the current obstacles, some of which were not substantial and therefore did not have to be solved immediately. Nita encouraged the members of the committee to extend their interests to other countries. Together with representatives of other Caribbean countries she led the committee to focus attention on the needs of the small states and include in the resolution some reference to them.

As a natural team-builder, Nita played a leading role in helping to create a cohesive and identifiable Caribbean entity at the UN. Caribbean states were represented at the UN at reasonable, if not affordable levels, but meetings of their permanent representatives seemed to be held only when crises were imminent. During Nita's period as Barbados' permanent representative she assisted in completing a process which had been attempted before her arrival. She shared the leadership in making the Caribbean group more identifiable, cohesive and a subgrouping which could no longer be ignored. As a result, the group began to meet regularly once a month with a specific agenda.

One item on the agenda was the contentious problem of candidatures within the Group of Latin American Countries and Caribbean countries (GULAC). Two most undesirable consequences arose from the closer association of the Caribbean representatives. One was that indecision, national self-interest and jealousy would not again adversely affect Caribbean government leaders and their permanent UN representatives, as they did in 1988 when Nita was a candidate for the presidency of the UN general assembly. Indeed it would appear that Barbados' unsuccessful attempt in 1988 to secure the presidency of the general assembly and the embarrassment to the whole Caribbean caused by the prevarication of some of the Caribbean governments strengthened relationships among the Caribbean states and contributed to their understanding of the importance of presenting a united front to the rest of the UN world. The 1992 nomination of the Ambassador of Guyana, Samuel Inshanally, by GULAC demonstrated that.

Another consequence was that the Latin Americans in GULAC found that they had to give greater consideration to Caribbean candidatures.

Other regional groupings in the UN had recognized that the GULAC group was in effect divided and had openly expressed their dissatisfaction with the obvious disunity between the large continental members of the Latin American subgroup and the small island Caribbean group to the point where Caribbean candidates would lack support.

When Nita became Barbados' permanent representative, it was a little over one year since Forum '85 in Kenya. She was therefore well placed to assist those members of subcommittees at the UN who were undertaking the follow-up action. In addition, because of her service with international bodies, she was quite well known. Her experience with the WCC, the World YWCA and in the EPG mission to South Africa enabled her to speak from personal experience on matters affecting African countries, as for example on the issue of the proposed lifting of sanctions against South Africa. The opinion which she expressed on behalf of Barbados was based on first-hand knowledge and carried some weight. As an experienced nurse, administrator, proponent of primary health care and a genuine feminist, Nita was often invited to leave one meeting for a short while to attend another, for example, that of a subcommittee of UNICEF, to give advice on matters affecting women and children. Her contribution to these meetings was as a resource, to inform opinion and avoid or resolve deadlocks.

As if to test Nita's ambition – and its companion, modesty – there came the time when a new president for the 1988–89 Session of the General Assembly should be chosen. The presidency of the United General Assembly is, by convention, rotated annually among the five regional groupings represented in the UN. When it is the turn of a particular region or regional group to assume the presidency, a suitable candidate is sought, preferably by consensus, from among the constituents of the group. Every effort is made to avoid more than one candidate being presented for election by the general assembly.

Following the defeat of the Bahamas by Panama in the contest for the presidency in 1983, there was an understanding that for the 1988 presidency, when GULAC would once again have its turn to nominate a candidate, that nomination would go to one of the 13 English-speaking countries. GULAC was therefore required to offer a candidate for the presidency of the 43rd session of the general assembly due to begin in September 1988. On nine previous occasions the Latin American subgroup had held the post, five of them since Barbados had become a member of the UN after it became Independent in 1966.

As early as 1986 Barbados had indicated its interest in offering a candidate for the office in 1988. This was done by means of a note to the members of GULAC. Barbados was therefore the first of the group to declare officially its intention to seek the presidency. The Bahamas, Jamaica and Argentina subsequently – and surprisingly – also declared their interest in pursuing the honour. The Bahamas named its permanent representative to the UN, Ambassador Davidson Hepburn who had been unsuccessful in 1983. Whether the gentleman's agreement of 1983 about the sole candidate for 1988 being English-speaking was forgotten or whether Argentina's policy had changed is immaterial: Argentina did declare its interest and its candidate was its foreign minister, Daniel Caputo. The candidacy came as a surprise to the Caribbean subgroup of GULAC.

The Jamaican government made no move to confirm its candidate. There were indications from well-placed informants that Ambassador Lloyd Barnett, the Jamaican Permanent Representative to the UN, would be the candidate, but there were also strong rumours that foreign minister, Hugh Shearer, was a contender. The confusion was intensified when the Jamaican delegate stated at a meeting of permanent representatives of CARICOM that the Jamaican candidate was indeed Lloyd Barnett. However, when the Commonwealth summit held in Vancouver in October 1987, provided the opportunity for a caucus of CARICOM heads of government to be held to resolve the issue, the prime minister of Jamaica, like the other prime ministers attending the CARICOM summit, was informed of the caucus, but was conspicuously absent, allegedly without apology. The result was that it permitted speculation among those who did attend the caucus that Jamaica was snubbing its smaller associates and members of CARICOM. Of course, since Jamaica had not yet formally identified its candidate, Seaga's absence might well have been a delaying stratagem.

The caucus agreed that Jamaica's foreign minister, Hugh Shearer, would receive the support of the Caribbean. If however, he declined, as was considered likely, the Caribbean would support as candidate Dame Nita Barrow. On returning from Vancouver, the prime minister of Barbados, Erskine Sandiford, informed the 18 members of the Latin American subgroup that the Barbados candidate was Dame Nita Barrow.

Sometime during the months that followed, foreign minister Shearer confirmed that he was not interested in the post. In a press release of February 1988 Shearer stated that Jamaica had withdrawn its ambassador, Lloyd Barnett, from the candidacy in favour of Dame Nita Barrow and the Bahamas had withdrawn its candidate, Ambassador Davidson Hepburn. Shearer also noted that when he had informed the Argentinian ambassador of the Jamaican position, he had also reminded him that the Caribbean subgroup had never had the honour:

> to provide a President of the United Nations General Assembly, and we are urging the Argentine Government to consider acting in the same way as Jamaica and withdraw its candidate in favour of Barbados.

This announcement left two candidates, Dame Nita and Daniel Caputo.

However, the decision to withdraw the candidature of Barnett was widely regarded as having come too late to be of benefit to Dame Nita and to Barbados. The reluctance of the Bahamas and Jamaica to defer to Barbados permitted Argentina to disregard a virtual understanding made earlier in the campaign that it would leave the pursuit of the post as soon as the Caribbean reached a consensus on its candidate. The continued presence of Jamaica offered Argentina the excuse that by February 1988 its own candidate had committed too much time and resources to the effort to withdraw.

A bizarre footnote was added to the sorry story some months later after Caputo had been elected to the presidency of the general assembly, when the newly elected government in Argentina did not permit him to return to the final session of his year as president and to hand over to his successor. That action caused many eyebrows to be raised. The Argentinians were reported to have spent excessively large sums of money on the campaign.

During the period of canvassing in which the several Caribbean missions took part, many matters which would not normally have been thought relevant to the issue were raised. Barbados' former colonial status did not enhance the chances of its candidate, for it was put about that the Barbados candidature was in fact sponsored by the British. Coming as it did so soon after the Falkland/Malvinas Islands war, such rumours did nothing to endear Barbados to Latin American states because of the defeat of Argentina in its attempt to secure the islands. Had the British given any obvious support to the Caribbean candidature it would have been counter productive and would simply have played into the hands of the Argentinians.

Barbados' limited resources could in no way compete with those of Argentina in terms of financial support for the conduct of the campaign. For example, Barbados could not afford to meet the costs of sending delegations of a suitable size to countries whose governments might not have made a commitment. But it soon became obvious that the greatest damage done to the Barbados candidature was that by our own Caribbean, in showing to the world our disunity and our inability to unite in a common cause.

Professor Rex Nettleford of the University of the West Indies at Mona, Jamaica, was not at all flattering when he reviewed his own country's role in the sorry matter:

> but there is now cause for relief to the chronic unease which attends our relations with our cousins. Jamaica has thrown its support behind Barbados' candidate Dame Nita Barrow for the Presidency of the 1988 United Nations General Assembly. The news came out of Bridgetown. The Barbadians are happy with the final solution of yet another storm in a teacup. . . .
>
> I commend the Government of Jamaica for its show of commonsense in the

> Dame Nita Affair. Once our proposed candidate, Hugh Shearer, indicated a lack of interest in spending months on First Avenue in Manhattan with a gavel in hand and a promise of nights of poring over official papers, we should have abandoned interest in the admittedly prestigious honour.
>
> News that we were thinking of putting up a career civil servant for it seemed perverse when someone like Dame Nita Barrow was the candidate with backing from all Caribbean countries except Jamaica. Even the Bahamas, albeit with alternative designs on a Security Council nomination, decided to withdrawn its candidate . . . We cannot go wrong on Dame Nita. She is the Caribbean. The fact that she is the sister of Errol Barrow, the late Prime Minister of Barbados, is not purely coincidental. She is, nonetheless, a person in her own right with a track record of international service unsurpassed anywhere in the region, including Hispanic, Gallic, Netherlands parts of it.
>
> . . . Jamaica needs to return to the old practice of treating our Commonwealth Caribbean cousins as part of the Caribbean family . . .[4]

The efforts of the Caribbean subgroup, mainly those of Barbados, already damaged by the display of disunity, were valiantly shored up by Sir James Tudor, Barbados' foreign minister, in his address of 18 June 1988 to an Extraordinary Meeting of the Latin American and Caribbean group. Referring to the colonial status of the group, albeit colonials of European countries of differing cultural backgrounds, Sir James regretted the isolation of the English-speaking Caribbean from its Hispanic neighbours. He considered that the historic, cultural and linguistic barriers, the systems of law and education, were all very real. Together with Haiti and Suriname, the Caribbean subgroup constituted 14 of the 33 members of the group, yet it frequently was not consulted on matters of importance to the region.

Referring by implication rather than directly to the apparently scant courtesy paid by the Latin American subgroup to the ambitions of its Caribbean partners, Sir James said:

> It is a matter of record that, on the nine previous occasions on which the Presidency of the General Assembly has fallen to the Latin American and Caribbean Group, no Caribbean state has ever had the honour of representing our region. . . . The last occasion on which the Presidency fell to our Group the Caribbean aspiration was not accepted by the Group and the matter had to be voted on by the General Assembly. It was the Caribbean's understanding then that the next time around we would be entitled to the Presidency. It was therefore in that context that three Caribbean countries, from as early as September 1986, announced to this Group their interest in serving the Presidency. We in the Caribbean sub-group knew all along that we would resolve our differences among ourselves and unite behind one of the three candidates. And this we did.

Sir James as strategist obviously hoped that his own acknowledgement of the disunity of the Caribbean subgroup, would prevent the Latin Americans taking advantage. But the damage had already been done.

Sir James dealt with the aspersions cast on the candidature of Barbados and its candidate, Dame Nita, namely: the small size of Barbados, the alleged sponsorship of Great Britain and the qualifications of the candidate. On the matter of size, Sir James assured the group that Barbados was capable of providing from its large pool of intelligentsia adequate support for the candidate if elected to the post. As regards the sponsorship of Great Britain, he considered that an old canard:

> which we in the English-speaking Caribbean have had to confront ad nauseam since we became independent and tried to assume our rightful place in this region . . .the governments and people of our sub-region are tired of these constant slights on our sovereignty and independence, particularly when the record is there for all to see . . .

As for the qualifications of Dame Nita, in refuting the last aspersion, Sir James used language chosen for its civility as well as for its power to reject firmly suggestions he regarded as being somewhat uncharitable:

> we assessed very carefully and realistically our ability to offer a person who could not only carry out the duties of the Presidency but would do so with great distinction. The reality of being small nations . . . of some five million souls is that we do not have the luxury that larger nations may have of an abundance of qualified persons among whom to choose. We Caribbean peoples therefore adhere strictly to the policy of presenting candidates only when we have candidates of great merit and high distinction.

Sir James concluded by saying that a female president would be the first in almost 20 years (ie since Mrs Angie Brooks of Liberia) and the first woman from our region, which he considered would be a fitting tribute by the UN General Assembly to the worldwide struggle for the rights of women.

Why did Argentina not withdraw its candidate in favour of the Caribbean candidate, Dame Nita? There are clearly several reasons including the prestige of the post involved. Any action which would increase its prestige would be most welcome in assisting Argentina in regaining some of its national pride after its conflict with the UK. Perhaps the fact that the Caribbean subgroup is English-speaking served to make victory in the contest, for that is what it became, more crucial to the prestige of Argentina. On a personal level, its foreign minister could ill-afford to be defeated by Dame Nita. Consequently, much effort and substance were expended in ensuring that the Argentinian candidate was elected.

The Argentinians claimed that the presidency of the UN General Assembly would help restore the image of their country. It would be regarded as international approval of Argentina's return to the community of democratic nations. It would also, according to their lobbyists, discourage the ambitions of the highly motivated officers of the Argentinian armed forces who were still unhappy about their recent setback. The more widely accepted explanation was that the campaign was Caputo's personal effort to enhance his chances of becoming president of Argentina. There were also indications that the governmental bureaucracy in Argentina was not fully committed to Caputo's candidacy.

Dame Nita's victory in the campaign depended on solid support from the African delegations where ethnic and cultural considerations bolstered the appeal of Barbados. Her prominent role in the international struggle against apartheid made her personally attractive to the Africans.

While the support of the English-speaking Africans was considered firm, the position of the French-speaking Africans caused concern. France's hold on its former colonies is known to be unshakeable. At the time of the campaign, Franco-Argentinian relations, always good, were at their best and it was feared that if it became necessary, Argentina would ask France to use its influence in Africa to weaken Dame Nita's support. This appears to have been done during the last fortnight of the campaign when surveys indicated that Nita Barrow held a firm 3–6 vote lead over Caputo. The resulting defection *en bloc* of the Francophone Africans a few days before the vote crippled Barbados' prospects.

The Commonwealth community at the UN, led by Canada, provided unflagging support for Dame Nita's campaign. However this was insufficient to offset the strong appeal of Caputo to European delegations whose extensive commercial ties with Argentina overcame all other considerations. Similar priorities accounted for the position taken by several Asian countries. Australia, influential in sections of South-east Asia, was alone among Commonwealth states in supporting Argentina and was candid enough to explain its position early in the campaign.

Barbados did not have diplomatic relationships with the Soviet Union nor with any but a few eastern European countries. Argentina not only had diplomatic relationships but also trading relationships with all of eastern Europe. Barbados had solid backing from the wider Caribbean, including Suriname, and at the last moment, the Dominican Republic. The countries of the South Pacific gave support. India's position was unclear.

Other factors believed to have harmed Barbados' chances were the Arab communities' dissatisfaction with Barbados' principled middle-of-the road stand in the Arab–Israeli conflict and some Islamic unease over the role of women in political affairs. It was well known all over the world that Dame Nita was herself a formidable champion of women's rights and a supporter of women who sought to be free of male domination, where such practices resulted in little or no credit being given to women's role in commerce and industry.

In the end Barbados was able to rely on 60 votes, although at the election 66 actually voted in favour. This permitted Daniel Caputo to gain the presidency by 25 votes. The lessons learnt in 1988 by the Commonwealth Caribbean from its dilatory tactics or lack of decision-making have been useful.

When the 48th Session of the General Assembly began in September 1993, the Caribbean had already agreed on one candidate, the Guyanese ambassador, Samuel Inshanally, who was nominated unopposed by any candidate from Latin America. The editorial of the Barbados *Nation* newspaper of 20 September 1993, referring to Inshanally's election to the presidency, included in its comment:

> While it is an historic achievement for CARICOM, it is a dream which was denied Barbados and its Governor General Dame Nita Barrow and which eluded a diplomat from the Bahamas. That achievement: becoming the first person from the Caribbean to occupy the Presidency of the General Assembly of the United Nations.
>
> The last time the Presidency was to go to someone from the Caribbean and Latin America, Dame Nita, at the time Barbados Ambassador to the U.N. went for it. But she became a victim of Caribbean indecision and Latin American chauvinism and selfishness . . .

---

1. 20 September 1986.
2. From 1912 to 1926 US armed forces were in Nicaragua protecting US interests. One year after their departure Augusto Sandino formed a locally recruited army which defeated US forces in 1934 during a second occupation. Sandino was later assassinated and Samoza became the US supported president. The group for national liberation, the FSLN, increased their challenge to the US-supported undemocratic government. Eventually the Sandinistas became the elected government of Nicaragua. The continuing attempts to topple it were taken to the World Court in June 1984.
3. Ricky Singh 'CARICOM's Vote on Nicaragua', *Nation* newspaper, Barbados May 1987.
4. From 'Ideas', *Money Index*, 1 March 1988.

Nita about to receive from Queens University, Canada, an honorary LLD degree, 1991

Dame Nita at Government House, the official residence, putting frosting on cakes, assisted by great-nieces

Dame Nita with primary schoolchildren on lawn of Government House, 1992

Dame Nita entertaining a group from Bishop's High School, Trinidad & Tobago, at Government House, 1994

Nita with her sister, Sybil

Dame Nita entertaining A.N.R. Robinson, Prime Minister of Trinidad & Tobago and Sir Hugh Springer, former Governor-General

Dame Nita dubbing Sir Harold St John, Knight of the Order of St Andrew, 1994

10

The People's Governor-General

Anyone who has ever asked Nita for the telephone number or address of one of her friends soon looks on in amazement at the address book which she produces. It is a brown, leather-bound volume, not address book, being twice as thick, wider and longer than the ordinary variety but nevertheless fits easily into any handbag which Dame Nita might carry. It is held together by an elastic band, not because of any fragility, but to keep it closed. That address book is Nita's link with the world, with her friends in the world, the world which has from time to time paused from its busy-ness to recognise and honour her for the continuing sharing of herself. Such acknowledgement was first made by the University of the West Indies at its graduation ceremony at the Cave Hill Campus in Barbados when she was honoured with the conferment of its degree of Doctor of Laws, *honoris causa*, and was the guest speaker. The University honoured her again by inviting her to deliver the graduation address at the graduation ceremony at the Mona Campus in Jamaica in October 1990.

That occasion was special for Dame Nita because Joyce Robinson, O.J.[1] would receive an honorary degree from the university. Joyce Robinson, a long standing Jamaican friend of hers, had made a major contribution to her country's literacy programme and with the support of Dame Nita, through the International Council for Adult Education (ICAE) to the international community as well.

Mention was made in an earlier chapter of the award of Dame in the Barbados Order of St Andrew. In addition, Her Majesty has created her a Dame Grand Cross of the Most Distinguished Order of St Michael and St George. Altogether she has received twelve honorary degrees, a Fellowship of the Royal College of Nursing of London and a Membership of the Order of the Commonwealth Caribbean[2]. Among other honours which she has received are: the Louise McManus Award of Columbia University; the Christine Reismman Award – International Council of Nurses, Geneva and the Women First Award of the YWCA of the USA.

Writing to Nita inviting her to accept the honorary degree of Doctor of Science, Dr. Alvin A. Lee, president and vice chancellor of McMaster University considered that her service had been based on her 'perception of health care as a fulfillment of the demand to visit and heal the sick in the gospels . . .'

Five years later, in 1987, on presenting her to the Chancellor of the University of Toronto for the award of Hon. LL.D., the orator having summarised Nita's career, noted that she had been a student at that University.

> [Nita] is one of hundreds who have come from all parts of the world during the 67 year history of the Faculty of Nursing at the University of Toronto. Alumni of this Faculty number more than 6000 . . . more than 300 of these are in countries other than Canada.

The University of Toronto's award of Doctor of Laws, honoris causa in 1987 was followed by similar awards: in 1988 from the University of Winnipeg in Manitoba and Mount St Vincent University; Spelman College in Atlanta, in 1989 and the University of York in 1990, the same year when Nita was appointed governor-general of Barbados.

For Barbadians, the period immediately before Nita's appointment had not been without an atmosphere of uncertainty about who would be the person to succeed Sir Hugh Springer. John Wickham, literary editor of the Nation Newspaper in the independence issue of 30 November 1990 wrote of Dame Nita's installation in June 1990:

> 'Dame Nita Barrow, GCMG, DA was welcomed and acclaimed on all three sides of the House of Assembly itself which was more than was promised for a rumoured candidate for the position.'

Wickham was referring to a rumour of a few weeks before Dame Nita's appointment, that Sir James Tudor, a founding member of the Democratic Labour Party (DLP), more popularly known as 'Cammie' (Cameron being his middle name), was likely to be recommended for the post of governor-general. In political circles Cammie was reportedly the 'king maker' of the DLP. He was generally regarded as having initiated the action which led to the appointment of Erskine Sandiford, then minister of education, to the post of prime minister of Barbados after the sudden death of Errol Barrow in 1987.

The most generous comment that can be made about the unease which filtered down to ordinary citizens and existed even among the DLP's faithful is that there seemed to have been some undesirable haste in the selection of Barrow's successor. It had also been reported that the basis for the 'king maker's' action was that Errol Barrow months earlier had stated his order of preference, if not of precedence, for the members of the inner circle of the DLP party. Errol was supposed to have said that after him there was Sandiford, then Philip Greaves, and after Greaves 'any one can play'.

It had also been reported that Sandiford had said that Sir James was worthy of the highest post in the land. When therefore Sir Hugh

Springer, then governor-general, gave notice of his intention to vacate the post because of failing health, a rumour more based on truth than otherwise rapidly spread that Sir James would be recommended for the post. The public became fearful that Sandiford might really think that the time had come for him to recommend Cammie for the highest post in the land which many other persons thought might be better conferred on some other person. The rumour appeared to have been well founded for it became the subject of a comment in parliament.

The views of several members expressed in parliament on the matter, were not flattering to Prime Minister Sandiford. They seemed however to have guided him more wisely towards the will and mood of the people. The subject was never discussed publicly in the press.

Barbadians are among those people who sometimes know when to be silent. There must be few Barbadians, if indeed there are any, who do not genuinely like and respect Sir James. Nevertheless, for some days the matter of a successor to Sir Hugh Springer was the topic of conversation at breakfast tables, in lunch rooms, in bars and restaurants and most certainly at dinner tables.

Every Barbadian resident and citizen of reasonably sound mind knew that there was always really only one possible successor to Sir Hugh Springer, and that person was well-known by name and fame: Dame Nita Barrow, Sir Hugh's cousin, a sister of the late prime minister. Indeed Barbadians had some ten years earlier let it be known that they were proud that the Barbados Labour Party (BLP) government of the late prime minister, J.M.G.M. (Tom) Adams, had recommended Nita to the Queen for the conferment of Barbados' highest honour, that of Dame of St Andrew. Adams' action placed the acknowledgement of Dame Nita's service to people in many parts of the world above considerations of party politics of Barbados. That Nita was the sister of Adams' political opponent and leader of the opposition at the time demonstrated his political maturity, judgement and freedom from pettiness.

Nita had long been considered, at least by many Barbadians, as a world citizen and at the time of national concern and unpublicised but genuine anger, was ambassador and Permanent Representative of Barbados to the UN. All that need be said has already been confirmed by the action of the Queen who appointed Dame Nita Barrow to be her representative in Barbados, governor-general and commander-in-chief.

One other portion of John Wickham's full-page article should be quoted, if only for its wit. It captured one of the chief interests of Dame Nita; it also identified the emotion of the many women in the large crowd which had assembled in the parliament yard and environs at the installation of the new governor-general.

> The feminist lobby rejoiced but happily stopped short of suggesting that Dame Nita ought properly to be regarded as Barbados first Governess-General. . . .

Dame Nita in her inaugural address, before acknowledging her debt to her relatives and to those persons who had guided her in her early years and contributed to her maturity, recognised that her appointment would be of more than ordinary importance to all women.

> I am aware that my appointment to this honoured office will be discerned as a gesture of civic deference to the women of Barbados. I consider this a most appropriate occasion on which to render my own tribute to the women of this Country.
>
> No one familiar with Barbados and its history will have to be told where lies the rightful place of women in our society. None need be told that it is to the Barbadian women that we owe the existence of much of what is modern in Barbados. All . . . know that it is from our women – grandmothers and sisters, mothers and aunts – that we derive the strengths which have carried us through the darkest ages of our history.
>
> I reserve my deepest gratitude for the honour of this dignity being placed on my shoulders as one of Barbados' women. I accept it as a tribute to their many sacrifices.

As if taking its cue from Dame Nita, the local press highlighted the achievements of Barbadian women of at least two generations in several fields of activity, the pioneers as well as the recent achievers and those who had brought their skills from the home into the open world and were working alongside men. Among them were Nellie Weekes, a committed social worker of the early 1930s and a strong political campaigner for her husband, C.N. Weekes, who pursued honours in local government; Ermie Bourne, the first woman to be elected to Barbados parliament; former senators -educators, Milroy Reece, Enid Lynch and Odessa Gittens; Gwen Reader, nurse and social worker, Madame Ifill and Carmeta Fraser, food promotion specialist.

Dame Nita soon made it clear to all that her new post provided her with new opportunities for 'people service'. Although she could not be an active member of local organisations, she would support many which sought her patronage or involvement. The local YWCA, of which her sister Sybil was at the time treasurer, supported by 'Friends of the YWCA' held a black tie dinner and cabaret on the grounds of government in December 1994. It was all part of an effort to raise funds to meet the cost of renovation of the organisation's headquarters.

For the past three or four years, on a Saturday afternoon in mid-February, the Government House grounds are used for a garden party for hundreds of Barbadians and visitors to the island. The annual garden party is sponsored by the International Women's Group of Barbados to raise funds for some of the local charities. Besides her official entertainment as head of state, Dame Nita has been host to several women's groups, but not exclusively so. She was host to about 15 students from a high school in Trinidad on a visit to the island, who in turn showed their appreciation by entertaining in song Dame Nita and a few specially invited guests. With similar ease she has also entertained groups from the Barbados Retired Nurses Association among whom are many respected members of Dame Nita's own profession.

Dame Nita has retained membership of several organisations. One of these is the relatively new 21st Century Leadership Development Programme (LDP) later (LEAD) which was established in 1990 by the Rockefeller Foundation to support, 'through on-the-job-training, the maturation of professionals in developing countries for the integration of environmental considerations into all activity of economic and national development'.

On the invitation of Peter C Goldmark Jr., president of the Rockefeller Foundation in July 1991, Nita had become a member of the Programme's International Steering Committee. The other members were: Sir Shridath Ramphal (Chairman), Oscar Arias Sanchez (Costa Rica), Manuel Solis Camacho (Mexico), Professor Jose Goldemberg (Brazil), Chief E.Y. Eke (Nigeria), Dr George Golitsyn (Soviet Union), Dr Gordon Goodman (Sweden), Professor Emil Salim (Indonesia). Nita was unable at attend the First International Session, Cohort of 1992–94 which was held in Thailand in March 1993. The issues of major focus for the LEAD cohort of 1992-94 were: Population and Natural Resources; Energy, Trade and Debt.

Associated with another leadership training group, not an international one, Dame Nita delivered the keynote address at the 'Women's Leadership Conference' held at Wills College in California in June 1993. On the local scene, besides official speeches, she willingly delivers addresses to those groups and organisations as for example that in 1992 to a Joint Meeting of the Faculty of Medicine and the Department of Women and Development Studies of the University of the West Indies, Cave Hill campus.

Continuing association with the World YWCA and units within the UN however required Dame Nita's attendance at a conference of the first and participation in a celebration of the second. In 1991 she attended the World Council of Churches Fourth Assembly held in Australia. As one of the organisation's Vice Presidents she was due to retire by the convention of rotation. Two years later the World YWCA celebrated its Centenary in London. Most of the associations affiliated to the World YWCA were represented. The presence of large delegations of the YWCAs of Uganda and Korea provided Dame Nita with the opportunity to reminisce and meet once again some of the pioneers of these two associations which had been formed during her period of service on the executive of the World Y. Many of those from Uganda were from rural districts of their country and had travelled overseas for the first time. Others remembered Dame Nita from 1985 when she was the Convener of Forum 85 in Nairobi, Kenya.

The UN General Assembly and its Secretary-General established a secretariat for the celebration of the 50th Anniversary of the organisation in October 1995. The Purpose was to: educate and inspire a new generation of UN supporters; to mobilise public opinion; to reflect upon the UN's past, to consider and strengthen its future; convey and celebrate its achievements and build public support for the UN worldwide. The theme for the celebration is: 'We The Peoples of the United Nations . . .United for a Better World'.

As part of the preparations for the celebration, the 'Friends of the UN' in 1993 created a programme called 'We the People: 50 Communities Award'. The object of the programme is to 'select 50 communities around the world which have used innovative models which demonstrate success in building just, sustainable, participatory communities which can cooperate with others'. In order to reach its goal, nominations were sought through UN agencies and NGOs. To make the selection, a Panel of 40 Advisors co-chaired by Dame Nita and Dr Pierre Marc Johnson, a medical doctor, lawyer and former Premier of Quebec have met.

Before relinquishing her post at the UN, Nita had made an official statement in 1990 on the proposed conference on the environment in Brazil in 1992. The conference was not the first of its kind which the UN would hold. The first global conference on the environment was held in 1972 in Sweden.

In her statement to the UN Nita said that it was no secret that the concept of sustainable development was viewed with some concern. While developing countries' debts were becoming burdensome, developed countries were practising protectionism and applying declining terms of trade, thus creating unsurmountable problems for the struggling countries. Quoting one author, Nita likened the paradox to a football match in which for most of the time one team dictated all the rules and was thus able to score most of the goals, by fair or foul means, and so build up a commanding lead. Then 15 minutes before the close of play the team calls 'time-out' and decides that the rest of the game should be played fairly. Nita suggested that the proposed conference of 1992 should encourage the removal of barriers between environmental preservation and protection on the one hand and the fulfillment of development objectives on the other. Reverting to her earlier football match of inequalities, it was her view that in the 'match' no one team could win regardless of any lead. She ended by quoting from a Kenyan proverb:

> Treat the earth well.
> It was not given to you by your parents
> It was loaned to you by your children.

In 1992 Dame Nita attended the Conference on Environment and Development (ECODEF) held in Rio de Janeiro, Brazil as one of the 10 Eminent Persons invited by the Secretary General Maurice Strong, who would ensure that important environmental concerns received the degree of attention which they deserved. Arising out of the UN conference there was agreement to hold the First Global Conference on Sustainable Development of Small Island Developing States (SIDS) in Barbados in May 1994.

At that conference it was also agreed that the conference would be strengthened by having available the views of an independent group of international experts on sustainable development, especially in relationship to small islands. It was hoped that in addition to providing ideas on sustainable development of small islands, the group would also make recommendations about the problems facing small islands trying to achieve the goal; suggest how to raise the level of awareness of all nations to the problems; advise how technology, human resources and the pooling of information related to the subject might best be used. The government of Barbados would provide a convener.

In accordance with the agreement, Dame Nita invited the following persons to form the group: President Abdul Gayoom of the Maldives; Prof. Tetsus Koyama, a specialist in Asian Economic Botany; Most Rev. Sir Paul Reeves of the UN; Sir Shridath Ramphal, former Commonwealth secretary-general; Haarlem Brundtsland, chairman of Committee on Environment & Development; Fetani Mataafa, High Commissioner of Western Samoa to New Zealand; Ian Cummin, Chairman Leneadia National Corp.; Ms Ella Cisneros President of Together Federation of Global Unity; Ms Hilda Lini of Vanuatu and Chief Emeka Anyaoke, Commonwealth secretary-general.

Immediately preceding the SIDS conference in May 1994, the group of eminent persons met in Barbados, shared their expertise and wisdom on sustainable development issues as they related to small islands. The report from their meeting was submitted to the Global Conference of SIDS immediately afterwards.

In her welcome speech to the Eminent Persons Group, Dame Nita suggested that there existed among the peoples of the south and the so-called third world, especially those island-based, the view that sustainable development was not in fact a new invention, it was a concept practised intuitively in traditional resource management and the life-styles of island peoples. It was the profligate and wasteful life-styles and consumption patterns of the North that had precipitated Earth's current crisis. The small islanders had themselves contributed through unquestioning acceptance of those patterns as appropriate models.

As is the practice when a UN sponsored conference of governments is to be held on specific issues, every attempt is made to hold a conference of Non governmental Organisations (NGOs) on the same issues simultaneously as a means of informing and supporting the governmental conference. Barbados would therefore be host country to both the governmental and the NGO conferences. It was the business of knowledgeable and willing Barbadian citizens and residents to assist, advise and where necessary lead in the organisation of the NGO conference. It was inevitable that some persons would see the NGO conference as a competitor of the governmental SIDS conference. The organisation of the NGO forum was a joint effort of UNDP and Barbados. Basil Springer, head of a management company and Sir Frank Blackman, retired Dean of the Civil Service of Barbados provided much of the leadership required and assisted in coordinating the contributions of local and visiting groups. Colin Hudson, an environmental activist and inventor directed the organisation of an exhibition appropriately named, The Village of Hope. Dame Nita as patron, was more than nominally involved with the progress of the activities of the forum and of the Village of Hope, but took care to ensure that her support for the preparations for the global SIDS conference did not appear to be any more than that.

Many of those who worked to ensure the success of the NGO forum and of other activities were glad to know that there was available to the organisers the advice of one who had herself successfully undertaken and directed the staging a number of NGO conferences, including one of a number of women, estimated at nearly 18,000.

But it was of some concern to Her Excellency, Dame Nita Barrow, that, for some time, all was not well with her people. Within some six months of her assuming duty as governor-general, the prime minister Erskine Sandiford, indicated that the elections due in 1991 would take place in January of that year. Through election he hoped to obtain his own mandate from the electorate to lead Barbados as its chosen prime minister rather than as prime minister by inheritance. The run-up to election was not as easy as he had hoped; the economy of Barbados was in serious trouble, since as a small island with an open economy it would, according to a wit, 'normally catch economic cold when North America sneezed' from the chill of recession. Barbados' economic health had been undermined through reckless living in the form of bad financial management. In denying the obvious, Sandiford was quoted in the press as having said in parliament that there was no runaway expenditure in Barbados and that the management of the economy was sound. However, a World Bank report stated that since 1989 fiscal management had faltered and that evidence pointed to a severe liquidity crisis.

Senator Wendell MacClean, an economist of considerable standing, stated that the Central Bank had incurred heavy losses in December 1990, an unprecedented situation. MacClean accused Sandiford, who was also minister of finance, of not taking competent local advice; further, that his failure to do so would result in his having to take the advice of the International Monetary Fund (IMF), an organisation regarded by third-world countries as lacking a human face. Perhaps severe and stringent measures imposed by the IMF are deserved by those third-world countries which find themselves led by arrogant, self-centred, real or potential tyrants who show little concern for their people's welfare and more for establishing the cult of the individual, erecting costly buildings as monuments to themselves or for extravagance. Sandiford dismissed all prophecies and warnings of approaching economic disaster as fantasies and those who projected them as 'prophets of gloom and doom'.

The 1991 elections did provide Sandiford with the mandate he required; no longer would he wear the shoes of his late mentor Errol Barrow, nor would he be regarded as Barrow's beneficiary. Within a few months, however, all the anticipated agonies were realised, and the greatest, not anticipated by any commentator, was that of humiliation. Barbados fell into the hands of the IMF. Barbados had never, even as a colony of the UK, been forced to play the part of mendicant. Part of the shame of Barbados and the anger of ordinary citizens resulted from the hasty sale of government-held shares in international companies at less than their market value. Commenting on the matter columnist Ralph Jemmott wrote:

> the agreement of government to sell its shareholdings in BET and BARTEL represent nothing less than privatisation on the basis of surrender, the hasty sale of the family heirlooms to foreign pawnbrokers, a birthright bartered for a mess of pottage.[3]

Within a few weeks it became quite clear that Barbadians had been deliberately misinformed of the state of the island's economy in late 1990 and early 1991 when they were being persuaded to vote the Sandiford-led party, the Democratic Labour Party, back into office for another five-year period.

As foretold by economist MacClean, Barbados was forced to approach the IMF for assistance with the restructuring of the island's economy. The IMF prescribed stringent methods for repairing the badly bruised and mismanaged economy which had been made worse by pre-election extravagant spending. One of the requirements was that the government reduce its expenditure. That resulted in lay-offs of many government employees. Other measures resulted in a contraction of the economy. There was one fear, however, which never materialised, that of the devaluation of the Barbados dollar (Bds$1=US$0.50). Sandiford fought valiantly to maintain the 2:1 relationship with the US dollar and in that he was successful, thus regaining some of the respect of the Barbadian people, since it made him appear to be making a real attempt to salvage as much as was possible from the economic catastrophe consequent upon his government's recklessness. By comparison, Jamaica, Trinidad and Tobago and Guyana, which were forced to seek IMF assistance, have not been able to escape currency devaluation and all the attendant miseries which befell the poor.

This is a brief outline of the conditions in the disturbed community of misled citizens, citizens whose elected leader also insulted them when, instead of giving them reasons for action, or appearing to know the meaning of accountability and the importance of communication, preferred to act the potential tyrant. He openly stated that if they, the people, did not like what he had done or was doing they could do what they liked. The colloquial language used was insulting, arrogant and outrageous.

The labour unions protested mainly the ill-effects which the structural adjustment would have on their members. The sympathy of the community for its poorer members was widespread. Finally, in response to the general feeling of bitterness and a desire for unity in adversity, the trade unions formed a coalition and organised a march in November 1991 in which people from all walks of life, many of them members of no union at all, joined to show their solidarity with the coalition and their own dissatisfaction with the Sandiford government. The demand most common on the placards was for the resignation of the government. One daily newspaper under the headline 'Solidarity' summarised the demonstration:

> all shapes, sizes and colours . . . echoed the same sentiments . . . they [the government] must go, clergymen, politicians, teachers, nurses, labourers, doctors, lawyers, businessmen all made their position abundantly clear. 18,000 are supposed to have participated [in the march] from early morning. . . . Coalition leader Leroy Trotman hinted that there was a possibility of intensifying the action . . . the coalition called for the resignation of the prime minister . . .

The demonstration, a faithful handful of determined non-partisan newspaper columnists, among them, known former supporters of the DLP, began or maintained in the island's two daily newspapers active and persistent criticism of the government and its obvious ineptitude.

As dissatisfaction with the performance of the government continued into 1992, many of Sandiford's cabinet colleagues became disenchanted with what they euphemistically called his 'leadership style'. (Indeed, minister of finance, Richie Haynes, had resigned from the cabinet on those very same grounds in 1986.) There was more than a rumour that a sizeable faction of the DLP representatives in parliament were going to inform the governor-general that Sandiford no longer enjoyed their confidence.

The beginning of 1993 brought little hope of improvement and ended with no indication of better days to come. Far from it: Sandiford's domination of his colleagues and his overpowering arrogance of silence increased the anger of the people in all walks of life. The distinguished newspaper columnist, Gladstone Holder, who had constantly warned of the danger to our freedom, continued to remind Barbadians that the price of democracy was eternal vigilance. Leonard Shorey listed breaches of principle and supported the call for the government's resignation.

Early in 1994 Sandiford chose to insist that Tony Arthur, a senior staff member of the (statutory) Board of Tourism, be appointed its executive director without recommendation of the board, although this recommendation fell under its authority. Sandiford's display of ruthlessness and violation of procedures caused the minister of tourism, Wesley Hall, to resign. He was succeeded by Evelyn Greaves who also failed to obey the demands of the prime minister. Greaves' appointment was withdrawn, a euphemism for 'Greaves was fired'. Sandiford took over the portfolio of minister of tourism and made changes to the membership of the board. Tony Arthur was appointed as executive director of tourism within two days.

Public opinion expressed in the local press and on radio call-in programmes reached new heights of protest. The minister of health, Keith Simmons, resigned from the cabinet in protest against the action and the leadership style of the prime minister. Sandiford ignored or appeared to care nothing for it all. Just, however, as Barbados had settled down once again to wait out the long months before 1996 when elections would be constitutionally due, Sandiford took upon himself to address the nation on the local TV station on 18 May 1994. Speaking about the appointment of Tony Arthur he said that the ministers who had resigned were diametrically opposed to the appointment of Tony Arthur:

> they felt strongly enough on the matter to resign from the cabinet. If their view had prevailed I would have had on principle to resign, which is what the plotters and schemers would have dearly wished to achieve.[4]

What Sandiford defined as a kind of power struggle was in fact a miserable and unseemly act of despotism, seasoned with arrogance and masquerading on the national TV screens as righteous indignation. The opposition Barbados Labour Party brought a no-confidence motion against the prime minister soon afterwards. The motion was passed with the support of the three former ministers and Leroy Trotman, leader of the Coalition of Trade Unions, who had earlier resigned from the Democratic Labour Party and was sitting in parliament as an independent. Owing to the absence from the island of one member of the opposition, the ballot fell short by one vote which was required in order for the governor-general to revoke Sandiford's appointment. The result provided Sandiford with one of two choices: calling a general election or quitting his post.

At that point Dame Nita as governor-general might have resolved the issue by dismissing Sandiford as prime minister, because resignation was one of the options consequent upon a successful vote of no-confidence. Gordon Matthews, a regular writer in the local newspapers declared that the dismissal of the prime minister of Australia, G. Whitlam, by governor-general Sir John Kerr in the 1970s was a precedent which Dame Nita might follow. He also said that precedents related to the Barbados situation which required the exercise of a governor-general's initiative existed in Canada (1926) and in South Africa (1939) when the respective governors-general had refused to dissolve Parliament at the request of their prime ministers.

Dame Nita sought the best possible legal advice available and considered that her wisest course of action was to take no action until Sandiford had decided what he would do. Philip Greaves, former deputy prime minister, confirmed that view recently and also said:

> I believe that Her Excellency acted in accordance with advice. If however the vote of no-confidence had been passed with a higher majority her hands would have been freer and she would have acted differently.

Keith Simmons, also a former minister supported Greaves' view:

> Besides having studied the Constitution of Barbados carefully, Dame Nita would no doubt have had consultations with persons who would have assisted her. I believe that in the final analysis she could have done nothing to prevent the situation from developing as it did, although I believe that she might have used some form of persuasion to achieve what she thought would have been a better result.[5]

Sandiford chose to call a general election. It did not require an experienced political analyst to forecast that the DLP, at the time most unpopular, would lose the ill-timed and unnecessary election.[6]

Simmons added to his earlier comment:

> Dame Nita came to the post of Governor General during a period of economic crisis which was not unique to Barbados but existed all over the world.
>
> ... in all the crises which were encountered since 1986 the word 'method' would always crop up. It was the method in which things were done[7] ... Barbadians saw Dame Nita not only as a leader in her own right but also as sister of a man who was revered by most Barbadians, if not all. So that if things went wrong and she had anything to say it would be in the interest of all Barbadians. She would be concerned that justice be done and that is why a lot of people felt that in the political crisis she would have done what was right. That was important.
>
> She was accepted by everybody as a genuine person. Her dignity comes naturally, she belongs to the people, so she feels that she can go to a calypso tent as a Barbadian and as Governor General signalling 'I am here, so what is the big fuss about, I can invite the kids to government House and play with them . . .'[8]
>
> I think that Dame Nita is seen as a mother figure in Barbados. As one who can settle disputes in a family setting. If we expand that to encompass the country, you will appreciate what I am saying. It is felt that once she speaks all will be well. In that respect she assisted us a lot. People did not see her as a supporter of any political party even though she was Barrow's sister. They saw her as a person of world-wide experience holding the highest post in the country. Many had seen her help to solve problems in Africa and in South Africa, therefore any problem in Barbados would not be too big for her.
>
> It is not possible in the situation to attribute success or otherwise to Dame Nita's efforts. I believe that she was able to use her influence to advantage. Had she not been there, things might not have turned out as they did in the sense that whatever people protested about, whenever they did it, it was quiet and dignified. I believe that she had a great part to play in that.

During the three years of unsettled feeling in the island, whenever Dame

Nita appeared in public, a special kind of silent communication between herself and her people took place. Her appearance of strength, her smile of undefinable quality and her full 'eye contact' conveyed a calmness and signalled that her inner strengths which were there, were still there. Her 'family Barrow' eyes of authority which had assisted her in maintaining order in many a forum across the world, as if by a magic of will, converted their power of command to that of persuasion, to persist with dignity whatever required persistence.

Our attention to the problems associated with the government of the country should not distract our interest from other events in the community which were influenced by Dame Nita's interests. Barbadians knew of her commitment to the welfare and advancement of the status of women and admired her for it. In 1991 for the first time there were six women in the senate. Two of them, Mrs Margaret Walcott, Chief Guider and Mrs Ada Straughan, former headmistress of a secondary school and social worker were appointed by Dame Nita. Once again and in the new senate of 1994, Dame Nita has appointed two women Mrs Peggy Rickinson, president of the Barbados Nurses Association and Mrs Viola Davis, social worker and social activist.

The number of women holding senior positions in the government service has increased and the National Union of Public Workers (NUPW) elected Ophelia King as its first female president. The Diocese of the Anglican Church in Barbados through His Lordship, Bishop Brome, appointed and ordained two young women, Sonia Juanita Hinds and Beverley Bernadette Sealy, deacons.

There has been talk about Dame Nita's exercise of the prerogative of mercy, but which is in fact vested entirely in the post of the governor-general, much as it is her right as governor-general to appoint some members to the senate.

Barbados has not escaped the wave of crime which has swept across the Western world in recent years during which an unusual number of murders have been committed. The public through the press and other media has persisted in calling for the use of the death penalty which is on the statute books of Barbados. But no official statement has been made on the subject. Some people believe that delays are not accidental, others that the governor-general is herself against capital punishment. Philip Greaves volunteered a comment on the subject less in explanation of how the prerogative of mercy is exercised than in defence of the post of governor-general.

The governor-general exercises the prerogative of mercy on the advice of the local privy council, the membership of which presently includes a bishop, ministers of government, members of the opposition and lay persons. Greaves himself a member of the privy council, said:

> We all sit and review each case, we give the Governor General the advice

which we think should be given and she acts on that advice. She has no constitutional right to take any action on her own. We can only advise her when everything is in place and all action prior to our sitting has been taken. The perception of her bias is false and unfair.

The beginning of the year 1994 was like that of the two or three before it, but by the end of the year there was an evident buoyancy of spirit. But perhaps it might all be better stated by our people's governor-general, head of state Her Excellency, Dame Nita Barrow, who in her Christmas message 1994, briefly reviewed the major events of the year, among them the SIDS conference although she found that it had not yet shown any lasting results. She reminded her people that they had displayed a high level of maturity which had led to the resolution of the nation's difficulties. The positive signs of economic recovery she considered were cause for gratitude. Dame Nita ended her message with a quotation from the national anthem of Barbados:

> The Lord has been the people's guide for the past three hundred years
> With Him still on the people's side we have no hopes or fears.

---

1. Order of Jamaica, that country's highest honour.
2. List of Honorary Degrees:

LL.D. University of the West Indies   1975;
D.Sc. McMaster University 1982
D.H.Lit. Morris Brown University 1987
LL.D. University of Toronto 1987
LL.D. University of Winnipeg, Manitoba   1988

D.Humanities Mt. St. Vincent University	1988
LL.D. Spellman College, Atlanta	1989
LL.D. York University, Ontario	1990
LL.D. Queens University	1991
LL.D. Smith College, USA	1991
LL.D. Adelphi University	1994
LL.D. Wilfred Laurier University	1994

OTHER AWARDS

Fellow of the Royal College of Nursing	1980
Order of the Caribbean Community	1994

3. *Barbados Advocate*, 30 November 1991. BET is Barbados External Telecommunications and BARTEL is Barbados Telephone Co.
4. Barbados Advocate newspaper of 27 November 1994 – Independence Anniversary Issue.
5. Discussion with the author.
6. The Barbados Labour Party gained 19 of the 28 seats in Parliament, the Democratic Labour Party, 7 and the National Democratic Party 1.
7. Keith Simmons did not wish to make further criticism of Sandiford. He differed with Sandiford over what he has publicly and somewhat euphemistically called the latter's leadership style.
8. Keith Simmons in discussion with the author.

Index

Aboriginal Women's Centre 87
Adams, J.M.G.M. (Tom) Prime Minister 171
Adams, Grace Lady (nee Thorne) 18, 29
Adiseshiah, Malcolm 113
Advanced Nursing Education 62
African National Council (ANC) 125, 135, 136
African Methodist Episcopal 10
Afrikaners 125, 128
Alexandra 131, 134
Alleyne School 9, 13
Alma Ata 88, 150
Amin, Idi President 146
Anstey, Bishop 8
Antigua 59
Anyaoka, Emeka Chief 131, 175
Arole, Rajanikant & Mabelle Drs. 70
Ashby, A.S. Dr. 26
Ashra Princess 96
Asquith Commission 45, 46, 58
Assad Marie 85
Astorga, Nora 158
Athenassion, Athena 146, 150
Audeh, Dora 149
Australia 95, 117, 124
Balfour Declaration 152
Bam, Brigalia 128, 147, 155
Banda, Hastings Dr., President 84
Bangkok 120
Bantu 126, 127, 129
Bantusans 130
Barbados Nursing Council 128
Barbados 54, 115, 164, 166
Barbados General Hospital 19, 22
Barber, Lord 124, 142
Barker-Welch, Maisie 107
Barnes, Lilace 144, 150, 154
Barnett, Lloyd 163
Barrow, Jonathon 4
Barrow, Sybil 4, 5, 13, 19, 172
Barrow, Bellingham 4, 5
Barrow, Lucy 5
Barrow, Graham 5, 13

Barrow, Reginald Revd. 5, 8, 9, 10, 12, 21
Barrow, Florence 4
Barrow, Ruth Nita Dame, Her Excellency 1–182
Barrow, Ruth, nee O'Neal 4, 5, 9, 13, 19, 21
Barrow, Errol, Prime Minister 1, 5, 13, 58, 165, 170
Barrow, Robert 4
Barrow, Ena 5, 13, 19, 38
Barrow, Griselda 5
Butler, Ivy 32, 42
Bayley, Evadne 48
Beckles John B. 17, 18
Behrhorst, Caroll Dr. 68–70
Beirut (Lebanon) 43, 144, 149
Belanger, Paul 116
Bequia 8
Biko, Steve 130
Bindley, Canon T.H. 8
Blackman, Frank Sir 170
Boers 128
Boesak, Alan Revd. 132, 142
Bom Jesus da Lapa 85, 86
Botha Pik 136
Botswana 74, 76, 126, 140, 159
Bowen, Hilda 57
Boyd, Doreen 150
Branford, Beresford 17
Brathwaite, Christopher A. 17, 18
Brazil 81, 115
Brodie, Erica 147
Brooks, Angie 166
Bryant, John (Jack) H. Dr. 66
Buenos Aires 114
Bullen, Nathaniel 17, 18
Burton, Norah 18
Bustamante, Alexander 54
Buthelezi, Mangosuthu Gatsha Chief 138, 139
Cameroon 75
Carter, Bertie Dr. 26
Canada 167
Caputo, Daniel 163, 164, 166

183

CARICOM 163
Catlow, Helen 18, 19
Cato, Arnot Sir 26
Catto, Isabel Hon. 144, 150, 154
Chandler, Eunice (nee Griffith) 22, 23
Chang-sha 117
Charles, Eugenia Dame 32, 33
Charles R. Dr. 26
Chengdu 117
Chipenda, Jose 142, 143
Chimaltengo, Guatemala 68, 77
China 117, 118
Christian Medical Commiss'n (CMC) 65, 66, 71, 87, 88, 148, 150
CICARWS 71, 78
Clairmonte, Nathaniel 17
Codrington College 8, 45
Codrington, Christopher 8
Colonial Devel. & Welfare Corp'n C.D. & W. 34, 37, 42, 52
Columbia University 52, 55
Combermere School 8
Cotton, Nora 28, 30
Cox, Berinda 3
Convergence 111
Copenhagen 93, 96, 101, 103
Crosby, Heather 148
Dash, Ruth 35
de Klerk, F.W. 139, 140
de Mello, Artaro 83, 84
Democratic Labour Party 2
Democratic League 17, 18
Deng, Cora Madame 119
Denmark 113
Department of Social & Preventative Med. 62, 79
Durant, Elliot 15
Dutch Reform Church 77, 127
Echeverra, Luis 111
ECODEF 174
Edinburgh University 42
Ellis, Pat Dr. 114
Eminent Persons Group (EPG) 107, 123, 125, 128, 136, 154
Ennever, Olive 58
Ethiopia 105, 136
Federation of the West Indies 53
Fiji 115
Forum 85, 93, 94, 95, 162
Foster, Marian 145
Francis Evelyn (Lady Standard) 27
Fraser, Malcolm 124, 131
French, Eleanor 145
Friendship Plantation 5
Gaborone (Botswana) 126
Garden, The 6, 13
Gardner, Robert 110, 112
Garvey, Marcus 17
Gayfer, Margaret 111, 112
General Nursing Council (GNC) 54, 55, 61

Gibel, Inga 103, 104
Gideon, Helen Dr. 77
Gittens, Dolly (Lady Springer) 25
Grassfield School 14, 18
Greaves, Philip Hon. 170, 180, 181
Greaves, Evelyn Hon. 179
GULAC 161, 162
Hall, Bud 111, 113, 121
Harare (Zimbabwe) 126, 141, 159
Harden, Ena 62
Harjula, Raimo Dr. 73
Harper, A. Washington 15, 17
Hart, Margeurite 145
Huslam, Phyllis 31, 145
Haugland, Birgitte 62
Hellberg, Haakan Dr. 77
Hepburn, Davidson Ambassador 163
Herald (Newspaper) St. Croix 10, 12
Herald (Newspaper) Barbados 16, 17
Hijab, Nadia 100
Holder, Candy 3
Hong Kong 117
Hope, Clyne 5
Horton, Miles 112
Hough, Henry Governor 10
House of Assembly 7
Huddlestone, Trevor Bishop 141
Hudson, Colin 176
Huddlestone, Trevor Bishop 141
Hudson, Colin 176
Hunte, Thomas Sir 46
Ibbotson, Dora 42
ICAE 95, 110, 118, 169
IMF 176, 177
India 124
Inniss, Clement 15
International Year of Literacy (IYL) 120, 121
Iran 96
Iraq 115, 120
Irvine, James, Sir 46, 47
Israel 153
Ives, Janet 63
Jackson, David Hamilton 11
Jaigge, Annie Justice 144
Jamaica 164
Jamaica Labour Party 54
Jamaica Democratic Party 54
Jamaica Nurses Association 49, 51
Jamaica 58, 59, 61
JAMAL 119, 120
Jamkhed India 70, 77
Jeliffe, Derrick Dr. 80
Jenkins, David, Bishop of Durham 68
Jobson, Katherine 86
Johnson, Pierre Marc Dr. 174
Joseph, Helen 135
Kempadoo, Peter 87
Kenya 96, 150
Kenya 115
Khan, Ivy 153

Khartoum 78
Khoikhoi 126
Khoury, Samia 154
Ki-Zerbo, Prof. 76
Kidd, Margaret 112
Kidd, Roby Dr. 110. 114
Kiplagar, Bethuel (Kip) 78, 95
Kingma, Stuart, Dr. 76
Kingston Public Hospital (KPH) 44
Klimenko, Antonia 62, 63
Kruyt, Sophia Dr. 66
Lambourne R.A. Dr. 68
Landauer, Stella 62, 63
Laurie, Peter 159
Lawrence, Enid 58
Lawrence, Ivy 32, 33
League of Nations 127
Legislative Council 17
Lesotho 140, 160
Liebrich, Ursula Dr. 85
Lilli Madame 119
London University 45
Lowe, Eva 48, 49, 52
Lusaka (Zambia) 126
Lusan, Carmen 39, 145
Lutheran 75, 147
Luthuli, Albert Chief 135, 136
Mac Gilvray, James Dr. 67, 71, 77, 79, 84
MacClean, Wendell 176
Mac Master University 170
Mahler, Karsten Dr. 77
Malan, David 127
Malawi 84
Malaysia 115
Malecela, John 124
Mandela, Nelson 125, 133, 135
Mandela, Winnie 133, 135
Manley, Michael Prime Minister 40
Manley, Norman Premier 51
Mao, Chairman 117
Maori 87
Marly-le-Roi 111
Matthew, Gordon Dr. 179
Matthews, Marie 63
McBurnie, Beryl 42
McNeil Madam 31, 32
McKay, Jean 63
Meru 73
Methodist Church 38, 39
Mexico 91, 98
Miller, Billie 107
Mills, Charles Mr. & Mrs. 33
Mirau 73, 74
Mitterand, Francois President 111
Moi President 95
Molale, Michael Dean 76, 77
Montreal 113
Moore, Donald 33
Mount Pleasant Estate 6
Moyne Commission 45

Mungherera, Joyce 146
Mussalem, Helen Dr. 56, 58, 59, 62
Nairobi 91, 96, 108, 173
Nairobi 148
Namibia 108
Narty Dr. 74
Nassau 123
Neilson, Agnes 43, 44
Nepal 115
Nesfield 6
Nettleford, Rex Prof. Hon. 164
New Delhi 123
New Zealand 87, 95
Nigeria 115, 124
Nightingale Home for Nurses 23
Northcote, Ann 151
Nursing Assoc'n of the Caribbean 54
Nyerere, Julius President 113
O'Neal, Ruth Alberta 5, 15
O'Neal, Thomas W. 5, 8
O'Neal, Ebenezer W. 5, 30
O'Neal, Inez Malvina 5, 15
O'Neal, Joseph Edwin 5
O'Neal, Thomas Prescod 5, 17
O'Neal, Joseph, J.C. 5, 13, 16
O'Neal, Catherine 5, 14
O'Neal, Charles Duncan Dr. 5, 16, 17, 22
Obasanjo, Olusegun General 124, 131
Ochoa, Emma 62, 63
Okot p'Biteke 79
Ontario Institute for Studies in Education 110
Ovens, Gerald Professor 47
PAHO/WHO 51, 52, 55, 61, 62, 145
Pakathi, Jane 157
Palestine 96, 101, 152
Palmer, Elizabeth 147, 149
Panama 7
Park Lodge 14
Parkinson, Rawle 15
Parks, Rosa 32
People's National Party 54
Peterson, Hector 130
Phillipines 115
Pilgrim, Alexander Revd. 7
Port Moresby 88
Potter, Philip Dr. 67, 72, 87
Pretoria 124
Primary Health Care (PHC) 87, 88, 110, 117
Principal Nursing Officer (PNO) 48, 51, 52, 56
Queens College 19, 21
Queens University 42, 63
Rajasthan, India 115
Ram, Eric Dr. 86
Ramdass, Lalita 120
Ramphal, Shridath Sir 173
Rastafarian Group (Rastas) 41, 42
Recife, Brazil 81
Reynolds, Betty 33
Robinson, Joyce Hon. 39, 119, 120, 169
Rockefeller Foundation 30, 31, 33, 52, 173

185

Rodney, Pat 114, 120, 121
Roosevelt, Eleanor 91
Royal School of Nursing 42, 169
Runcie, Robert Archbishop 142
Russel, Kathleen Dr. 30, 33, 35
Sainikito Mirau Massari 73
San 126
Sandiford, Erskine Prime Minister 163, 170, 176
Sao Paulo 83
Scandinavia 42, 95
Scott, Edward, W., Most Revd. 124, 155
Scroxton, Joyce 147
Seroke, Joyce 128, 134, 148
Shanghai 117
Shankland, Alfred, Dean 18
Sharpville 130, 136
Shearer, Hugh Hon. 165
Sheel, Martin Dr. 98
Shen-yang 117
Sherlock, Philip Sir 45, 46
SIDS 175
Simmons, Keith Hon. 179
Simmons, Gilmary Dr. (Sister) 77, 84
Singh, Sardar Swaran 124
Siu, Phoebe Madame 119
Skipper 3
Solo, Indonesia 71, 77
Somers Gordon, Frank 38
South Africa 43, 44, 108, 123
South African National Party 127
Soviet Union 118
Sovik, Ruth 147
Sovik, Arne 147
Soweto 134
Spanish Town/St. Jago 41
Spring Garden 6
Springer, Basil 176
Springer, Charles Wilkinson 4, 8
Springer, Charles R. 4
Springer, Robert C. 4
Springer, Hugh Sir 2, 4, 35, 46, 171
Sri Lanka 115
Srour, Heiny 101
St. Croix Benevolent Society 13
St. Lucia 115
St. Michael Girls School 14, 19, 21
St. Vincent 4, 8
Standard, Kenneth Sir 62, 63, 79
Stewart, Ilene (Murray-Ainsley) 26
Stewart, Marjorie 38
Stock, Arthur 114, 115
Stowe, John Sir 1
Strong, Maurice 174
Stuart, Lionel Dr. 26
Sudan Christian Council (SCC) 78
Sudan 78
Sumatra 71
Susuli, Walter 135, 136
Swaby, Gertrude 44, 48, 52

Swaziland 140
Taitt, Nella 14, 18, 19
Talbot, Sylbot Dr. 77, 85, 86, 88
Tambo, Oliver 136, 139
Tanzania 74, 124
Thompson, Janet 51, 52, 55, 62, 63
Togo 144
Tokyo 110
Tonga 115
Toronto 113, 114
Trench Town 42
Trotman, Leroy 179
Tubingen 65
Tudor, James Sir (Cammie) 165, 166, 170, 171
Turkey (Balikli) 89
Tuskegee Institute 15
Tutu, Desmond Archbishop 132, 142
Udell, Florence 57
Uganda 105, 146
UK 95
UNESCO 110
United Kingdom, UK 136, 144
United Nations (UN) 94, 99, 104, 107
United Methodist Women 94
UNHCR 78, 150, 153
UNICEF 162
UNIFEM 107
University of Ibadan 76
University of Nairobi 106
University College Hospital of the W. Indies 44, 46, 47
University College of the West Indies 46
University of the West Indies (UWI) 62
University of Otago, N.Z. 87
University of Ghana 76
University of Toronto 170
Uppsala 90
Vancouver 146
Venezuela 115
Verwoerd Dr. 129
Wedderburn, Courtenay 51
Wesley Hall (Boys) School 15
West Indies School of Pub. Health 42
Wickham, John 171
Wickham, Clennel Wilsden 16, 17
Williams, Maggie (nee Sealey) 22
Wolfe, Mary 154
Wolpert, Betty 134
World Council (YWCA) 146
World Health Organisation (WHO) 99
World YWCA 43, 94, 99, 127, 145, 154, 173
World Council of Churches (WCC) 66, 93
Xencle 44
Xhosa 127
Xhuma, Maide Hall Mrs. 43, 44, 154
YWCA 38, 43, 119, 145
Zaire 93
Zambia 137
Zulu 127, 129, 138